W9-ASZ-155

INDIANA
ONE PINT AT A TIME

A TRAVELER'S GUIDE TO INDIANA'S BREWERIES

Funding for printing has been generously provided by
Monarch Beverage in honor of Edwin T. French Sr. and Edwin T. French Jr.,
the founders of the company.

ONE PINT
INDIANA
AT A TIME

A TRAVELER'S GUIDE TO
INDIANA'S BREWERIES

DOUGLAS A. WISSING

INDIANA HISTORICAL SOCIETY PRESS
INDIANAPOLIS 2010

Printed in China

This book is a publication of the
Indiana Historical Society Press
450 West Ohio Street
Indianapolis, Indiana 46202-3269 USA

www.indianahistory.org

Telephone orders 1-800-447-1839
Fax orders 1-317-234-0562
Online orders @ http://shop.indianahistory.org

The paper in this publication meets the minimum requirements of American
National Standard for Information Sciences—Permanence of Paper for Printed
Library Materials, ANSI Z39.48-1984 ∞

Library of Congress Cataloging-in-Publication Data

Wissing, Douglas A.
  Indiana : one pint at a time : a traveler's guide to Indiana's breweries / Douglas
Wissing.
     p. cm.
  ISBN 978-0-87195-283-7 (alk. paper)
  1. Bars (Drinking establishments)--Indiana--History. 2. Breweries--Indiana--
History. 3. Brewing--Indiana--History. I. Title.
  TX950.57.I6W565 2010
  647.959772--dc22
                                    2009048950

Table of Contents

. . . .

CRAFT BREWING

CHAPTER THIRTEEN

Favorite Indiana Draft Houses 221

CHAPTER FOURTEEN

Indiana Home Brewing 229
Organized groups of Indiana home brewers.

CHAPTER FIFTEEN

Recipes 233
Broad Ripple Brewpub's Beer-Cheese Crock—Heartland Beer-Cheese Soup—Carbonnade a la Flamade—Coq à la Bière—Hoosier-Gaucho BBQ Beer Chicken—Indiana Pork Loin with Kriek and Dried Cherry Sauce—Jets de Houblon—Lager Pancakes

Appendix 243
Indiana Breweries Operating at the Onset of Prohibition, April, 1918—Indiana Breweries, 1933–1997

Acknowledgments

· · · · · · · · · · · ·

BOOK THAT MINGLES HISTORY with contemporary times is bound to be a team effort. Dozens of folks have labored to help illuminate this story of Indiana brewing. My sincere thanks to all of them.

I am forever in the debt of reference librarians, curators, and scholars of diverse interests who carefully steward the tomes, tales, and ephemera of our past so history can be lit into glowing color. Anderson Public Library reference librarian Beth Oljace provided important information about that city's brewers, as well as critical suggestions on eighteenth- and nineteenth-century Moravian missionary brewing. Reverend Otto Dreydoppel and Doctor Paul Preucker of the Moravian archives in Bethlehem, Pennsylvania, were also helpful. In Bloomington, Doctor Barbara Truesdell of the Indiana University Center for the Study of History and Memory assisted with oral histories of Dubois County bootlegging days. Indiana University Wells Library reference librarian Sarah Mitchell tracked down an elusive article. Kevin Grace, head archivist of the Archives and Rare Books Department at the University of Cincinnati, helped with the role of Cincinnati in early Indiana brewing. Kenneth Lee, brewmaster at the Sam Adams brewery in Cincinnati, provided insights into mid-twentieth-century and modern brewing. Reference librarian Sharon Olson at the Evansville Public Library went an extra mile to deliver a lode of historical material on Evansville's brewing industry. Evansville's historic preservation officer, Dennis Au, offered an architectural-sociological perspective. Jennifer Greene, reference librarian at the University of Southern Indiana, supplied a wealth of early Evansville brewing photos. In Fort Wayne, journalist and historian Scott Bushnell was kind enough to share his own impeccable research on local brewing, as well as providing an anecdote-filled tour that brought Fort Wayne's long history to life. Bushnell also waded into the photo archives to glean wonderful images for this book. Walter R. Font, curator of the Allen County–Fort Wayne Historical Society's History Center, was also a great resource for information and photos. John Beatty of the Allen County Public Library provided a vital overview and contacts. Fort Wayne's Susan Berghoff Prowant and Patricia Centlivre Bonahoom passed on family stories and their books about their families' long brewing traditions. Huntington Library's Joan Keefer supplied archival material on Huntington's lively brewing history. In Indianapolis, Bob Ostrander of www.indianabeer.com generously shared his voluminous historical and contemporary research posted on his fine Web site. Reference librarians Susan DesJean and Lois Laube of the Indianapolis–Marion County Public Library helped untangle some of the conflicting information in Indianapolis's early brewing history. Eberhard Reichmann of the Indiana German Heritage Society offered his insights into the role of German brewers in Hoosier history. Jessica Pollitt, Tippecanoe County Public reference librarian, helped connect me to experts on Lafayette brewing. La Porte County historian Fern Eddy Schultz supplied material about the La Porte breweries, and La Porte librarian John Mundy was equally accommodating. In Lawrenceburg, Joyce Baer, Chris McHenry, and David Steigerwald helped sort out the historic record. Janice Barnes of the Madison–Jefferson County Public Library sent extensive information about this early Indiana brewing center. Marion historian

Louis E. Ebert regaled me with his tale of Marion's drunken Prohibition-era fish. Karen Rettinger of the Marshall County Historical Society scoured the archives to locate information on Plymouth-area brewers. Peter Guetig, coauthor of the magisterial book on Falls Cities breweries, *A History of the Brewing Industry in Louisville, Kentucky, New Albany and Jeffersonville, Indiana,* supplied encouragement and a rare copy of his book. Under the able leadership of Historic New Harmony director Connie Weinzapfel, New Harmony continues to offer utopian hopes in today's world. Weinzapfel and former curator Dan Goodman were generous with their time and resources, helping me unveil the lives of Indiana's first commercial brewers. At the New Economy historical site in Ambridge, Pennsylvania, former curator Ray Shepherd and curator Sarah Buffington were instrumental with clues to Indiana's first beer recipes that were hidden in Harmonist archives. Corry Cooper assisted with vital translations. At Purdue University, Distinguished Professor of Agronomy Herb Ohm shared his knowledge about Indiana barley, and Jule Janick, distinguished professor of horticulture, enlightened me about the complexities of hops in Indiana. Marilyn Nobbe of the Morrisson-Reeves Library supplied great reference material about Richmond's colorful brewing past. In the South Bend-Mishawaka area, several scholars assisted: Scott Schuler of the Northern Indiana Center for History, John Kovach of the Saint Joseph County Public Library, Andy Beckman, archivist of the Studebaker National Museum, and Gabrielle Robinson, author of the incisive *German Settlers of South Bend.* In Terre Haute, reformed brewer and brewing historian Mike Rowe described his city's long brewing history and took me in search of the Lost Speakeasy through an imaginary tour of the Terre Haute Brewing Company's catacombs. Through his meticulous records, Vincennes historian extraordinaire Richard Day provided insights into early Vincennes brewing. Vincennes University reference librarian Richard King provided access and direction in the university's historic archives, and VU reference librarian Jill Long supplied a number of wonderful visuals and clips. Brian Spangle of the McGrady-Brockman Annex unearthed vintage court records and newspapers that illustrated pioneer brewing in Indiana. Vincennes educator and breweriana expert William Hopper kindly shared his wealth of knowledge about Vincennes beer culture. Vincennes polymath (and brother-in-law) John Ostendorf started me off on this project with his own Indiana brewing archives, as well as disclosing the Indiana apprenticeship of the famous German brewer, Heinrich Beck, founder of Hamburg, Germany's international Beck's brewery. West Union, Indiana, Shaker experts Cheryl Bauer, Katherine Rowland, and Mike Anderson shared their understanding of distilling and brewing in the early midwestern Shaker communities.

Contemporary Indiana brewers and authorities have likewise been generous with their expertise. My thanks to Omar Castrellon and Belinda Short at Alcatraz Brewing Company; Back Road Brewery's Chuck Krcilek; Jon Lang and Mike Hess at Barley Island Brewing; Jeff Mease and Floyd Rosenbaum with Bloomington Brewing Company; Brass Monkey's Andrew Lewis; the Broad Ripple Brewery's John Hill and Kevin Matalucci; Ted Miller at Brugge; Jim Cibak at Crown Brewing; Justin Dirig of Granite City in Fort Wayne; Steve Kotsianis at the Mishawaka Granite City; Larry Chase at the Iowa worthouse; Dan Valas at Great Crescent Brewery; Chris Roegner and John Templett at Half Moon; Lafayette Brewing Company's Greg Emig for both his knowledge of historic brewing and contemporary craft brewing; Tom Peters, former brewmaster at the Indianapolis Brewing Company; Mishawaka Brewing Company's Tom Schmidt; Mad Anthony Brewing Company's Blaine Stuckey and Jeff Neels; Jack Frey of the Main Street Brewery; Roger Baylor of the New Albanian; the Oaken Barrel's Kwang Casey and Mark Havens; Jon Myers at Power House Brewing Company; Dave Colt and Clay Robinson at Sun King Brewery; Jon Simmons at the Ram; Jerry Sutherlin at the downtown Rock Bottom Brewery, and Liz Laughlin at the Rock Bottom in College Park; Sam Strupeck of the Shoreline Brewery; The Three Floyds's Nick Floyd, Michael "Doc" Floyd, and Barnaby Struve; Doug Dayhoff, Caleb Staton, and Eileen Martin of Upland; Vigo Brewing Company's Micah

Weichert; and Doctor David Holmes of Warbird.

Additionally, Jim Schembre of World Class Beverages shared his broad experience in the craft beer industry. Anita Johnson of Great Fermentations opened the doors to Indiana home brewing with her convivial insights and connections. Home brewers Bat Bateman, Ryan Clarke, Bruce Deters, Paul Edwards, Tom Ferguson, Chris Ingerman, Marvin Keenan, Bruce Kehe, Jim Matt, Sean Reeves, Justin Rumbach, Ron Smith, Brian Steurwald, Tom Stilabower, and Andy Walton were generous with their time. Former Hoosier Jamie Emmerson, now of Full Sail, talked of the early days of Indiana craft brewing. Keith Lemcke of the Siebel Institute discussed Indiana's barrel-aging success. Indiana native Tonya Cornett, now a vaunted brewster at Oregon's Bend Brewing, and Teri Fahrendorf of the Pink Boots Society mused on women's roles in brewing.

A special thanks to the Indiana Historical Society Press, especially Senior Director Paula Corpuz, Senior Editor Ray Boomhower, and Editor Kathy Breen. Hoosiers owe a tremendous debt of gratitude to the generations of IHS historians and staff who have preserved our past and celebrated our living culture. A particular thanks to the visionary designers and *bon vivants* at Dean Johnson Design, Inc., including Bruce Dean, Scott Johnson, Pat Prather, and Indiana beer enthusiast Mike Schwab, who championed this project. And a thanks to my son, Seth, who started all this by introducing me to Westvleteren 12 Trappist ale. And to my son, Dylan, who listened patiently to my beer mania. Research should always be so much fun.

Introduction

. . . .

THIS BOOK HAS BEEN a beer trek across Indiana, a chance to understand the long Hoosier brewing tradition and experience today's remarkable craft beers. As I explored Indiana brewing history and discovered today's exciting microbrewing industry, the long drives gave me time for reflection.

I wondered, what is beer? Yellow lagers and amber ales connect to golden fields of grain. The bite of hops sends my mind up towering poles where hop cones nod against the blue sky. Cooking beer mash smells like a celestial porridge. Food, I thought. Maybe beer is essentially food.

I realized science is part of the picture. Brewers have struggled for a very long time to master the organic mysteries of beer. Brewing history is rife with tinkerers and industrial designers who rationalized the process, refracted forward into twenty-first-century craft brewers' tiny laboratories and neo-industrial tubs, tubes, and racketing grinders.

Then I began conjecturing that beer is art—some conceptual, performative work. I thought of the brewers' boot-footed dances, choreographed by each brewhouse's idiosyncratic setup—a jitterbug for some as they twist and turn with their manual systems; stately waltz-like routines in the more automated places; jagged hip-hops when things get chaotic. The elegance of well-crafted lager is hard to not find aesthetic; the high-wire act of deftly balanced ale is as artful as chamber music. And I remembered conceptual artist Tom Marioni's famous *The Act of Drinking Beer with Friends Is the Highest Form of Art*, a piece of social art he performed countless times in museums and public places across the globe. The art is—you know—drinking beer with friends.

Thinking about this Beer with a capital B, I considered the social chemistry involved—the Friday-night thrum of a happy brewpub, the clink of bottles at sports gatherings, and the welcoming hiss of bottles uncapped at family picnics. Perhaps concentrated conviviality is part of the equation. But then I pondered the quiet enjoyment of beer: the comfort of ale by the fire, the sensual excitement of a high-hopped IPA, and the intellectual stimulation of a lambic—so maybe it's liquid solace, too.

In some contemplative moments, I thought about beer as religion, conjuring up thousands of generations of yeast priests stewarding mysterious metabolic processes into a mind-altering sacrament. Before Louis Pasteur, brewers had a name for the unknown substance that changed grain into a transcendental liquid. They called it Godisgood—part of the alchemy that transformed base grain into a higher calling.

But having finally reached the end of my zymurgic journey across Indiana, I at last concluded it is something far more elemental than all of these things: it's beer.

INDIANA: ONE PINT AT A TIME covers a lot of historic ground. To place Indiana brewing in a larger context, there is an overview of brewing from prehistoric times through industrial brewing to the emergence of the American craft-brewing industry. The book then unveils Hoosier brewing history, including pioneer brewers, the Indiana German brewers who dominated the industry until Prohibition, and the twentieth-century decline of the state's industrial breweries that overlapped with the 1990s rise of Indiana's craft breweries. This is Indiana history seen through the bottom of a beer glass, a little distorted, but easily recognizable. The big subjects of Indiana pioneer agrarianism, immigration, nativist reaction, cultural and hot wars, urbanism, industrialization, consolidation, and the renaissance of localism all get played out in this beer-soaked history.

Then there is the amazing story of Indiana's many contemporary craft breweries. At the time of this writing, there are thirty-two breweries operating in the state, more than any time since Prohibition, giving Indiana a ranking of seventeenth among the states in number of breweries. *Indiana: One Pint at a Time* profiles the Hoosier craft brewers, telling the tales of their triumphs and tribulations. These brewers form a wildly diverse crowd: three philosophy majors, a psychiatrist, a professional soccer player, a Yorkshire publican, a grade-school teacher, skinheads and frat guys, lefty activists, and social conservatives among them. They are variously irascible, genial, and morose; some are taciturn, some almost perky; a number are garrulous, a couple almost inarticulate—letting their beers do the talking. This book also celebrates their extraordinary beers that have brought the state both international fame and a renewed pride in our Indiana beer. Among the more than twenty-eight thousand barrels of beer produced in Indiana last year, there was enormous diversity in style, from rigorously traditional brews to beers creatively concocted for every palate. So, here is *Indiana, One Pint at a Time*. And here's hoping you enjoy the trip as much as I have.

Douglas Wissing
Bloomington, Indiana
December 2009

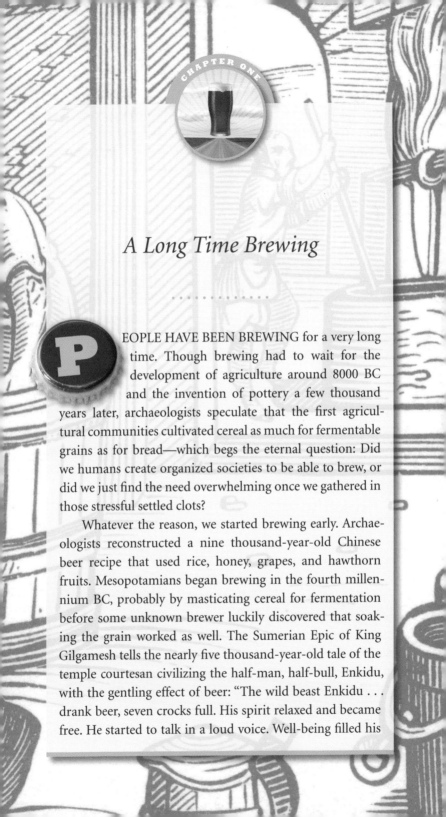

CHAPTER ONE

A Long Time Brewing

P EOPLE HAVE BEEN BREWING for a very long time. Though brewing had to wait for the development of agriculture around 8000 BC and the invention of pottery a few thousand years later, archaeologists speculate that the first agricultural communities cultivated cereal as much for fermentable grains as for bread—which begs the eternal question: Did we humans create organized societies to be able to brew, or did we just find the need overwhelming once we gathered in those stressful settled clots?

Whatever the reason, we started brewing early. Archaeologists reconstructed a nine thousand-year-old Chinese beer recipe that used rice, honey, grapes, and hawthorn fruits. Mesopotamians began brewing in the fourth millennium BC, probably by masticating cereal for fermentation before some unknown brewer luckily discovered that soaking the grain worked as well. The Sumerian Epic of King Gilgamesh tells the nearly five thousand-year-old tale of the temple courtesan civilizing the half-man, half-bull, Enkidu, with the gentling effect of beer: "The wild beast Enkidu . . . drank beer, seven crocks full. His spirit relaxed and became free. He started to talk in a loud voice. Well-being filled his body, and his face turned bright. He washed his matted fleece with water and rubbed his body with oil, and Enkidu became human." Babylonian clay tablets from 4300 BC detail twenty different beer recipes—a diversity that ambitious contemporary craft brewers have embraced. At Godin Tepe in western Iran, one of the world's first urban settings, shards of drinking vessels from 3500 to 2900 BC have the oxalate ion traces indicating beer. Assyrian tablets noted the crocks of beer that Noah loaded on his ark for his voyage escaping the Great Flood.

The Egyptians began brewing almost as early as the Mesopotamians, like them, using bread as the raw material. The Upper Egyptian site of Hieraconpolis has remains of a 3500–3400 BC brewery, presided over by Hathor, the goddess of dance and drunkenness, who also invented beer. Made of barley and spelt (a subspecies of wheat), ginger- and honey-flavored Egyptian beer was everyday sustenance for the common man, so much so that the hieroglyph for "meal" was the combined glyphs for "bread" and "beer." When brewed to a blood-red color and dosed with the narcotic Mandrake root, beer was the psychedelic path to the other world for Hathor's temple worshippers. By the Middle Kingdom, around 1800 BC, Egyptian brewers were delivering 130 jars of beer daily to the royal court, including 5 jars for the queen herself on one—clearly memorable—day.

Classical Brewing

In prehistoric northern Europe, beer drinking was also a social activity. Throughout Europe, archaeologists have found sets of beer-tinged amphorae dating back to parties in the third millenium BC. Based on archaeological digs in Scotland, Neoliths and Bronze-Agers were getting down on a brew that contained cereal, honey, meadowsweet, and the psychedelic, but also poisonous, henbane—unique admixtures that had no comparable beverages in the vine-growing regions of southern Europe.

There was little brewing among the wine-drinking Greeks—*and* they were downright snooty toward those beer-drinking barbarians. In the eighth century BC, Homer sniffed at the tribe of one-eyed Cyclopes in his *Odyssey*, depicting them as hopelessly déclassé with their cannibalistic, beer-drinking ways. It was a prejudice that has lived on.

The *vino*-smitten Romans also had little respect for the brewing culture of the Germanic and Celtic tribes they encountered after launching the centurians' great military ventures north of the Alps in 500 BC. The Germanic and Celtic tribes had begun making beer in the latter part of the Bronze Age, sometime before 1000 BC, when breakthroughs in metallurgy allowed them to improve their agricultural implements and culinary gear, including the giant pots essential for tribe-sized brewing. Around the beginning of the Christian era, the Greco-Roman historian Strabo saw a bronze brew kettle that the Germanic Cimbri tribe used to brew 130 gallons of beer at a time.

> In the eighth century BC, Homer sniffed at the tribe of one-eyed Cyclopes ... depicting them as hopelessly déclassé with their cannibalistic, beer-drinking ways.

Within their central European homelands, the Germanic tribes, such as the Alemans, Swabians, Bavarians, and Saxons, tilled the deep glacial soils, growing grain for bread and beer. Made of wheat and barley, the beer was a dark, sour, swampy beverage, sometimes flavored with oak bark, aspen leaves, and an occasional gallbladder of ox—small wonder the Romans roundly disparaged the brew. Nonetheless, the historian Tacitus tactfully wrote of the *Germanii* brewing "an extract of barley and rye as a beverage that is somehow adulterated to resemble wine" and noted their enthusiasm for inviting guests into their homes to share their brew and provender. "No other people indulges more extravagantly in feasting and hospitality," he declared. While the *Germanii* impressed Tacitus with their vigor and martial zeal, he found their work ethic a touch lax, excepting the labor needed to cultivate their brewing grain: "they cultivate the grains of the field with much greater patience and perseverance than one would expect from them, in light of their customary laziness." Figuring the legions could use the Germans' "addiction to drink" to their advantage, Tacitus counseled the Romans to give the tribesmen as much beer as they wanted, as "we could defeat them as easily by this vice as with our weapons."

Ironically, German mercenaries serving as Roman legion auxiliaries popularized beer in the empire, including Britain after Julius Caesar's campaigns in 55 and 54 BC. Numerous excavations of subsequent Roman camps in Britain point to the widespread brewing of *cervisia* among the soldiers. The Latin word *cervisia* reflected beer's improved reputation among the latter-day Romans, who came to view it as the gift of strength given them by the goddess of agriculture, Ceres—*vis* meaning strength. The word formed the root for Spanish *cerveza* and all its Romance-language derivatives. Some linguists find the origin of the word *beer* in the Old English *beor*, which Anglo-Saxon warriors swilled from long, curling auroch horns in the great halls of Beowulf, part of the Germanic warriors' drinking-hall culture—a deep atavistic strain that is played out on game day in every sports bar in America.

The northern European Celtic tribes were also brewers, making "a wine of barley rotted in water, a foul-smelling juice," according to the Greek historian Dionysius of Halicarnassus, who confused yeast fermentation with "rotting," as did many Roman commentators. Dionysius's disdain for Celtic beer was not unique. One fourth century AD emperor, Flavius Claudius Julianus, wrote a poem about Celtic beer: "What makes beer smell of goat, while wine has the scent of nectar. The Celts invented it from ears of barley, because they have neither grapes nor a nose." In spite of the Roman antipathy, the Celtic Gauls happily imbibed beer, Plinius the Elder writing, "the Gauls generally drink barley wine, as they always have. They understand how to brew different varieties, with which they get inebriated."

The Romans also gave the Celts of southern Gaul a taste for Italian wine. Through that bustling trade we owe the Celts a debt for inventing a crucial brewing implement: the barrel. In the last couple of centuries BC, the ancient port cities of Tolosa (today's Toulouse) and Cabillonum (Châlon-sur-Saône) were the great entrepôts of the wine business, so much so that the cities rose on the detritus of countless clay amphorae used to ship the wine. With its pointed end, the amphora was ideal to ship from Italy in ship holds, but a lousy, fragile container for hauling wine into the thirsty interior of Gaul. The clever Celts hit on the idea of fastening staves of wood together into a cylindrical shape, creating the sturdy, relatively light, rollable barrel we know today.

> **"The Gauls generally drink barley wine, as they always have. They understand how to brew different varieties, with which they get inebriated."**

The Monks' Brew

Beginning in the first century AD, the ale-quaffing Germans began to turn the tide against the wine-drinking Romans. The Germanic Cheruscans, Visigoths, and Vandals all took whacks at Rome over the next five centuries, with tribesmen sacking the Eternal City again and again, culminating in 455 with the Vandals' climactic rampage.

Vercingetorix (beer drinker) surrenders to Julius Caesar (wine drinker) ending the Gallic Wars.

Rome's death rattle ended in 476 AD, when the last emperor, Romulus Augustulus, abdicated to the Germanic general, Odoacer.

Thus began the Medieval Age, when Germanic feudalism held sway, and the newly empowered Christian monastic orders developed their sprawling monasteries that housed Europe's first large-scale breweries, supplanting the female alewives who had previously brewed the household beer. With the aim of supplementing their austere meals with a nutritious, sprightly drink, monks began brewing in the fifth century AD, first centered in British and Irish monasteries. In the sixth century, the energetic Irish missionary, Saint Columban, introduced brewing to French monasteries, where he promulgated strict penances for spilling beer, including lengthy prostrations while "moving no limb." Stories of beer miracles began to circulate, such as Saint Columban magically replacing the contents of a barrel at the monastery of Luxeuil, where a monk had left the cask unbunged. Or the tale of Saint Columban shattering the barrel of beer that pagans were offering as a sacrifice to their god, Wodan, by breathing on it. The chronicler contended, "It was clear that the devil had been hidden in this vessel, and he would have captured the souls of the participants through the heathen offering." There were many tales of the miraculous Irish missionary/bartender Saint Brigid, who used beer to heal her wet nurse and transmuted dirty bathwater into "red beer" that cured lepers. In a kind of brewing loaves-and-fishes story, Saint Brigid made a small amount of grain provide beer for eighteen parishes for a whole week after Easter.

> There were many tales of the miraculous Irish missionary/bartender Saint Brigid, who used beer to heal her wet nurse and transmuted dirty bathwater into "red beer" that cured lepers.

Charlemagne's successor, King Louis the Pious, reigned from 814 to 840 AD, a crucial period for monastic brewing when monks codified rules for both brewing and imbibing. Two synods at Aachen decreed that monasteries should provide their monks a *sextarius* (about a pint) of beer a day, about double the prescribed alternate of a *hemina* (half pint) of wine. Monasteries in Brabant in today's Belgium began to brew with wild-gathered hops, *Humulus lupulus,* a perennial climbing plant that is related to marijuana. By the 820s and 830s, northern French monasteries in today's Normandy and L'île de France systematized its use. The monks learned that the hops plant's female flower (cone) had a resin, *lupulin,* with the oils *humulone and lupulone.* These oils preserved, sterilized, and clarified the ale, outweighing the bitter flavor and aroma that medieval palates, accustomed to sweet beer, had to grudgingly learn to appreciate. In the twelfth century, the Abbess and composer Hildegard of Bingen dismissively wrote about hops: "In its bitterness it prevents spoilage in those drink is to which it is added so that they can last much longer." No fan of extreme ales, she.

One after the other, the great monasteries of northern Europe built large breweries to handle their ecclesiastic and mercantile needs, the monasteries having become the medieval travelers' hostels and caravanserais. The famous Plan of Saint Gall dates back to 820 AD, when the monastery in today's Switzerland had three breweries—one for the monks, one for pilgrims, and one for guests—with large storerooms filled with casks and barrels. Through the Middle Ages, the monks' daily beer allowance crept up, to as much as five liters per day, according to some historians (though the monastic rules indicate that a good portion of that was supposed to be shared with paupers or sold to guests). With universal abbey rules codifying the right of monks to have "good" beer, it was natural that there would be complaints: a ninth-century Irish monk living in what is now Belgium lamented to the local bishop: "Indeed I am not able to live in such misery, not having to eat and drink except very bad bread and a very little small amount of very bad beer. Oh miserable me!"

Changes in Brewing

As the Medieval period began to wane, beer was still primarily a viscous, often-sour beverage—"muddy, fulsome, puddle, stinking," as one thirteenth-century commentator put it. The use of hops had brought some degree of preservation to brewing, though some continental brewers resented that monastic-controlled hops supplanted the so-called Flavorings License, or *Grut* ("*Grutrecht*" in old German). *Grut* was a flavoring mixture of herbs, such as juniper berries, aniseed, bay leaves, yarrow, gentian, rosemary, tansy, Saint-John's-wort, caraway seed, oak bark, wormwood, spruce chips, pine roots, and hallucinogenic henbane—a "Witches Brew" in the parlance of the day. Prior to the monastic use of hops, each brewer's unique assemblage of *Grut* was like a patent that monopolized an area. Hops replaced *Grut*, weakening the old-style home breweries—particularly those operated by women.

British brewers resisted the addition of hops to their ales long after their continental brethren, though the Hundred Years War (1337–1453) introduced Dutch and Flemish hopped beers to England, where brewers in the southeast began to utilize hops. But the English were still chary in 1524, when a ditty stated:

> *Hops, Reformation Bays and Beer*
> *Came to England in one bad year.*

Until the 1300s, the church dominated brewing beer for travelers and festivals. But change was coming. With the late medieval revival of trade, fairs and markets began to flourish. And where there is business, there is beer. Alewives and other commercial brewers proliferated. Inns, taverns, and alehouses sprouted across Europe. In 1309 the city of London had 35,000 residents—and 354 taverns and 1,330 brewhouses. The Black Death, the four-year pandemic that began in 1347, killed more than forty million in Europe and revolutionized brewing economies. With the sharp decline in population, survivors saw an increase in wages and wealth. Outside of London, there were few English inns in the 1300s, but by 1577 there were seventeen thousand inns across the island, where traders and locals could congregate to heft a flagon or two.

As always, there was the issue of taxes. In the late Middle Ages, sovereigns began to covet the wealth generated by the monasteries' brewhouses, which were exempt from beer taxes. Often under "royal license," the nobles encouraged the growth of commercial brewers, who could fill the royal coffers with levies. Emperor

Sigismund (1368–1437) was the first ruler to close the tax-exempt monastery breweries so his royal breweries could generate more revenues.

As brewers proliferated across Europe, authorities continued to issue controls. In a legislative tradition that dates back to Hammurabi, King John added ale standards to the Magna Carta that he signed in 1215. But the most important law governing beer quality was the *Reinheitsgebot*, the German Purity Law that William VI, Elector of the duchy of Bavaria, issued in 1516. Intending to prevent a price war between bakers and brewers for scarce wheat and rye, the famous decree eliminated troublesome *Grut* by allowing only water, malted barley, and hops in beer. (Yeast was yet an unknown element, await-

> **Yeast was yet an unknown element, awaiting Pasteur's groundbreaking nineteenth-century research. Early monastic brewers called the mysterious invisible element, "Godisgood."**

ing Pasteur's groundbreaking nineteenth-century research. Early monastic brewers called the mysterious invisible element, "Godisgood.") The *Reinheitsgebot* decree read: "Furthermore, we wish to emphasize that in the future in all cities, markets and in the country, the only ingredients used for the brewing of beer must be Barley, Hops and Water. Whosoever knowingly disregards or transgresses upon this ordinance, shall be punished by the Court authorities' confiscating such barrels of beer, without fail." The law slowly spread through Bavaria, and with the unification of Germany in 1871, became the law of the land, effectively barring the *auslander* British and Belgian ales from the Fatherland. The law also banned many regional Teutonic beers, such as North German spiced and cherry beers, accelerating the expansion of pilsner-style lagers throughout Germany.

Early in the eighteenth century, British brewers began using brown malt to craft a strong beer for the London river porters. The first beer that could be made in large quantities, porter brought prosperity to London brewers, such as Whitbread, Truman, Parsons, and Thrale. In Ireland, the Dublin firm of Guinness began to brew porters in 1778. In 1810 it launched a "stouter kind of porter," an inky, muscular beer that Guinness first called Superior Porter, then boosting it to Extra Superior Porter, before finally settling on Extra Stout.

Early in the eighteenth century, British brewers began using brown malt to craft a strong beer for the London river porters.

Lager, the light, golden beer that came to dominate the world's breweries, had its origins more than five hundred years ago in the Austrian, Bavarian, and Bohemian mountains of central Europe, where the brewers learned that storing their beers in caves for a few weeks mellowed them out—*lager* meaning "to store" in German. A special strain of yeast was critical. Sometime during the latter days of the Holy Roman Empire, it appears that the yeast associated with ale, *Saccharomyces cerevisiae,* had a chance mutation into *Saccharomyces pastorianus,* the yeast that is critical for lager production. Lager yeast ferments at colder temperatures and flocculates on the bottom of the fermenting vessel, while ale yeast bubbles along at warmer temperatures at the top of the fermentation tank.

In the early nineteenth century, Gabriel Sedlmayr of Munich and Anton Dreher of Vienna began to refine and correlate seventeenth- and eighteenth-century scientific discoveries about yeast with the practicalities of brewing. Sedlmayr convinced the Kaiser to establish a brewing school in 1836. By 1840 the two men were the premier European lager producers, as the market celebrated the translucent, delicate-tasting lagers made by Sedlmayr's Spaten Brewery in Munich and Dreher's Schwechat Brewery in Vienna. In 1842 brewers in the Bohemian towns of Pilsen and České Budějovice began brewing a lighter style of lager, which became known as Pilsner.

In an act of extraordinary largesse in the 1880s, Gabriel Sedlmayr supplied pots of lager yeast to his colleague Jacob Christian Jacobsen, who transported the fragile yeasts the six hundred miles from Munich to Copenhagen by carrying the pots under his stovepipe hat, cooling the pots in streams at each stagecoach stop. Back in Copenhagen, Jacobsen gave the pots to the Carlsberg Brewery chemist Emil Hanson, who isolated the strain of lager yeast and developed techniques to semicontinuously propagate the cultured lager yeast, which became known as *Saccharomyces carlsbergensis*. Carlsberg began to distribute Hanson's yeast free to other breweries around the world, where it still forms the basis of lager production today.

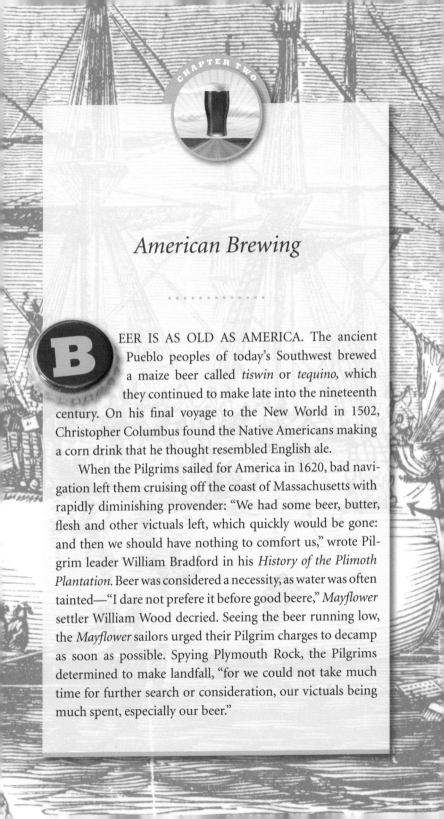

CHAPTER TWO

American Brewing

BEER IS AS OLD AS AMERICA. The ancient Pueblo peoples of today's Southwest brewed a maize beer called *tiswin* or *tequino*, which they continued to make late into the nineteenth century. On his final voyage to the New World in 1502, Christopher Columbus found the Native Americans making a corn drink that he thought resembled English ale.

When the Pilgrims sailed for America in 1620, bad navigation left them cruising off the coast of Massachusetts with rapidly diminishing provender: "We had some beer, butter, flesh and other victuals left, which quickly would be gone: and then we should have nothing to comfort us," wrote Pilgrim leader William Bradford in his *History of the Plimoth Plantation*. Beer was considered a necessity, as water was often tainted—"I dare not prefere it before good beere," *Mayflower* settler William Wood decried. Seeing the beer running low, the *Mayflower* sailors urged their Pilgrim charges to decamp as soon as possible. Spying Plymouth Rock, the Pilgrims determined to make landfall, "for we could not take much time for further search or consideration, our victuals being much spent, especially our beer."

A brewhouse was one of the first structures the Pilgrims erected that bleak winter. Under the tutelage of Wampanoag chief Samoset, the Pilgrims learned to grow corn, which quickly got tossed into the brew pot. A 1630s Pilgrim poem celebrated the New World substitutions:

If barley be wanting to make into malt,
We must be content and think it no fault,
For we can make liquor to sweeten our lips,
Of pumpkins, and parsnips, and walnut-tree chips.

But the Pilgrims were not the first brewers in the New World. Virginia colonists brewed with corn as early as 1587 and celebrated the arrival of the first beer shipment from England in 1607. Within two years, the Virginians were advertising in London for brewers. But the southern colonies faced a major problem: the climate was too hot for decent beer. Beer ferments at 70 degrees and lower. Above 70 degrees, the yeast produces fusel oils, which impart a solvent taste. Until ice making became widespread in the nineteenth century, the South generally had to import its beer.

In 1612 New Amsterdam's Adrian Block and Hans Christiansen established the first commercial brewery in the New World on Manhattan Island's Brouwer (Brewer) Street, in the heart of what is now the Wall Street district. Utilizing grain grown along the Hudson River, the brewers concocted a fine drink. "Beer is brewed here as good as in Holland, of barley and wheat," averred the sheriff of New Amsterdam, Nicasiums de Sille. A couple of years after the New Amsterdam brewhouse was established, it became the birthplace of the Dutch colony's first American-born son, Jean Vigne, who went on to become the first brewer born in the New World.

Up in Boston, Samuel Cole started the town's first tavern in 1634, and three years later Captain Robert Sedgwick established the Massachusetts Bay Colony's first brewery. John Harvard's plans for his namesake college he founded in 1636 included a brewery—beginning the connection between beer and American higher education that persists to this day. The first Harvard president, Nathaniel Eaton, failed to provide the necessary lubricant for academic amity, and the embittered students complained that "they often had to go without their beer and bread," presumably listed in order of importance. The beer shortfall was a prime cause of Eaton's dismissal. Renowned Boston cleric, Increase Mather (Cotton's father), described alcohol as "a good creature of God." Named Harvard president in 1686, Mather codified prompt beer delivery, ensuring it with the construction of three campus brewhouses. Carousing undergrads burned down the last one in 1814.

Deep in the heartland of America, Jesuits were brewing ale on the upper Mississippi River in the 1760s at the French trading post of Kaskaskia in what is now Illinois. When the Jesuits were thrown out of the country in 1763 after the Papal Bull that suppressed the order, the local French commander auctioned off their brew cauldron. Records indicate the kettle ended up with a wealthy local landowner and judge named Vitol Ste. Gême Beauvais, who presumably kept brewing. The Jesuits were some of North America's original beer evangelists: Canada's first brewer was a Jesuit, Brother Ambroise, who established his brewery in 1647 near Quebec City.

> John Harvard's plans for his namesake college ... included a brewery—beginning the connection between beer and American higher education that persists to this day.

William Frampton began Philadelphia's first brewery in the 1680s. The Blue Anchor tavern was Philadelphia's first tavern, and reportedly the first structure in the town, hosting William Penn when he came to scout out his territory. Built in 1759, the appropriately named Man Full o' Trouble Tavern is the only pre-Revolutionary tavern still standing in the City of Brotherly Love.

Benjamin Franklin was a great fan of beer, credited with the oft-quoted phrase, "Beer is living proof that God loves us and wants us to be happy." While his authorship of that axiom is unclear, he definitely did pen the ditty, "For there can't be good living/ Where there is not good drinking." Franklin lauded American resourcefulness, including the early brewers who utilized corn, wheat, molasses, and sassafras in their beers. (While campaigning during the French and Indian War, even George Washington had a recipe for small beer that mixed bran hops with molasses, "Let this stand till it is little more than blood warm then put in a quart of yeast.") Franklin's American Philosophical Society offered a recipe for pumpkin ale (a notoriously tangy beverage unless aged for a couple of years):

> Let the Pompion be beaten in a Trough and pressed as Apples. The expressed juice is to be boiled in a copper a considerable time and carefully skimmed that there may be no remains of the fibrous part of the pulp. After that intention is answered let the liquor be hopped culled fermented &c as malt beer.

Colonial beers most often followed the English style of ale, a dark, cloudy brew made of barley with a hit of hops, weighing in at about 6 percent alcohol. Small beers—low-alcohol ales—were most often brewed at home and consumed soon after brewing. Left to ferment longer, the higher-alcohol ales were known as strong beer or table beer. The colonies also had access to India Pale Ales, originally brewed in England for its colonists in India. Lighter in malt content and color, the India Pale Ales were dosed with extra hops to help with preservation during the long sea voyage. Washington was a big fan of dark, creamy English Porters, only switching to American-brewed ones when things got restive between the colonists and Mother Britain.

Revolutionary Ferment

A barley shortage in Boston precipitated one of the first revolutionary acts by the previously quiescent American colonists. In

1711 Bostonians faced a severe beer crisis because of a barley shortfall. When they heard that a local merchant, Andrew Belcher, was readying a ship to sail with a load of the grain, the proto-revolutionaries did what any right-thinking patriot would do: they blockaded the harbor. Don't tread on us, or mess with our booze.

But the British failed to heed the warning signs. The Revenue Act of 1764 imposed a direct tax on liquor, which incited those ever-idealistic Yale students to switch to beer. The *New York Gazette* commented, "The Gentlemen of the College cannot be too much commended for setting so laudable an example." In 1765 the British instituted the pernicious Stamp Act, which, among its many taxes on trade, levied additional taxes on taverns, causing them to raise prices. Homebrewing became the *au courant* thing to do for many colonists. For the more activist Americans, agitating at the taverns became the order of the day. Long the colonies' center of life, taverns were where Americans conducted business, talked up friends, gossiped—and organized. (With their breweries on premises, taverns were also the first American brewpubs. Being only a few yards from tun to tummy, colonial taverns provided food-miles that would impress the most contentious locavore.) By 1756 there were 156 taverns in Boston alone. Among them, the Green Dragon Tavern was a bubbling cauldron of rebellion, the place where the Sons of Liberty gathered to plan their actions against the perfidious empire. Incited by their tavern seditions, the colonists boycotted English imports and destroyed the hated British stamps.

Responding to the unprecedented rebellion, Parliament repealed the Stamp Act, only to enact the repressive Townsend Acts of 1768. Equally reviled, the Townsend Acts taxed imports rather than domestically produced goods, which provided an unexpected boon for American brewers. With English beers now taxed at a high rate, local brewers had a heyday.

Within two years, the British bowed to the widespread resistance and repealed the Townsend Acts—except for the tax on imported tea. At the Green Dragon Tavern on the night of December 16, 1773, the Sons of Liberty steeled themselves with rum and the strong ale donated by John Hancock. Following the plan hatched by Hancock and patriot brewer Sam Adams, the Sons donned their faux Indian gear to toss a shipload of English tea in the harbor. While more a kegger than a tea-and-crumpets event, the Boston Tea Party ignited the colonies. The Revolution was on.

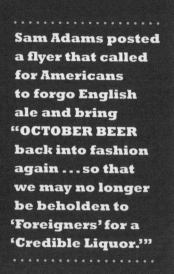

The influential southern colonies joined the North in protesting the British retributions. The Virginia Assembly in Williamsburg, led by Patrick Henry, Richard Lee, George Mason, Thomas Jefferson, and Washington, declared June 1, 1774, as a day of "fasting, humiliation and prayer" in support of their northern brethren. When the piqued Royal Governor dissolved the assembly, the members reconvened in the nearby Raleigh Tavern. Emboldened by ale, the assemblymen allied themselves with all of the British colonies, proclaiming, "That we will not hereafter, directly or indirectly import, or cause to be imported, from Great Britain, any of the goods hereafter enumerated, either for sale or for our own use . . . beer, ale, porter, malt."

· · · · · · · · · · · · · · · · · ·
Sam Adams posted a flyer that called for Americans to forgo English ale and bring "OCTOBER BEER back into fashion again ... so that we may no longer be beholden to 'Foreigners' for a 'Credible Liquor.'"
· · · · · · · · · · · · · · · · · ·

Another smoky alehouse, Philadelphia's City Tavern, served as the rendezvous point for the northern rebels John and Sam Adams to meet the firebrands of the South, Henry and Lee. There they forged the nonconsumption accord that was intended to end imports from England, including ale. Back in Boston, Sam Adams posted a flyer that called for Americans to forgo English ale and bring "OCTOBER BEER back into fashion again . . . so that we may no longer be beholden to 'Foreigners' for a 'Credible Liquor.'"

After the violent years of war, the peace treaty with Britain was still not signed in 1787 when the Constitutional Convention convened in Philadelphia. The long days of debate and oratory at the Pennsylvania Statehouse most often led to impasse. But after the formal deliberations, delegates hastened to the Indian Queen, Black Horse, and City taverns, where rum and ale helped the members hammer out essential compromises. At the City Tavern on the momentous night of June 30, 1787, Roger Sherman of Connecticut and John Rutledge of Virginia wrestled with the ultimate accord between the large and small states that yielded the bicameral Congress we know today. Following the signing of the Constitution soon after, convention president Washington penned in his diary: "The business being closed, the members adjourned to the City Tavern."

The Germans Arrive

Almost from the start of the republic, there were German American brewers. As early as the 1790s, visitors noted the high quality of the alt-style beer in the German settlements. French traveler Louis Phillipe noted in his *Diary of My Travels in America,* "Beer is always available in these German homes, and theirs are the only inns where we have been able to buy it."

The great German migration began in 1817, when royal authorities drove out students revolting against the decaying political structure of the Fatherland. Through the early nineteenth century, hundreds of thousands of immigrants—primarily conservative farmers and tradesmen seeking to rebuild their traditional lives in a new land—joined the earlier transplants. In the 1820s and 1830s almost one in three immigrants were German. The flood reached a new level after the Revolutions of 1848, when authorities crushed the left-wing rebellions, causing thousands of intellectuals and progressives to relocate to the burgeoning cities of America. The Germans of the great migration came to be known as *auswanderers.*

The German influx included hundreds of brewers, many trained in the smooth, lagered style of beer that had swept Germany. Lager beers arrived in America soon after Sedlymayr and Dreher's mid-nineteenth-century breakthroughs. While the historical record is controversial, it appears that Johann Klein and Alexander Stauz had a small lagering cellar in Alexandria, Virginia, in 1838. According to lore, Johann Lemp arrived in Saint Louis the same year and began selling lager-type beer from his neighborhood grocery, opening his stand-alone brewery two years later (which evolved within a few decades into Lemp's behemoth Western Brewing Company). The record is clear that in 1840 John Wagner brewed lager beer in Philadelphia with lager yeast he imported. In 1844 a Philadelphia sugar baron, Charles C. Wolf, became the first to brew lager on a large commercial level, as did Cincinnati's Franz Fortmann, who converted the Agneil and Fleishman Bavarian Brewery to lager production under the name of Fortmann and Company the same year.

As it had through the colonial era, beer continued to play second fiddle to cheap rum and corn whiskey. By the early nineteenth century, there were fourteen thousand distilleries producing twenty-five million gallons of whiskey annually—six to seven gallons per adult. In contrast, there were only two hundred American breweries, making English-style ales for the most part. But lager changed all that. With fast clipper ships speeding lager yeast to brewers, lagers began to dominate American beer production and palates. By the 1840s the consumption of spirits dropped to two and a half gallons per adult. By the 1850s beer was outselling spirits, and the Germans controlled the brewing business—when the Brewing Association met in 1862, the official language of the convention was German.

In the 1870s the Bohemian-style of lager entered the American market. Originating in the Pils region of the Austrian empire, the lemon-hued, low-alcohol Pilsner style was much lighter than the Bavarian and Prussian lagers that the German American immigrant brewers were trained to brew. At the Vienna International Exposition in 1873, representatives of the Missouri brewing industry tasted some of the award-winning Bohemian brews, including one made with Moravian barley and Saaz hops from the ancient royal city of Budweis. Its brewers called it the "Beer of Kings." Saint Louis brewer Adolph Busch inverted the slogan when he rolled out his American version, which he called Budweiser.

The new, mass-produced glasses filled with clear, bright beer helped make Bohemian-style lager become the modern thing to drink in America. Within twenty-five years, spirit consumption was under a gallon per adult. In the same period, beer consumption skyrocketed from one gallon per person annually to fifteen gallons per capita. The German American "lager beer" saloons and biergartens certainly helped the trend. While a colonial might sip a few pints of ale in his tavern, lager drinkers could toss back considerably more. One lithograph of a biergarten included a sign that limited patrons to forty-eight glasses, with trenchermen reputed to be able to down sixty glasses without intoxication. "Rushing the growler" became a common phrase in American life, the growler being the container used to carry beer from the saloon to the quiet confines of home (and also a way for women to drink discretely).

But the same beer glasses that helped grow America's love of lager also highlighted every wisp of yeast and glob of protein floating in the clear brew. The problem was American six-row barley, which had far higher amounts of protein than Bohemian barley. It took Bohemian-born chemist Anton Schwarz to crack the code. He discovered that mixing "adjuncts"—rice and low-protein white corn—into the mash solved the clarity problem. The result was a translucent, yellow beer with a foamy head and unctuous body. American brewers found adjunct brews cost more than all-barley Bavarian lagers, but with the enormous popularity of Pilsner-style beers, they quickly learned to live with the expense. Beginning an attack on adjuncts that continues today, early Prohibitionists in the 1870s and 1880s pilloried the use of adjuncts, claiming "corn and rice beer" caused temporary insanity. But in spite of the invective, light lager beers ruled supreme in America from the 1870s on. Most imbibing Americans considered dark beers to be inferior to their clear, light lagers, excepting a few notable, often seasonal, brews, such as springtime bock.

Through the Gilded Age into the new century, German American breweries continued to flourish, as the nascent beer companies of the 1860s blossomed into mighty consolidated industrial corporations. Saint Louis's Anheuser-Busch Company and Milwaukee's Schlitz, Pabst, and Miller companies competed for top rankings with immense plants, sophisticated distribution systems with refrigerated warehouses, and elaborate rail arrangements, while thousands of neighborhood saloons and lavish biergartens made their owners some of America's wealthiest families.

The Great Experiment

Anti-German sentiment dated back to at least the Know-Nothing Party, a nativist movement that burgeoned in the 1850s as a reaction to the swelling tide of immigration. While there had been only six hundred thousand immigrants to the U.S. in the 1830s, by the 1840s the number more than doubled to 1.7 million. In the next decade, more than 2.6 million foreigners clambered off the ships—75 percent of them from Ireland and Germany. In cities with large German populations, tensions mounted through the 1850s, climaxing in 1855.

In April 1855, joining many other cities' drive against the foreigners' alcohol, Cincinnati nativists campaigned for anti-German prohibition laws. During the election, anti-German rioters destroyed voting stations and a thousand ballots in the German neighborhood of Over-the-Rhine. German Americans barricaded a bridge into the area, but the mob, armed with a cannon and muskets, stormed the defenses. The anti-German riots in Chicago could only be suppressed with the help of the National Guard. In Louisville, incited by anti-foreign editorials by *Louisville Journal* editor George D. Prentice, local mobs killed nineteen people on Bloody Monday, August 6, 1855, and wounded hundreds. Armed with muskets, bayonets, and cannons, crowds also attacked institutions synonymous with German culture, swarming William Armbruster's brewery and destroying six thousand dollars worth of equipment and inventory. The rioters set fire to Adolf Peter's brewery three times.

Temperance-minded women picked up the banner of the Prohibition movement, which had dipped in the years following the Civil War. Throughout the 1870s, "visitation bands" of temperance women harassed saloons by relentlessly demonstrating outside the swinging doors, praying on their knees, and warbling hymms. One Hillsboro, Ohio, *biergarten* owner, Charley Beck, was determined to withstand the pious assault. But after two weeks of round-the-clock prayer outside the garden, Beck tossed in the towel, howling, "Ach, vimmins, shut up vimmins, I quit." In 1874 the Women's Christian Temperance Union first convened with seventeen states represented, but soon had chapters in every state. They were the firebrands against the "liquor interests," tirelessly leafleting and demonstrating.

Primarily run by men, the Anti-Saloon League was one of the most effective Prohibitionist organizations, utilizing newly developed scientific business techniques and canny lobbying at both the state and national level to move Prohibition forward on a number of fronts. Beginning in 1895, with the core of its membership coming from rural and small-town America, the ASL had great support from evangelical religions, particularly the Methodist Church. ASL members inundated the country with temperance tracts, flyers, and even sheet music, which included,

> "The Saloon Must Go:"
> I stand for prohibition, the utter demolition
> Of all this curse of misery and woe,
> Complete extermination, entire annihilation
> The saloon must go.

America's entry into World War I against Germany in 1917 again uncorked anti-German furies. Cincinnati, with more than 30 percent of its population German, withdrew all books in

German from its public library shelves. Milwaukeeans posted a machine gun in front of a theater showing *Wilhelm Tell*. Authorities suppressed German American papers, and some states banned the teaching of the German language. Even speaking German could have dire consequences. A Minnesota gang tarred and feathered a minister overheard praying in German with a dying woman. A mob in Collinsville, Illinois, lynched a German American, believing him to be a spy—wrongly, as it turned out. The jury found the accused innocent by reason of patriotism.

> Prohibition ushered in a lawless era of bathtub gin and hooch, alley brew, speakeasies, and Al Capone's tommy-gunning gang. For the brewing industry, it was a disaster.

As before, the rage extended to German American brewers. Brewing in 1917 was still primarily a German occupation in the United States—even the brewing publications were most often in German, as were brewers' union cards. In a speech decrying the "German enemies," a former lieutenant governor of Wisconsin, John Strange, thundered, "And the worst of all our German enemies, the most treacherous, the most menacing, are Pabst, Schlitz, Blatz and Miller. They are the worst Germans who ever afflicted themselves on a long-suffering people." Under draconian anti-German "Trading with the Enemy" laws, American authorities began to attack the Busch family's fortune, as well as attempting to seize a forty-million-dollar estate of George Ehret, the German-born beer king of New York who owned the Hell Gate Brewery. Ehret had been an American citizen for forty years.

The war provided an ideal opportunity for the determined prohibitionists, who had been laboring mightily since the 1840s. They could form an alliance with the Protestant nativists, who still harbored a deep-seated antipathy toward the foreign born. In the years leading up to the war, Congress had passed a constitutional amendment banning alcohol. The proposed amendment began winding its way through the forty-eight state legislatures for vote—with the amendment needing thirty-six aye votes to become law. The majority of the states were already dry by 1917, as were thousands of towns under "local options." By 1918 the prohibitionists had linked "German brewers" with the hated Huns in the mind of the American public. Railing against "Kaiser brew" became the order of the day. There were hysterical hearings on Capitol Hill, which culminated on September 6, 1918, when President Woodrow Wilson (himself a temperance supporter) ordered the nation's breweries to close by no later than December 1—ostensibly to save precious grain and fuel. On January 16, 1919, it was official: Nebraska became the thirty-sixth state to ratify the Eighteenth Amendment. Prohibition was the law of the land.

Prohibition ushered in a lawless era of bathtub gin and hooch, alley brew, speakeasies, and Al Capone's tommy-gunning gang. For the brewing industry, it was a disaster. Some companies limped along on investments, soft drinks, nutritional yeast, and near-beers—soupy, unpleasant stuff, such as Pabst's Pablo, Schlitz's Famo, and Anheuser-Busch's Bevo. Most breweries just closed their doors.

A New Brew

President Franklin Roosevelt repealed Prohibition, effective April 7, 1933, when 3.2 percent beer could again be legally sold. The day became a *de facto* national holiday. Streams of cars and trucks waited outside of the surviving breweries—a mile long at the Anheuser-Busch plant in Saint Louis. In Milwaukee, ten thousand people milled outside the Miller plant, where the lineup of vehicles included forty with Indiana plates. When the vast countrywide party tottered to halt that rapturous night, America had consumed a million gallons of beer.

By June 1933 there were 31 breweries back in operation, making more than eleven million barrels of beer. The next year, 756 breweries produced almost thirty-eight million barrels. The nation's appetite for beer seemed insatiable. In 1935 the Krueger

Brewing Company of Newark introduced a new-fangled invention: canned beer, designed for the brand-new "home market," as the beer moguls decreed the old saloon to be defunct. The same year as the first beer can, the Falstaff Brewing Company of Saint Louis leased the Krug Brewing Company in Omaha, unleashing a frenzy of acquisitions by large brewers. Buoyed by healthy profits (Americans drank almost eighty-eight million barrels of beer in 1948, more than eighteen gallons per person), the big boys went on a buying binge. By 1950 there were only 407 breweries in operation. Consolidation picked up steam through the 1950s, with 185 breweries selling out or ending business, leaving only 230 in operation by 1961.

The post-World War II desire for blander beers exacerbated the consolidation. The president of the Master Brewers Association warned his membership to abandon old styles of nasty bitters and Commie-looking dark malts, and rather aim for pale, "steamlined" beer with an "agreeable, mild hop flavor." Modern Americans wanted nice, and the brewers—preferably very large, heavily standardized brewers—gave it to them. And so it went. Beers such as "sparkling clear" Knickerbocker and "extra-light" Miller High Life, the Champagne of Bottled Beer, captured the market, followed by even blander Lite beers. By 1983 there were only fifty-one brewery companies in America, operating eighty breweries. The top six brewing companies controlled 92 percent of the nation's beer. It was to prove the nadir of flavorful American brewing.

But it was darkest before the dawn. Concurrent with the consolidations and the dumbing down of American beer, another trend was frothing up. In 1969 a rather scholarly scion of old Midwestern money decided to purchase a near-defunct brewery in San Francisco's crusty North Beach neighborhood. When Fritz Maytag bought the Steam Beer Brewing Company and its oft-sour Anchor beer, few would have guessed that it was to be a scismic event in American brewing. Maytag took his cerebral nature and focused it on brewing. He attended brewing schools and talked endlessly with brewers. He replaced his decrepit equipment. Maytag was determined to make beer that resembled the expensive imported beers he saw his friends ordering in the trendy clubs of San Francisco. With pricy two-row barley, whole hops, and his hard-won knowledge, Maytag began brewing a better beer—a complex, full-bodied, bronze-red beer with a taut hoppiness that quickly found a clientele. Maytag proved there was a market for robust American beers that were made with care and high quality.

In 1977, at the height of the *Whole Earth Catalogue* self-reliant craze, a former submarine repairman who had learned to love ale while stationed in Scotland, decided to patch together a brewery in Sonoma, California. With fermenters made of fifty-five-gallon drums that were installed in a building so basic water had to be trucked in, long-haired Jack McAuliffe brewed some eye-opening English-style ales in his New Albion Brewery. Attracted to the story of fine American beer being brewed in what was basically a roadside stand, the media beat a path to New Albion's door. Giddy reviews were soon appearing in places such as the *New York Times* and *Washington Post*. With little more than word of mouth and media coverage, McAuliffe sold everything he brewed. "If you make good beer," he told a *Washington Post* reporter, "you don't have to pay for advertising." While New Albion succumbed to capital deprivation after only five years, McAuliffe's small operation opened a world of possibilities to a ragged group of home brewers and iconoclasts searching for a way to brew commercial world-class beer on a less-than-conglomerate-sized budget. Half-hippie entrepreneurs suddenly had a model to follow, a way to

The president of the Master Brewers Association warned his membership to abandon old styles of nasty bitters and Commie-looking dark malts, and rather aim for pale, "steamlined" beer with an "agreeable, mild hop flavor." Modern Americans wanted nice.

cobble together an affordable microbrewing operation.

All across the country, passionate brewers began wildly diverse beer operations. Out in Albany, New York, English-trained brewer Bill Newman established Newman Brewery in 1981, selling his Albany Ale in plastic jugs that his patrons could return when they wanted more. Newman's was the first microbrewery in the East and had a hardworking young employee named Bill Koch, who went on to some small success as a brewer. In the college town of Chico, Calfornia, Ken Grossman was one of the microbrew believers, selling his first bottle of Sierra Nevada in 1981, when he sold 950 barrels. The next year he sold double that amount, beginning Sierra Nevada's phenomenal growth.

Up in Yakima, Washington, ex-brewery executive Bert Grant began serving his Yakima Brewing and Malting Company ales, porters, and stouts in 1982 in his brewpub—often considered the nation's first. The next year the Mendocino Brewing Company in Hopland, California, rolled out its copper-colored Red Tail Ale in another early brewpub. The short tun-to-tummy model so prevalent in colonial times was again in fashion.

The number of brewpubs and microbreweries began to multiply like healthy yeast: Boulder in Colorado; Columbia River, Widmer Brothers, and Full Sail in Oregon; Riley-Lyon in Arkansas; Kessler in Montana; Gritty McDuff in Maine; and Manhattan in New York's Soho district.

In Boston, the earnest Newman's brewery employee, Koch, began the Boston Beer Company in 1985. A descendant of six generations of American brewers, Koch was a high-powered business consultant when he noticed Yuppies buying expensive craft beers from the by-then fifty-odd American microbreweries. Recognizing a trend in the making, Koch decided to brew Sam Adams Boston Lager, reportedly made from his great-great-grandfather's Bavarian-style recipe that he had dug out of the family's Cincinnati attic. Drawing on his family's large-scale brewing experience, Koch realized he did not need a brewery, he just needed to control the formulas and processes in established breweries with excess capacity. The market demand for craft beer and Koch's contract-brewing concept allowed him to expand rapidly across the country.

By the mid-1990s there were five hundred microbreweries in America; eighty-four in California alone. Each week three or four new ones opened. As the new industry shook out the weaker strains through the late 1990s, quite a number closed. But the strong continued to prosper. Sierra Nevada was brewing almost a half million barrels annually by 1999; Sam Adams was over a million. In 2000 the two were both among the top ten brewers in the country. Two years later the Institute of Brewing Studies announced that the year before 1,458 American microbreweries (999 of them brewpubs) produced 6.2 million barrels of beer worth $3.4 billion. With its idiosyncratic operations and exuberantly creative beers, microbrewing had gone big time.

CHAPTER THREE

Indiana's Pioneer Brewers
1814–1829

U TOPIAN GERMAN COMMUNARDS in New Harmony were Indiana's first significant brewers. Arriving on the wild Wabash River frontier in 1814 under charismatic Father George Rapp, the eight hundred Swabian Harmonists began erecting a prim, brick town of shady lanes and myriad industries when most Hoosiers were still hunkered down in log cabins. The celibate Harmonists were millennialists, drawn to the Indiana frontier to await the end of the world. Meanwhile, they labored ceaselessly to "make of the wild country fertile fields and gardens of pleasure," as Rapp wrote.

And indeed the Harmonists did. Within a few years, they had planted thousands of acres of barley, wheat, and other grains. Vineyards and orchards lined the hillsides. Lemons and oranges flourished in portable greenhouses. They built 180 sturdy buildings, including two large churches. The Harmonists had the region's only steam engine, six mills, a printing press, and workshops producing shoes, bricks, rope, and textiles, including silk from their own silkworms. They sold their goods to twenty-four states and ten foreign countries. Although the Harmonists drank moderately, they ran a distillery, a winery, a tavern, *and* Indiana's first commercial brewery.

Though beer was an essential part of their diet at their previous home in Harmonie, Pennsylvania, the Harmonists did not initially brew in Indiana. Father Rapp wrote his son, Frederick, in 1815, "We do not have any use for beer, for our men, but whiskey and water will be good enough for a while because we do not have cellars to keep it." But with the brewing supplies they brought and their daunting work ethic, the Harmonists most likely had their brewery in operation by the fall of 1816, or soon after.

The Harmonist brewery was a large frame-and-plank building about forty by sixty feet in size. Frenchman Victor Colin Duclos described the brewery in 1824, "At the northwest intersection of Brewery and North streets was a frame building used for a brewery. In connection with this was a tread wheel built on a platform about twelve feet high. With the wheel a dog or some other small animal was used to furnish power to pump water." Today, the lobby of the New Harmony Inn occupies the site of the Harmonist brewery.

Behind the brewery, there was a frame malt house that was smaller than the brewery, with a well between them. At the east edge of town, a tall, brick *höpfenhaus* housed the Harmonists' hops, which they sometimes sold when there was a surplus. A Shawneetown agent asked, "If any hops could be spared Mr. Oldenberg of this place wishes you to send him two or three pounds." The hops house was moved in 1974 to the corner of Brewery and North streets, where it still stands with its utilitarian Harmonist rectitude.

The Harmonist brewer and cooper, George Bentel, was born November 3, 1781, in Iptingen, the same village in the Swabian kingdom of Württemberg where George Rapp was born. Bentel lived at the northeast corner of Brewery and Grainery streets, where his house remains today, as upright as when Indiana's first brewer marched out to make his beer almost two centuries ago.

According to accounts, the Harmonist brewers made pretty good beer that included wheat beer, a type of porter, and a heavier, dark beer akin to a *dubbel*. In July 1819 an educated German, Ferdinand Ernst, stopped in New Harmony. "They served me a stein

The Harmonists' hops house (*höpfenhaus*) stands at the corner of Brewery and North streets. RICHARD SPAHR

of beer," Ernst wrote, "and I was not a little astonished to find here a genuine, real Bamberg beer." Ernst gushed that the Harmonists "must be the happiest people of entire Christiandom." (When Ernst referred to Bamberg beer, it is unlikely he was referring to Bamberg's famous *rauchbier,* a beechwood-smoked brew so smoky it is known as "a sausage in a glass." He was probably referencing the Franconian city's excellent beer. Bamberg today still has a hundred breweries, the world's most densely breweried region.) With their patterns of numerous beer breaks, the Harmonists needed to brew a lot of beer, the brewers calculating the needs of a tin of beer per day for six hundred to seven hundred people. In late April 1823 Father Rapp wrote, "the brewer has quit making beer. He has more than 600 barrels, so that will be enough for our people until October; also 50-60 barrels are to be sold."

By 1819 the Harmonists were making enough beer to satisfy their internal needs and began selling their surplus in a territory that eventually stretched along the Ohio River from Shawneetown in the Illinois Territory up to Wheeling in what is now West Virginia. A colony of British nobs in the nearby English Settlement around Albion, Illinois, were good customers. Albion

Indiana's First Beer

The rediscovery of Indiana's first beer was serendipitous. Former Historic New Harmony's Collections Manager, Dan Goodman, is a home brewer and an authority on the Harmonists' brewing operations. Goodman mentioned that he'd talked to the curator at the Harmonist historic site at New Economy, Pennsylvania, where Father George Rapp's followers had moved after they sold their Indiana operation to the Owenites. The New Economy curator told him there were original Harmonist beer recipes in the archives.

From that point, it took some investigation. Several phone calls eventually yielded the number of the now-retired curator, Ray Shepherd. He told me about the two brewing volumes the Harmonists most likely brought from Indiana: *Handbuch der praktischen Technologie oder Manufaktur- Fabrik- und Handwerkskunde für Staatswirthe, Maunfakturisten, Fabrikanten und Handwerk* (Handbook for Practical Technology), and *Die Kunst des Bierbrauens, nach richtigen Gründen der Chymie und Oekonomie betrachtet und beschrieben* (The Art of Brewing). The books were carefully preserved in the New Economy archives. No photocopying; very expensive photographic charges.

So I journeyed to the New Economy historical site in Ambridge, Pennsylvania, a declining little Ohio valley industrial town that grew up around the old Harmonist structures. New Economy curator Sarah Buffington brought out the two books, the pages yellowed with age. After she oriented me to the contents (and helped with some of the German translation), I photographed the pages, hoping I could find a German beer historian to help decode the contents.

Keith Lemcke of the Siebel Institute of Technology, the country's foremost brewing school, directed me to Conrad Seidl, an Austrian journalist and authority on beer. Seidl pointed out that brewing books from the period typically gave directions as to how to brew a "standard" beer, and then suggestions as to how to vary the standard to produce specialty beers. Rather than listed recipes as we know them, eighteenth- and nineteenth-century brewing books offered narratives. But that was as much as he could help. He noted he'd recently given a talk to the Bavarian Brewers's and Maltsers's Association in Munich, "encouraging them to do more research about historic brewing recipes—and to try to brew according to them." At least someone else thought tracking down the first Indiana beer recipe was worthwhile.

Lemcke also suggested contacting Horst Dornbusch, a German who had authored a number of books on beer, including *Altbier, History, Brewing Techniques, Recipes.* Dornbusch leapt into the project. The first step was transliterating the old Fraktur script into some sort of modern German script he could read. Dornbusch called on Sabine Weyermann and Thomas Kraus-Weyermann of Bamberg, Germany's Weyermann Malting Company. The Weyermanns arranged for the Fraktur transliteration into a type the Dornbusch could translate. After looking over books and the historic records I had unearthed, Dornbusch decided the "porter" the Harmonists' customers enjoyed was most likely a type of Bavarian Dunkel or Thuringian Schwarzbier—a *rot* (red) or *braun* (brown) beer, as opposed to a *weiss* (white) wheat beer. "German dark beers are very difficult to make because the requirements of color and flavor are contradictory," Dornbusch wrote. "Essentially, unlike in a British porter, you need to get the opaque color from highly kilned grains, but WITHOUT the roasted flavors that normally came from very dark barley or wheat malts. One way to achieve this today is through the malting of de-husked barley." He noted that since the Harmonists' home district of Baden-Württemberg was one of the first German states to adopt the Beer Purity Law from neighboring Bavaria, the brew was probably made the Bavarian way. "This means it was a lager (bottom-fermenting yeast)—unlike the London porter, which is a top-fermented ale," said Dornbusch. He thought Cluster was an appropriate hops choice, as it was a cross between cultivated English hops and a wild American variety that was widely grown across the country. Having cracked the code, Dornbusch then concocted a recipe that approximated an antique Dunkel with modern ingredients. It was a thrilling moment when I opened the e-mail: We had a recipe for Indiana's First Beer!

And then the baton passed to the Harmonists' modern-day successors: Indiana's craft brewers. The Brewers of Indiana Guild (B.I.G.) agreed to brew Indiana's First Beer as its 2010 Replicale project. (Each year, the Hoosier brewers all brew one type of beer—the Replicale.) After tapping the results at Broad Ripple's annual Microbrewers Festival, the brewers offer their versions at their microbreweries across the state. So 185 years after the Harmonists steamboated down the Wabash with their brew kettles and recipes, Hoosiers again have the opportunity to drink some Indiana history.

innkeeper James Jackson ordered twenty barrels for his cellar in 1819: "Beer is the principal thing among the English in this settlement, & a good stock of that is absolutely necessary for me to keep on hand." An influential French trader in Vincennes (more a whiskey and *eau de vivre* town) sent an order: "Michel Brouillett requests that you send him two Barrels of Beer by the first opportunity, which he will pay for on delivery." Down in Louisville, the local Harmonist agent reported, "Mr. Breeden, the most celebrated porter seller in the place says the strongest part of it would almost pass for porter and is the best beer he has ever seen in this country."

The Harmonists' brewing knowledge appears to have come from diverse sources. While their original home in Swabia was more of a wine region, Württemberg, home of scores of later Hoosier brewers and the ancient Maulbronn monastery, certainly had a brewing tradition they could draw upon. The Harmonist library also included a couple of books with brewing information. *Handbuch der praktischen Technologie oder Manufaktur- Fabrik- und Handwerkskunde für Staatswirthe, Maunfakturisten, Fabrikanten und Handwerk* (*Handbook for Practical Technology*) was written by Johann Christian Gotthard and published in Hamburg und Mainz in 1804. Among detailed instructions for vinegar, tobacco, and indigo factories, there was information on establishing and running a brewery. Marked with a handwritten note on the binding that read *vom Bierbrauen,* the dog-eared and notated book discussed beer ingredients, types of beer, and brewing procedures. The second book, *Die Kunst des Bierbrauens, nach richtigen Gründen der Chymie und Oekonomie betrachtet und beschrieben* (*The Art of Brewing*), was written by Johann Christian Simon and published in 1803. Simon's book explained different types of beer from various locales and how to brew them. Various jottings inscribe the volume, including five pages at the back where an early brewer wrote lists of ingredients in an old German script.

As was most likely the case from the earliest days of brewing, the beer business was not without travail. "The last casks I had were not well secured, which occasioned me some loss. Please inform the cooper of this," innkeeper James Jackson complained, later writing he had lost half a load to bad barrels—"the loss of the beer is a very serious injury, as I am not in a situation to supply my customers with that article." A Shawneetown tavern owner worried in the summer of 1824 that he had been sent casks of bad beer: "On examining the Beer there appears to be twenty one Bbls marked with a black cross, & twenty seven not marked but four of which have sustained some injury from fermentation on its first arrival." The Harmonist business manager, Frederick Rapp, dryly replied that the twenty-one barrels were a "Common Kind of Beer" that were worth four dollars a barrel, but "the others are one third Stronger and ought to bring five dollars per Bbl, it was made for our own use and is of excellent quality, it will be well if possible to effect an early sale else it might sour at this Season of the year."

> As was most likely the case from the earliest days of brewing, the beer business was not without travail. "The last casks I had were not well secured, which occasioned me some loss. Please inform the cooper of this," innkeeper James Jackson complained.

And then there was competition. Jackson complained to the Harmonists in 1821 that one of the English Settlement's founders, Morris Birkbeck, was horning in on his inn business, and even started a brewery cobbled together by a carpenter. Though Jackson contended Birkbeck made an inferior beer, the Albion market appeared ready for the novel brew: "Already the satellites of Birkbeck cry up this new brewed beer & vaunt how much superior it is to any that is brewed at Harmonie."

In 1824 Father Rapp decreed the Harmonists needed to move on—for a number of reasons. With their Indiana development work complete, his followers were getting restive. River transport was erratic on the shallow Wabash River. Besides the domestic and environmental problems, the wealthy, insular Harmonists were beset by some pretty tetchy Hoosier neighbors—in spite of the annual Fourth of July party the Harmonists threw for their neighbors with "plenty of beer," as a Michigan paper of the day noted. In a time when whiskey-soaked inebriation was at its zenith in America, the Harmonist tavern was known for its "cleanliness, neatness and good order," according to one English traveler. He contended the tavern keeper, Frederick Eckensburger, while civil to his guests, "effectually prevents excessive drinking." The English Settlement engineer Elias Ryan (who later laid out Indianapolis) reported, "The country people hate the Harmonists very much, because they permit no drunkenness in their tavern." One day in 1820, twelve hard-drinking backwoodsmen rioted in the town, perhaps in resentment against the Harmonists' sober ways. The one person the mob attacked was Eckensburger.

Rapp put New Harmony up for sale, advertising far and wide. Among an impressive list of acreage under cultivation, fifteen hundred bearing fruit trees, two granaries, mills, and dozens of buildings, the inventory included "2 large distilleries, 1 brewery." Far away in Scotland, a wealthy utopian industrialist, Robert Owen, read about the opportunity in Indiana and decided to launch *his* great utopian dream on the banks of the Wabash. For $150,000 Owen bought out the Harmonists' entire operation, including the brewery buildings. But the temperance-minded Owenites most likely did little brewing, as the Harmonists shipped most of their remaining beer, brewing equipment, barrels, and supplies back with them to their new home in Economie, Pennsylvania. Until his death on October 14, 1838, the Harmonist brewer, Bentel, lived in Economie.

The Quaker Brewer

A one-eyed Quaker brewer named Ezra Boswell was accepted into the Society of Friends monthly meeting in the young town of Richmond late in 1817. Boswell had learned his trade in his native Britain, before immigrating first to North Carolina, then transferring to a Quaker meeting in Ohio's Miami Valley. The year following his acceptance into the Richmond Quaker meeting, Boswell opened his brewery in a shop on Front (Fourth) Street, where a steady stream of townspeople and visiting country folk sought out his beer and gingerbread cakes. The local court fixed the price of Boswell's beer at twelve and a half cents a quart "and allowed no extortion," according to an early county history.

Boswell must have made a positive impression amongst the primarily Quaker citizens of the newly incorporated town, as they elected him town clerk in their first town meeting. Later in the year, the citizens voted Boswell onto the board of trustees. The first town ordinances, which prohibited, among other things, profanity after the age of fourteen, horse galloping, the discharge of "any gun, pistol, fuzee or any other kind of fire-arms," also banned the drinking of "ardent spirits to excess." So there was some scandal a few years later when straight-laced locals contended that the councilmen were drinking Boswell's beer at the town's expense, subjecting the solons "to the tongue of slander," as a nineteenth-century town history recounted. After serving as a town father while also fathering eleven children, Boswell died in 1831.

Steamboat Brewing

In 1823 Virginia flatboatman Jacob Salmon decided to trade the floating world for a brewer's life in the bustling entrepôt of Madison, Indiana. When Salmon started his brewery, Madison was Indiana's largest city. Founded in 1810 in a bend of the Ohio River where it curls farthest to the north, the town sat astride the great conduit of trade pouring down the valley on the recently developed steamboats. Madison soon became one of the hot spots of the trans-Appalachian West—a trendy destination for second sons of wealthy Easterners, who built an extraordinary array of classical Greek Revival- and Federal-style homes and commercial buildings, many of which are still standing. Along with the tony Easterners, polyglot hordes of homesteaders looking for cheap land passed through the town. The Treaty of Saint Marys in 1818 had opened the lands to the north to settlers, who used Madison as their place for provender and trade, helping the town blossom as a frontier industrial center. All that work made for a thirsty crowd.

Salmon built his brewery at the east edge of Madison, at what is now Second Street, where a spring of pure water burbled to the surface of the hill. Conveying the water down to his brewery with a wooden trough set on posts, Salmon constructed at the base of the hill a hefty thirty-foot by sixty-foot stone structure with walls thirty inches thick. Extending into the bluff, the building served both as his family home and storage vault. Beside it, he erected a rough-hewn, two-story, log-and-plank brewery. The upper floor was used for grain storage, while the lower one housed the malting floor, mash tubs, and cooling floor. About five years after Salmon began brewing, the state began construction on the Michigan Road (State Road 421 today), a massive public works project that connected the Ohio River at Madison with the Great Lakes at Michigan City. It became a favored route for settlers into the interior and helped bring new customers to the brewery. Salmon operated his brewery until about 1841. At some point the brewery took on his name to become known as Old Salmon Brewery.

> Brewers were also an idiosyncratic lot. Creative, innovative, determined to contribute—in many ways, Indiana's pioneer brewers set the standard for those who followed.

The Beginnings

From the start, Hoosier brewers had to deal with the Indiana government's complicated, often contradictory, attitudes toward alcohol. While Indiana's leaders coveted the tax revenues that alcohol generated, they were often chary of liquor's pernicious effects. The very first regulation passed by the Territorial Legislative Council and House of Representatives, which Territorial Governor William Henry Harrison signed in the capital of Vincennes on August 24, 1805, regulated taverns. The law also raised funds for the state through the sale of permits for "any sum not exceeding twelve dollars," a dollar of the fee going to the county clerk issuing the license. But just a few months later, Harrison harangued the legislators to better control taverns: "The design of those houses of entertainment countenanced by law can, I should suppose, be no other than that affording rest and refreshment to the weary traveler. This does not however appear to be the object of the majority of those who now have availed themselves of the facility of procuring licenses. Their houses are in fact the nurseries of vice and are daily exhibiting scenes which must shock every friend of his species."

While most of the trouble in the rip-roaring territorial capital related to whiskey and other spirits, beer began showing up in Vincennes taverns and inns as early as 1814. A lawsuit filed in Vincennes over one Peter Jones's unpaid room and board noted a "bottle beer" among Jones's lengthy bar tab that included brandy, bounce, sling, toddy, cider, eggnog, whiskey-and-bitter, and punch. (Beer bottles in those days were often corked whiskey bottles.) In 1820 another innkeeper, Christian Graeter, sued James Johnston in Vincennes for an unpaid inn bill of $114.12 $\frac{1}{2}$, which also included a tab for brewed beer.

But whether dealing with government intervention, poor transportation and shortages of equipment, supplies, and even hard money, Indiana's first brewers persevered. Out in the far western hinterlands of the United States, they reflected the rich diversity of the young state: Harmonists, Quakers, frontiersmen, and settlers in complex religious and secular societies, all striving to succeed in Indiana's nascent economy. Seeking to maintain a connection to their pasts, they reached back to their traditions for their beers—ales and old-style *alts,* mainly. But the brewers were also an idiosyncratic lot. Creative, innovative, determined to contribute—in many ways, Indiana's pioneer brewers set the standard for those who followed.

CHAPTER FOUR

The German Brewers of Indiana
1830–1918

"**B**REWERS HAVE A GOOD BUSINESS," Johann Wolfgang Schreyer wrote his Bavarian family in 1843 from his home near Plymouth, Indiana. "The products, barley, hops, and wood are cheap and there are almost no expenses. The beer brings a good price, six cents a quart, but there's not enough demand for it. The people here are not accustomed to beer drinking, often at a distance of from twenty to thirty miles. Distilleries are more profitable than breweries, for whiskey is a common drink; it is made of corn and rye. In summer during the harvest time a wagon loaded with whiskey and water is constantly taken to the field to supply the harvesters with something to drink."

Schreyer was part of a great nineteenth-century German immigration that dramatically changed American drinking habits. The vast exodus began in 1817 when rebellious students fled the wrath of royal authorities. In the wake of the economically devastating Napoleonic wars, hundreds of thousands of conservative German farmers and tradesmen left the Fatherland in hopes of reestablishing their traditional lives in America. The flood reached a new level after the Revolutions of 1848, when authorities crushed left-wing rebellions that erupted across Europe, prompting thousands of intellectuals and progressives to immigrate to America, particularly to the burgeoning cities of the Midwest. In the 1840s, 27 percent of total immigration to the United States was German, surging to 34.7 percent in the 1850s and 34.8 percent in the 1860s, the decade when more than 700,000 Germans arrived in America. After the Civil War immigration leapt to new levels, with 751,769 Germans entering the United States in the 1870s, followed by 1,445,181 in the 1880s. Many of the German immigrants were "leaving old world oppression to seek new homes in the wilds of America," as South Bend resident Otto Knoblock wrote, forced to immigrate because of onerous laws and reduced economic possibilities.

From Baden, Bavaria, and Bremen; Alsace, Hesse, and Holstein; Oldenburg, Pomerania, and Prussia; and Westphalia, Wittenberg, and Saxony, large numbers of Germans began immigrating into Indiana early in the 1830s, many floating down the Ohio River to the German redoubt of Cincinnati, before moving on to their Indiana home. Some immigrants clustered into informal agricultural colonies, such as the strong German areas in Dubois, Spencer, and Franklin counties, where towns such as Jasper, Huntingburg, Saint Meinrad, and Oldenburg still retain a Teutonic air. One historian counted seventeen such German communities in southern Indiana alone. Others settled in Indiana's growing cities, including Indianapolis, Evansville, Terre Haute, Lafayette, South Bend, and New Albany. For example, in 1880 immigrant Germans constituted half of the foreign born population in Indianapolis's Marion County. At one point in the nineteenth century more than 80 percent of the population of Fort Wayne was German born. By 1910, when Fort Wayne's population was more than eighty thousand, two-thirds of the citizenry were still German. The vast immigration lived on in Indiana. In 1990 more than two million Hoosiers claimed German heritage, the largest ethnic group in the state.

The Germans had a distinct impact on Indiana. In the agricultural areas and small towns, the German farmers and tradesmen utilized their thriftiness, work ethic, and ethnic cohesion to build sturdy institutions that buttressed their conservative ways. Hoosier cities, particularly following the arrival of post-1848 German progressives, blossomed with Teutonic cultural institutions, including choirs, orchestras, gymnasiums, and friendship societies.

But whether city or countryside, the German *auswanderer* brewers took over the state's beer industry. Even before the Civil War, Indiana Germans operated dozens of breweries—sixty-one by 1860. Even as late as 1880, German-born brewers and maltsters constituted more than half of Indianapolis's total number, with American-born Germans constituting the vast majority of the balance. Until Prohibition in 1918, brewing in Indiana remained a German business. One historian estimated that 90 percent of the Indiana brewers were German.

> **Until Prohibition in 1918, brewing in Indiana remained a German business. One historian estimated that 90 percent of the Indiana brewers were German.**

Eastern Indiana

Germans began arriving in the Quaker town of Richmond in 1827, seeking work on the National Road. Primarily from the kingdom of Hannover, the Germans stopped in Cincinnati before traveling to Indiana via the Whitewater Valley, the state's first developed corridor. They shared with the Quakers an adamantine work ethic, plain living, and progressive views on abolitionism and pacifism. The German preference for beer over hard liquor also sat well with their neighbors.

Twenty-five-year-old Christian Buhl came to Richmond from Germany in 1830, when he established a tavern. His imposing three-story, Federal-style brick structure sat on the south side of Richmond's Main Street, between First and Second streets near the National Bridge. In the fall of 1832 Buhl ran an ad in a Richmond paper urging farmers to plant barley for a brewery he planned to start the following year. Buhl installed his brewery's large tanks and vats in the tavern's commodious cellar. Local German families and road workers were Buhl's best beer customers, and housekeepers sent their children with small tin buckets and "a large copper cent" to buy the yeast he skimmed from the bubbling vats. It was all good money, which Buhl invested in a fertile farm near town.

Draymen and settlers heading west often stopped at Buhl's tavern for a libation. One Richmond lady remembered a road-weary settler leaning against the brewery wall with a pipe in his mouth. When a passerby asked what he thought of this western country, he called back, "It's Heaven for men and dogs, but Hell for women and horses."

Buhl died of apoplexy in 1861 at his comfortable farm, where he had retired years before. His brewery drifted through other hands until 1873, when Emil Minck and Anton Bescher of Columbus, Ohio, bought it from under the sheriff's hammer for four thousand dollars. By 1885 Minck's Brewery was booming: "A good-sized engine has been put in, and everything so enlarged that they will hereafter be fully able to supply the demand," a Richmond paper reported. In the following years the Richmond Brewery, as it was then known, advertised, "Pure, unadulterated beer by the keg or bottle," touting that "Physicians pronounce it the PUREST, and prescribe it for MEDICAL PURPOSES." There must have been a lot of healthy people in Richmond: the *Evening Item* noted in 1895 that "Richmond is quite a beer drinking city, and there is more of the amber colored fluid guzzled yearly than one would naturally suppose." The article calculated that the 5,030 beer drinkers in the town (one in four people) consumed 1.32 million quarts of beer the year before, or 264 quarts per drinker.

Perhaps enticed by the statistics, a group of businessmen purchased the brewery in 1897 with a $100,000 stock offering. By 1903 the company reorganized under new management with a $175,000 capitalization. One Minck ad trumpeted the arrival of "Famous Bock Beer" that was aged for nine months. Another touted, "For nursing mothers and for women who have household duties to perform, there is nothing that will nourish both nerve and muscle and give you backbone and energy like Richmond Export Beer." A newspaper article praised Minck's pure lager beer, stating, "The city of Richmond possesses its full share of the many good things of life and not the least of them is The Minck Brewing Company."

In Fort Wayne, two Frenchmen, Comparet and Coquilard, had the Fort Wayne Brewery going by 1834, when the *Fort Wayne Sentinal* advertised, "Good, strong beer for sale at the Fort Wayne Brewery, by the barrel or gallon, *cheap.*" The brewers also expressed their willingness to buy wild-gathered hops. Comparet was part of the early French families who settled the old fur-trading post of Fort Wayne in the eighteenth century. The French brewery, the town's first, was destined to be the father of a long Gallic brewing tradition in Fort Wayne, counterintuitive for a town that later became so influenced by Germans.

When Carl Phenning founded his brewery in 1853, there were already a number of tiny breweries operating in the city. Two years later an immigrant from Munster, Germany, Herman Nierman, opened what became known as the Ale and Lager Beer Brewery. The following year Francis J. Beck built his brewery, which provides an interesting footnote to Indiana brewing: son Heinrich Beck practiced his craft for ten years in Fort Wayne before starting what became the international German brewing corporation, Beck's, in Bremen, Germany.

In 1862 Alsatian Charles Centlivre established his French Brewery on the west bank of the Saint Joseph River beside a feeder canal, where ice could be cut and canal boats tied up to deliver grain and take on beery cargo. From a wealthy cooper family in Valdieau, Alsace, Centlivre had already established his first French Brewery in a cavern in northeastern Iowa, where he learned under a second-generation German *braumeister*, Christian Magnus. Centlivre initially brewed ales that appealed to Fort Wayne's French, English, and Scottish drinkers. The city's other six brewers focused on the Germans in town, though Centlivre soon learned to serve the Teutonic market. By 1871 the *Fort*

Wayne Daily Sentinal reported the city had twelve lager breweries, including Centlivre's: "All are doing a thriving business."

Located near today's Spy Run Avenue and State Street, Centlivre brewed five hundred barrels its first year for the city's ten thousand people. Quantities soared to twenty thousand barrels by 1880. Under Chicago *braumeister* Peter Nussbaum, who was to direct brewing operations for thirty-seven years, Centlivre eventually brewed more than a hundred thousand barrels a year. As the decades passed, the company utilized Canadian malt, imported hops, and "rock water" from the brewery's deep wells to brew fine lagers that included Kaiser, Kulmbacher, and Bohemian.

The original Centlivre building burned on July 16, 1889. The firemen almost had it under control when an ammonia tank blew, sending flares and debris a hundred feet into the air. Five thousand people thronged the streets to watch the spectacle. It was a total loss. The following December 28, the rebuilt brewery reopened. Like many of the period's brewers, Centlivre set up a

Centlivre Brewery. COURTESY OF SCOTT BUSHNELL

shady *biergarten*, though his was replete with a horse track and boat rides. Known as the Gentlemanly Brewer, Centlivre did not tolerate excess. His Fort Wayne descendant, Pat Centlivre Bonahoom, recounted Centlivre's technique for handling drunks in his rathskeller: "He'd take a fiery poker from the fireplace and stick it in the man's stein—'Out!' was all he'd say."

In 1895, the year after founder Centlivre died, the brewery was renamed the C. L. Centlivre Brewery. In May 1905 a band of seven pistol-wielding robbers crept into the plant about one in the morning. After subduing the night watchmen, the bandits blew the Centlivre safe, escaping into the night with the firm's cash as the watchmen wiggled out of their bonds.

As the city's German population grew, so did the number of brewers. Through the 1870s, breweries run by L. J. Horning (sometimes spelled Hornung), Henry Hurbach (Hubach), Fred Kley, and J. M. Reidmiller dotted the neighborhoods, along with the Certia and Rankert firm (later to be Lutz and Company), and Linker, Hey and Company. Some of them, such as Riedmiller, folded up their operations as Centlivre expanded, joining his firm.

In the early 1880s Prussian brothers Herman and Henry Berghoff from Dortmunder, Westphalia, were on a train passing through Fort Wayne. When Henry stepped off to buy a pretzel, the cook offered him a job. Berghoff grabbed his brother from the train, and a Fort Wayne dynasty began. By 1882 two other Berghoff brothers, Hubert and Gustav, arrived. After purchasing the East End Bottling Works, the brothers opened the Berghoff Brewing Company in June 1888. But before they made their first beer, the brewery burned down. Family lore states that even as the fire raged, Herman stayed at the helm in his office writing telegrams to equipment companies asking for help with repairs. As the firemen were hosing down the last embers, skilled craftsmen were rushing from Chicago, Cincinnati, New York, and Milwaukee. The Berghoffs promised the city they would be brewing within a month, and exactly four weeks later production resumed. The Berghoffs' rebuilt brewery was a stolid brick four-story structure that resonated Prussian restraint. Inside, the brothers brewed lager with German hops, malt, and filtered water from two-hundred-feet deep wells.

Success came quickly. By 1890 the Berghoffs added a 50-by 170-foot addition to the plant to house a new beer vault and ice machine. Under Dortmund *braumeister* William Breuer, the Berghoffs produced a deep-golden Dortmunder-style lager, a mid-nineteenth-century style that was fuller than pilsners and dryer than Munich's *helles*. Berghoff also brewed a strong Salvator for the springtime. Berghoff beer was a big seller at the Chicago World's Fair in 1892, prompting one of the Berghoffs to open the famous and long-lived Berghoff Restaurant in Chicago's Loop in 1898. In its heyday, the Berghoff Brewing Company brewed ninety thousand barrels a year.

In 1910 the (renamed) Berghoff Brewing Association and Fort Wayne German cultural societies established Germania Park. It was a canny defensive move by the German community to dodge the onerous Proctor Laws that the Indiana legislature had passed earlier in the year. Temperance advocates had long assailed the German communities' Sunday *biergarten* traditions as an insult to the Sabbath and had finally exerted enough pressure on the legislature to pass the measure. Written to curtail consumption, especially on Sunday when the Indiana Germans gathered for their socializing, the Proctor Laws prohibited breweries from selling directly to the public in their own saloons or *biergartens*. Responding to the new law, the two Fort Wayne *gesangverieines* (singing societies), the *Turnverein Vorwarts* (gymnasium society), and *Plattdeutcher verein* (low-German society) banded together with the Berghoff brewery to build a stronghold for German culture: a now-legal *biergarten* with the requisite oom-pah-pah band.

As the century moved on, the Prohibitionists continued to fan anti-German sentiments—particularly after World War I erupted in Europe. When the United States finally entered the war, breweries had to bow to the prevailing winds—the Berghoff brewery changed its slogan from "A Real German Brew" to a "Real Honest Brew."

Southern Indiana

In prosperous Madison, Phillip Scheik began a brewery on Jefferson Street near Fourth Street in 1841, about the time pioneer Jacob Salmon stopped brewing. Scheik's brewery produced beer until the 1890s under the names of Ross Brewery and Belser and Company, before eventually becoming a canning factory. In 1852 Mattias Greiner started his brewery on the site of Salmon's brewery at Second and Park streets, where a stream of excellent water tumbled out of a bluff. Brewing ale and common beer, Greiner's brewery was renamed the Madison Brewing Company in 1882. Its handsome brick plant with its twin belfries, fuming smokestack, and snapping American flag produced the coveted Madison XXX ale that was shipped as far away as New Orleans, as well as Old Madison, which falsely advertised it was brewed by "The First Brewery West of the Alleghenies." The Madison brewery also brewed a porter, lagers, and, near the end of the company's life, the Bon Ton, advertised as an "old-fashioned" beer. The *Madison Courier* reported in early 1918 when state prohibition was looming, "While the brewing company, which is one of Madison's oldest industries, at one time did a prosperous business, the brewing business in general has lately become so demoralized by reason of adverse legislation and the high cost of materials of all kinds as to make the business unprofitable." The company was conveyed to trustees soon after.

The Civil War was still raging when Alsatian entrepreneur Peter Weber formed the Union Brewery at Main and Vine streets in Madison. Before immigrating to America in 1850, Weber had learned the brewing trade in France. He first worked at the Scheik Brewery for three years, then in Cincinnati and Vernon, Indiana, before returning to Madison. By 1864 he had his brewery in operation, which grew over the next few decades into a grand, six-story (three of them underground) factory that was pilastered and embellished to full Victorian glory. A narrow-gauge railroad ran through the plant. The deep cellars were chilled with three thousand to four thousand tons of ice annually, which kept Weber's lagered beer in fine shape for the summer season.

Cook and Rice City Brewery. COURTESY OF THE UNIVERSITY OF SOUTHERN INDIANA

In 1882 Weber transformed one of Madison's four pre-Civil War breweries, George Appel's on lower Third Street, into the Union Brewery's malt house. Weber died of apoplexy in 1891, though his concern continued on until approximately 1910.

Down in Evansville, Fred Kroener and Jacob Rice (also spelled Reis) began their Old Brewery in 1837 in the German neighborhood of Babytown, so named because every time a particular traveling salesman came through, there was a new baby. With its canal- and river-trade connections, Evansville was booming. One historian counted seventeen Pocket City breweries operating in the mid-nineteenth century—mostly tavern-sized places in the northside Lamasco and westside Independence neighborhoods, where the working-class Germans congregated. The Old Brewery was located at the northwest corner of Fulton Avenue and Indiana Street in Lamasco, near the terminus of the Wabash and Erie Canal.

In 1853 Rice's stepson, Frederick Cook, and Rice's brother, Louis, founded the City Brewery in a cornfield at the edge of town on Seventh Street between Main and Sycamore streets. Born in Washington, D.C., in 1832 to Christiana Kroener Cook, F. W. Cook moved to Evansville when he was four, just as the city was entering its heyday. Though scarcely educated by his eighteen months of formal schooling, ambitious Cook found Evansville to be the right place. It was the era when Evansville touted itself as "the city of Northern Vitality, Southern Hospitality and German Frugality." With his brewery prospering, citizens elected Cook to the city council in 1856, then sent him to the state legislature in 1864.

In 1857 Louis Rice sold his interest in the City Brewery to his brother, Jacob. The following year the City Brewery built a large malt house and began producing lager, arguably the first lager in Indiana. Upon Jacob Rice's death in 1872, Cook ran the now-sprawling plant by himself, renaming it the F. W. Cook Brewery in 1885. Within five years, 110 Cook workers were producing 75,000 barrels a year, consuming 175,000 bushels of malt and 115,000 pounds of hops. The *Evansville Courier* bragged, "Purity, brilliancy and deliciousness of the flavor, together with its sparkling, foaming qualities, is what has made the Pilsner of the F. W. Cook Brewing Company so popular wherever it has been introduced."

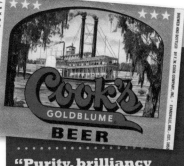

A fire in 1891 necessitated the construction of a new plant, which was erected in fifteen months. The result was a massive brick plant anchored with a belching smokestack and a soaring beflagged cupola. Waves of Romanesque-arched windows rippled down the side of the factory. When the electric era arrived, a huge rooftop sign with a flickering American flag championed Cook's famous Goldblume beer. Inside the new plant, Cook's German *braumeisters*

"Purity, brilliancy and deliciousness of the flavor, together with its sparkling, foaming qualities, is what has made the Pilsner of the F. W. Cook Brewing Company so popular wherever it has been introduced."

The Fulton Avenue Brewery. COURTESY OF THE UNIVERSITY OF SOUTHERN INDIANA

coddled his great polished kettles, frost-encrusted pipes, and powerful churning engines that could produce three hundred thousand barrels of beer a year. Each day, muscular dray horses tugged the beer wagons out to the local areas, while entire trains of bottled and kegged Cook beers headed south. "The tawny beverage made in Evansville quenched the thirst of millions from the Mason and Dixon line to the Gulf of Mexico," the *Evansville Courier* crowed.

Clear-eyed and bewhiskered in his Edwardian frock coat, Cook became one of Evansville's wealthiest men. Beyond his brewing company, Cook was also president of the Evansville, Newburgh and Suburban Railway and the telegraph company, along with managing his extensive real estate holdings that included Cook's Park, a sixteen-acre *biergarten* and retreat at Maryland Street and Pigeon Creek that was decreed to be "one of the finest resorts in the country." When Cook died in 1913 at the age of eighty-one, his son, Henry, took over as brewery president.

The Evansville Brewing Association was the result of the 1894 consolidation of the Fulton Avenue Brewery, the Evansville Brewery, and the Hartmetz Brewery. The Fulton Avenue Brewery began in 1877, when Wilhelm Ulmer of Russia and Ferdinand Hoedt of Baden joined together. They soon had the capacity to

Hartmetz Brewery. COURTESY OF THE UNIVERSITY OF SOUTHERN INDIANA

brew eighteen thousand barrels a year. Their "export" beer was considered particularly fine, possessing reputed "health-giving and preserving" properties: "there is scarcely a family, no matter how temperate, that has not at some time experienced its pleasant and beneficial effects."

The Hartmetz Brewery occurred because John Hartmetz lost a coin toss with his brewer brother in Louisville over who had to relocate to Evansville. In 1877 Hartmetz bought Henry Schnieder's old brewery, which dated back to 1863. Though located in Babytown, Schnieder's sales were flat, and the business had passed through a number of hands and under the sheriff's hammer in 1869 and 1876. After about fifteen years of modest success, Hartmetz moved back to Europe, leaving the brewery to his son, Charles.

Soon after, the turmoil of an 1894 price war with Cook allowed Hartmetz to convince two other smaller brewers to band together. The Fulton Avenue Brewery became the main production plant, and the others closed. In its early twentieth-century prime, the Evansville Brewing Association's most popular brands were Rheingold and Columbia, though the brewery was to have another long, embellished chapter that lasted well into the twentieth century.

The Union Brewery, located at Sycamore Street and the canal, had a short run before the Civil War. When the German brewers who ran the place gave it up, the place became a crash pad for lowlifes. The city fathers arranged for the local medical society to take over the large brick building, where the good doctors and their students dissected cadavers. One local history gossiped, "While no one ever charged that graves were robbed to furnish specimens for the numerous young students that flocked there, yet it is a fact that the crop of 'stiffs,' as they termed them, was always exceedingly large." Being a little lax with housekeeping, the students tossed the bones in the basement. When the Civil War hit, the building became a hospice for refugees from the South. When some of the guests went to the cellar for firewood, they

The Indiana-Cincinnati Brewing Connection

There is a strong brewing connection between Indiana and Cincinnati, the longtime bastion of midwestern Germania. Quite a number of early Hoosier brewers practiced their trade in Cincinnati before moving on to their destinies in Indiana. Among them are Madison's Peter Weber, New Albany's Paul Reising and Hew Ainslie, Terre Haute's Anton Mayer, Wabash's F. A. Rettig, and Indianapolis's August Hook. While George A. Bohrer's experience in Cincinnati was with shoes, horses, groceries, hotel guests, and corpses, undoubtedly sampling all that great Cincinnati beer while working must have prepared him for his Lafayette brewing career. Many Hoosier brewers attended the thirtieth annual American Homebrewers Association conference, held in Cincinnati in June 2008, reforging the brewing link between Indiana and the Queen City.

MIKE SCHWAB

encountered the bones, precipitating a flight that was likened to "worse than a stampede or a herd of Texas cattle."

In New Albany, an iconoclastic young Scotsman, Hew Ainslie, bucked the German trend when he opened New Albany's first brewery in 1840. An imposing six feet, four inches tall, with a craggy face and heavy brogue, Ainslie was already a published author and poet when he moved his family to Robert Owen's utopian experiment in New Harmony. Father George Rapp's Harmonists had left little more than the brewery buildings standing when they left for Pennsylvania, as they steamboated all of their brewing equipment and supplies to their new home. While the Harmonists' brewery buildings might have intrigued Ainslie, he spent his time in New Harmony as a community teacher. When Owen's utopian fantasy collapsed in acrimony a year later, Ainslie and his family moved to Cincinnati, where he started a brewery. By 1828 Ainslie had relocated to the Falls of the Ohio, operating breweries in the Louisville area. When Ainslie opened his New Albany brewery with Englishman John Bottomly, under the name of Bottomly and Ainslie, at Fourth and Spring streets, they made ale, porter, and stout. Ainslie was said to have been a conscientious brewer, who never lost the poesy of his time in Scotland and on the Wabash River.

The Bottomly and Ainslie plant burned down after some years. John Yager operated a rebuilt 20-foot by 60-foot brewery at the same site from 1856 to 1857. Bath and Rickle took control in 1859 and D. Bath in 1860. A year later, brewer Paul Reising of the City Brewery took over the Spring Street plant in order to expand. At the time Reising bought the facility, it had a capacity of fifteen hundred barrels of common beer a year. Many of the early Indiana Falls Cities brewers also had operations in Louisville. They included Ainslie, Reising, Julius Gebhard, J. H. Pank, Frank Senn, and John Kirchgessner. Within seven years, Reising had expanded his brewery to a 115-foot-by-50-foot, two-story size, with an icehouse, malt cellar, and four large cellars. His five German employees produced thirty barrels of beer a day, about three thousand to four thousand barrels a year. By 1891 Reising was producing twelve thousand barrels annually. An 1890 photo of the Reising employees shows a group of walrus-mustached men sitting on barrels hoisting glass mugs of dark beer. A sampling of names belie their origins: Alt, Huber, Nirmaier, Kleer, Botts, Orst, and Bertricht.

Through a consolidation after Reising's death in 1897, the Paul Reising Brewing Company incorporated the assets of the Indiana Brewery, then known as the Pank-Weinmann Brewery. Advertising their brew "Strengthens the Weak, Relieves the Dyspeptic, Soothes the Nerves and Cheers the Depressed," as well as providing "A Boon for Mothers," the company sold their Kaiserpale and dark Culmbacher beers in Louisville and a wedge of southern Indiana counties that were east and west along the Ohio River, and north into Orange, Washington, Lawrence, and Dubois counties.

In 1914 the company suffered a disaster: the brewers produced a large amount of bad beer, which they distributed. The backlash was immediate. Soon the company was filing for bankruptcy, "owing to the general dullness of business, and the enormous loss suffered on account of the bad beer distributed," according to the *New Albany Daily Ledger*. Reorganized under brewmaster Michael Schrick in 1915, the company was renamed the Southern Indiana Brewing Company.

Reising's City Brewery location was taken over by Martin Kaeling of Einseidlen, Switzerland, who brewed about three thousand barrels a year until 1872. Ten years later, one of Reising's former brewmasters, Louis Schmidt, opened the Main Street Brewery at Eighteenth and Main streets. Jacob Hornung and George Washington Atkins absorbed the operation the following year to brew and bottle lager, doing business under the names of the Jacob Hornung Brewery and the Indiana Brewery. By 1900 the Indiana Brewery had grown to a five-story complex, where the brewers produced twenty-five thousand barrels a year. The brewmaster was Moritz Eck, who had "learned his trade in the large brewing establishments of Germany," according to a local history. Other early New Albany breweries included the Market Street

Beer and Ice

COURTESY OF VINCENNES UNIVERSITY

When John Ebner opened his Eagle Brewery in 1859, he also started an ice plant, cutting the ice from the Wabash River when it froze. Brewers knew the vital importance of ice, particularly for the lagers that came to predominately quench Hoosiers' beer thirst. Up to the 1860s, when Australian James Harrison offered his revolutionary ice-making machine at the International Exposition in London, there was no other way to brew lager year-round than to harvest ice from mountains, rivers, lakes, and ponds.

In the pre-refrigeration days, ice harvesting was a gargantuan industry with highly evolved tools and techniques to score, cut, store, and transport ice until needed. Across most of the cold-climate states, immense icehouses stood beside lakes and streams, ready to receive the frozen largesse of winter.

The brewing industry was among the first to recognize the advantages of mechanical refrigeration. Utilizing the basic physics of evaporation and expansion of gases, inventors began to use plain air volatile gases such as ether and ammonia to make ice. Ice wars ensued, pitting refrigeration men and ice harvesters against one another. The ice harvesters claimed that "artificial" ice was softer and brittle, indeed was unnatural and close to diabolical. (Some of the early ice machines did indeed have a propensity to leak gas, and occasionally explode.) Conversely, the mechanical-ice men pointed out that the rivers and lakes the ice harvesters counted on were increasingly polluted and subject to the vagaries of weather, such as the mild winter of 1890–91 that caused a traumatic "ice famine."

The future was crystalline clear. Mechanical ice-making took off in the latter part of the nineteenth century. In 1889 there were only two hundred mechanical ice plants in the country; two decades later, there were two thousand. In 1890 Ebner's old brewery, Hack and Simon, installed a refrigeration machine. Though the Ebner Ice Company cooled Vincennes into the 1950s, home refrigerators and freezers finally did them in. Today, Ebner's giant, windowless brick icehouse stands beside the Wabash River on the Vincennes University campus, where it serves as an office building.

Brewery, the State Street Brewery, and the Spring Brewery, which also brewed under the name of Engle and Nadorff Brothers.

In Jeffersonville, Louisville brewer Franz Rettig opened a brewery in the 1860s. Henry Lang began the City Brewery in 1875, and five years later John Kirchgessner and a partner bought it to produce ale, porter, lager, and cream beer, a popular pale brew that took little cellaring time. Before closing in 1899, the brewery added a Pilsner export beer to its production of about ten thousand barrels per year.

COURTESY OF THE VINCENNES UNIVERSITY

Vincennes saw its first brewery in 1836, when William Ehrle announced in the *Vincennes Sun,* "VINCENNES BREWERY. The subscriber informs the citizens of Vincennes and its vicinity, that he has now got his Brewery in complete operation. Grocery and tavern keepers are particularly desired to call on him." Ehrle noted customers could purchase at either the brewery or a confectionary shop on Market Street. Jacob Kautz advertised another Vincennes brewery in 1858 offering, "An extensive supply of Ale and Beer constantly on hand."

In 1859 Alsatian John Ebner Sr. founded the Eagle Brewery (also called the Harrison Brewery) in Vincennes near the Wabash River. A veteran of the French army, Ebner had served five years in African campaigns before heading off to America, where he spent two years steamboating on the Ohio. When he first opened the brewery, Ebner, who had been trained as a miller and baker, operated the plant. But Ebner soon leased the plant to others, "who made but an indifferent success of the business," according to the early-twentieth-century history of American beer, *One Hundred Years of Brewing*. By 1866 Ebner was advertising his brewery for sale in Cincinnati, Chicago, Saint Louis, and Pittsburgh: "Description—Brick building 119 feet long and 56 feet wide; good cellars underneath—1 for Lager Beer, 2 for Gerring [*sic*], 1 for Schrank Beer, 1 for Common Beer, and 1 large malt cellar. Over the Lager Beer Cellar there is a good BEER SALOON." The property included a residence with extensive fruit trees and gardens, including room for a beer garden. In the meantime, Christopher Frist started the Vincennes Beer Garden just north of the city between the Wabash River and Second Street, a shady twenty-four-acre park where families could enjoy strawberries, ice cream, cake, lemonade, and cigars, as well as beer, of course. "Everything will be kept in perfect order, and no card-playing will be allowed on the grounds," Frist promised, along with barring "strong drinks" on Sunday.

> **In 1875 Ebner finally rented his brewery to Eugene Hack from Württemberg and Alsatian Anton Simon, who quickly put the business on solid footing.**

Ebner soldiered on as he tried to sell his brewery. An 1871 *Vincennes Weekly Western Sun* article noted the lunch offering at Ebner's Beer Hall on Second Street: "Two glasses cool, fresh Beer for five cents. None but the best liquids kept and everything done up in splendid style."

In 1875 Ebner finally rented his brewery to Eugene Hack from Württemberg and Alsatian Anton Simon, who quickly put the business on solid footing. The two partners bought into the property two years later, with Ebner staying on as a junior partner. The men commenced on a total refit that eventually included new refrigeration units, a boiler house, cellars, and stock houses constructed over two city blocks at the north end of town. Constructed of brick and trimmed in stone, the brewery was considered one of the most attractive in the state. Under the direction of brewmaster George Mueller, an Austro-Hungarian native, Hack and Simon brewed twenty thousand to twenty-five thousand barrels a year, including porter, lager, and a brew they called "alf and alf," evidently a conjunction of "half and half" porter and lager. The firm's bottled beers included Export, Erlanger, and Elite (pronounced "Eeee-lite"—this is southern Indiana, after all) that were sold primarily in southern Indiana and Illinois, with some shipments to Indianapolis. "The beer that boomed Vincennes," one ad bragged.

It appears that Hack and Simon garnered an impassioned allegiance. During an 1885–86 beer war with Aurora plutocrat Thomas Gaff's upstart Crescent Brewing Company, the *Vincennes Commercial* published a ten-stanza poem from a Hack and Simon supporter from Washington, Indiana, Mrs. Henry B. Jones:

> There are drinks of various colors,
> And also various make,
> But Hack & Simon's beer, my friends,
> Is the drink that takes the cake.

Testifying that imbibers never get drunk on Hack and Simon beer, though "You may drink, and drink, and drink," Jones further offered a distaff endorsement:

> The ladies, too, just love this beer,
> And tho' they look so nice
> If they can get it on the sly
> They will drink it in a trice.

The rural German areas of southern Indiana also saw their share of brewers, though most were relatively small. There were a number in southwestern Indiana's Dubois and Perry counties. E. A. Hockgesang started a Jasper brewery just after the Civil War.

When he passed away, his widow, Cecilia, took over in 1875. She brewed until 1884, when her brother, Anton Habig, and Martin Eckstein took it over. Habig bought out his partner in 1899, when the brewery became Habig Brewery, later known as the Excelsior Brewing Company. The firm, which lasted until close to Prohibition, brewed about fifteen hundred barrels a year in a rustic frame structure located in what is now the Jasper Memorial Park.

In nearby Huntingburg, Joseph Schubler and J. F. Strickfaden each brewed for a year in the mid-1870s. In 1894 Huntingburg's Moenkhaus, Fritch and Company began brewing. The firm lasted until 1918 under the names of Moenkhaus and Seubold and the Huntingburg Brewing Company. Tiny Teutonic Ferdinand had four brewers, beginning in 1875 with Henry B. Ruhkamp, who brewed until his death in 1884, when his widow, Elizabeth, took over the vats, continuing the brewery until 1891. The Stallman and Haug brewery began in 1888. The brewery operated under a number of names, concluding in 1916 under the name of the Ferdinand Brewing Company.

Tell City, the small Swiss-German town on the Ohio River, had two breweries. The Tell City Brewing Company had its start in 1858, when Charles Becker and Alois Beuter began brewing. Beuter left the next year and Becker continued, building a three-story brick brewery on Ninth Street between Washington and Pestalozzi streets for lager brewing in 1870. It was named the Charles Becker Lager Beer Brewery. In 1884 his son, Alois Becker, took over and ran it until 1894, when Gustavus Huthsteiner became the owner. The brewery lasted until Prohibition. A mural of the Tell City Brewery decorates the city's Ohio River flood wall. Fred Voelke's brewery in Tell City operated from 1875 to 1884. At Troy, scarcely an eyeblink on the Ohio River, the Heinze and Thaney brewery lasted from 1874 to 1914, also operating under John Winterath and as the Troy Model Brewery.

In the southeastern Indiana German heartland, a Bavarian tailor named Christopher Roe Balthasar Hammerle started a brewery on a homestead near New Alsace in the 1830s, when he found tailoring on the frontier to be unrewarding. With a brewmaster named Seibel, Hammerle produced twelve barrels of beer two to three times a week until 1856, when his son took over. At some point, Martin Wilhelm purchased the brewery properties. In 1865 Joseph Zix, an immigrant from Baden-Baden, bought the brewery, running it for a dozen years until he leased it in 1877 to his sons, Michael and Joseph, who also ran a distillery. The Zix family ran the brewery until it closed in 1893. Just south of its long brick brewery, the Zix family raised hops that climbed the towering poles in its garden.

Peter Weltner established New Alsace's second brewery in the 1850s. When Confederate cavalryman John Hunt Morgan made

Barley in Indiana

From pioneer days up to the 1950s, there was substantial barley production in Indiana, but today there is little except for a small winter crop in southern Indiana. Herb Ohm, distinguished professor of agronomy at Purdue University, discussed the factors that affected brewing barley in the Hoosier State. Beginning in the World War II era, hybrid corn and soybeans took over acreage where barley previously grew. Barley is probably not the best crop for Indiana, in any case. Ohm noted, "High rainfall in Indiana, especially in the spring and early summer, results in poor malting quality of much of the crop, rendering most of the barley production as feed, spring barley produced in Indiana yields very low and winter barley is not sufficiently cold tolerant most years." Further, the modern practice of reduced tilling has increased the devastating fusarium head blight disease, which affects barley and wheat. The Fusarium graminearum fungus produces a vomitoxin, deoxinivalenol, which ruins barley for brewing. Given our moist, frigid climate and the no-tolerance rule for vomitoxin, it appears the vast majority of our brewing barley will need to come from other regions.

MIKE SCHWAB

New Alsace Brewery. COURTESY OF THE AUTHOR

his lightning raid into Indiana in 1863, Weltner's brewery was one of the places Morgan hit. Martin Meyer bought Weltner out after the Civil War and ran the brewery until his death in 1897. Meyer's New Alsace Brewery produced seven barrels of common beer per brew, selling in the immediate neighborhood and as far afield as Shelbyville, with draymen sometimes hauling the barrels over plank roads. At the bottom of bad hills, the draymen would be forced to unload half the barrels, returning for them after the laboring horses had hauled the remaining load up the hill. When the Zix Brewery went under in 1893, the Meyers bought its boiler, but never got it installed. After some years of rusting in the brewery yard, the boiler shell and flues were recycled into local road culverts. Meyer's New Alsace Brewery itself closed in 1898, the year after his death.

In 1856 French immigrant John P. Garnier started a brewery in Lawrenceburg, but quickly shuttered it to purchase one that Kosmos Frederick began in the 1840s. Operating under the John P. Garnier Brewery and later the J. B. Garnier Brewery names, the company brewed lastly at Third and Shipping streets, with Victor Oberting as a partner. Balthasar Roell ran his brewery in Oldenburg from 1878 to 1901. Schneider's brewery operated near Penntown. The farming hamlets of Saint Peter's and Saint Leon each had a brewer, John Busold (also spelled Busalt) and L. Bischoff, respectively. Beginning in the mid-1870s, both men brewed for about six

John Garnier and brewery. COURTESY OF DAVID STEIGERWALD

years. In 1876 Bischoff had the distinction of heading the state's smallest brewery, with a total production of thirty-six barrels.

Beginning in 1843 Scottish distiller Thomas Gaff built a solid business in Aurora, producing bourbon, rye, and scotch whiskey in his plant on the Ohio River. In the 1870s Gaff saw the opportunities that brewing offered. With Württemberg native Charles Bauer serving as the brewery contractor and stockholder, Gaff began his Great Crescent Brewery in 1873. Within three years Gaff's brewery was the state's largest, with thirty thousand barrels of production. Gaff transported large amounts of the beer down the Ohio and Mississippi rivers on his fleet of steamboats to southern markets. The brewery was renamed the Crescent Brewing Company in 1877, as Gaff prepared to pass the entity into a joint stock company. The next year Prussian Herman Bartels and others invested in the brewery. Its flagship brand was Aurora Lager Beer, which was even exported to Germany.

With his beer-swollen profits, Gaff accumulated extensive farmlands, two Louisiana plantations, two Columbus mills, the Nevada Treasure Hill silver mine, a Cincinnati jewelry store, banks, utilities, canal-construction firms, and a turnpike. An 1880 biography of Indiana luminaries trumpeted Gaff: "As a financier, he is regarded as one of the best in the country. His executive ability is remarkable. No transaction within the range of his complicated affairs escapes his observation." In spite of immense success and later sale to an English syndicate, the firm fell on hard times. In 1899 its assets were sold in Cincinnati for the bargain-basement price of fifty thousand dollars. Gaff's grandiose steamboat-gothic Hillforest Mansion still stands above the Ohio River in Aurora.

Northern Indiana

With its substantial German population, northern Indiana had several pre-Civil War breweries. There were two in La Porte, one that began in 1831 in the "Ten-Mile Strip" north of the courthouse, and Matthias Kreider's that started in 1854. Beginning about 1859, Nicholas Bader of Baden produced one of Indiana's first lagers at his brewery and malt house on La Porte's Lake Street, between Tyler and Chicago streets. He brewed until the 1870s. Other brewers in La Porte included Gans Bader, August Zahn, and Urban Gaeckle. In 1880 Clement Dick fathered the brewery that later grew into the Puissant Brewery (sometimes spelled Pisant). Dating back to the 1870s, the Guenther and Zerweck Brewery on Lake Street was a substantial brick landmark, where brewers produced about ten thousand barrels a year by the 1880s. The company was known for its "Indiana Gold" beer and its handsome white workhorses that led the Fourth of July parade. After the brewery's demise during Prohibition, the building was used as a county garage, before being demolished in 1932.

In South Bend Johann Christoph Muessel of Arzberg, Bavaria, commenced in 1852 what proved to be a very long-lived brewery. Known as Christopher in South Bend, Muessel was among the many Arzberg natives who immigrated to Indiana because of the glowing descriptions written by Johann Wolfgang Schreyer, the Bavarian who extolled the wide-open market for breweries in 1843. Located in northern Bavaria, near Bohemia, Arzberg was in the heartland of fine brewing. Muessel came from a wealthy Arzberg family that owned extensive real estate as well as the town's major brewery, the *Bergbrauerei* (Hill brewery).

Muessel's original South Bend brewery produced both vinegar and beer. In the years following the Civil War, the company's

Arzberg Export and Bavarian beers served a thirsty market, which allowed the company to prosper. In 1870 the Muessel firm moved to an imposing industrial brick complex of steam-powered brewery, malt houses, bottling works, and stables on 136 acres on Portage Avenue, where gushing artesian wells provided excellent water for brewing. The company's ice machines disgorged forty-five tons daily.

Over the next three decades, the company was known as Muessel Brothers, M. and W. Muessel, and Muessel Brewing Company, producing Nine-Star Lager and Silver Edge beer. Until late in the nineteenth century, the company utilized locally grown grain, but came to rely on grain from Wisconsin and Minnesota as the new century dawned. For a number of years, the Muessels hired out some of their bottling to the Zipperer family bottling works, which also bottled mineral water, soft drinks, and Husting's Milwaukee Weis Beer in their Zipperer-embossed bottles. According to one writer, the family's bottling works were so well regarded in South Bend "that early 20th century sipperers weren't accepted nipperers unless the bottle they quaffed from was a Zipperer."

In 1913 the Muessels hired a Notre Dame college senior named Knute Rockne to coach the company's professional football team for $10 to $25 per game. It was a good hire, as the team went undefeated the first year. The kid had promise—so much so that Muessel had him also coach its second pro team, the Huebners (later the catchier Silver Edge), while Rockne also served as Notre Dame's assistant coach. Ever the innovator, Rockne would hop in his little Overland auto to motor between the various practices.

During the winter holiday season of 1915, a tragedy struck the brewery. Late in the day as the Muessels tallied the final beer receipts, two gunmen—one masked, one stuttering—muscled into the office, each carrying two pistols. When Frank Chrobot, a burly Muessel teamster, tried to subdue one of the robbers, a gun went off and Chrobot fell to the floor. The office manager, thirty-three-year-old Henry Muessel, threw himself at the robber, but was quickly shot. His twenty-five-year-old brother, William, struggled with the bandits, who smashed his face and then shot him. Before fleeing with the loot (less than one hundred dollars), the robbers bound and gagged seventeen-year-old Robert Muessel, the son of company president Walter Muessel. A third man joined them in their flight into the woods of Muessel Grove. Chrobot and Henry Muessel both died; William Muessel suffered a grievous wound. Four years later, a forty-one-year-old maid and former prostitute, Estella Schultz, told police that her estranged husband, Gus Schultz, was one of the robbers, along with South Bend bartender Jack Wright and a gambler named Charles Danruther. When the police apprehended Schultz a few days later, he named Wright and Danruther as the murderers. Wright was convicted of first-degree murder and got a life sentence; Schultz received a second-degree murder conviction and life imprisonment. Danruther was never found. A few years after the robbery, the Muessel Brewing Company closed its doors when Prohibition was declared. The closing proved temporary, as the brewery had another long, colorful chapter after Repeal.

In 1900 a group of tavern owners banded together to form the South Bend Brewing Association, which later became the South Bend Beverage and Ice Company. (Not to be confused with the short-lived South Bend Brewing Company at 1622 Michigan Avenue, which brewed from 1895 to 1897.) The South Bend Brewing Association's enterprise was a success. In 1903 the company built a four-story brick brewery on twenty-two acres at 1636 Lincolnway West, where the building, listed on the National Register of Historic Places, still stands today. With local Italians serving as the primary workforce, the South Bend Brewing Association's main brands were Tiger and Hoosier beers—"Good Old Hoosier Beer," advertisements read.

Mishawaka's John Wagner opened his five-barrel, wood-fired brewhouse on the south bank of the Saint Joseph River in 1839. A German immigrant who had relocated from Detroit, Wagner prospered until a fire ravaged the plant in 1851. But two years later Wagner had the brewery back in business in a new location on the north side of the river, just west of the village. In 1870 he sold part of the business to Clems Dick for the capital to be

Hops in Indiana

The pioneer brewers of Indiana relied on wild hops for their brews, and there is some evidence that the Harmonist brewers had a hops garden in New Harmony prior to 1824. The Harmonist hops house remains. Other early Hoosier brewers also grew their own. A local remembered the hops garden at the Zix Brewery in New Alsace: "To the south of the brewery, they had high poles, forty or fifty feet high, with the hop-vines all the way up, having the appearance of silver poplar trees." Up in La Porte County, the Shepard Crumpacker family cultivated hops on its farm in the 1870s. Crumpacker traveled to Wisconsin for the rootstock that he planted on ten acres. He also built a drying house, an essential part of hops production. For several summers, local families picked the hops to earn some cash in a convivial atmosphere. At night as the drying went on, there was memorable chicken roasting and dancing—a "continual round of hilarity," one La Porte picker recalled. According to the historic record, the boisterousness of the hops season finally wore on Crumpacker, who packed it in when a windstorm took down his drying house. He did, however, proudly report that he made $2,500 from the crop, a substantial amount in those days.

With the current hops crisis due to poor harvests, a catastrophic warehouse fire, and increased demand, many are pondering local hops production. Indiana still has ample wild hop, which some Hoosier brewers use in specialty beers. Greg Emig of the Lafayette Brewing Company treks down to Burnett Creek to gather wild hops for the pioneer brew that he makes for local festivals. Ted Miller of Brugge noted wild hops growing along the Monon Trail.

Commercial production of Indiana hops is not yet a reality. According to Jules Janick, Purdue University distinguished professor of horticulture, there is currently no commercial hops production in Indiana. While hops plants can grow in a wide range of climatic conditions, they like early ample moisture (or irrigation), followed by dry conditions, something seldom seen in Indiana's humid summers. Downy mildew is still a big problem in areas with high spring rainfall, though many varieties such as Cascade, Nugget, and Fuggle have greater resistance to the disease. Hops aphids, spider mites, and cutworms are villains that have to be controlled. But with today's fluctuating hops cost, the market demand for highly hopped beers, and the current obsession for local products, there may yet be a return to the days of Hoosier hops.

able to expand to a fifteen-gallon brewery, changing the name to the Wagner-Dick Brewery. Later in the year Adolphus Kamm, an immigrant from Württemberg, bought out Wagner, and it became the Dick and Kamm Brewery. In 1880 Kamm's brother-in-law, Nicholas Schellinger, bought out Dick, renaming the business as the Kamm-Schellinger Brewing Company. (Kamm and Schellinger were brothers-in-law two different ways, as their brides were each man's sister.) Successful millers back in Württemberg, the Schellinger family's impressive mill and home was known as the *Schlössle*—Little Castle.

By the time the business incorporated in 1887, Kamm-Schellinger was a hundred-barrel brewery. Drawing water from the nearby Saint Joseph River, the brewery had its own malting house, cooperage, and charcoal production for filtering. The company's dam on the river provided hydropower. In 1918 the company was brewing seventy-five thousand barrels a year, including its flagship Arrow brand beer. As a 1970s-era conversion into a shopping and entertainment destination, the Kamm-Schellinger Brewing Company complex still remains on the banks of the Saint Joseph River.

Plymouth, the home of Johann Wolfgang Schreyer, did not actually get a brewery until 1857, when John Hoham from Strasbourg, Alsace, opened his brewery. Arriving in Marshall County in 1844, Hoham initially lived alone in a log cabin in the old Indiana reserve at Lake Maxinkuckee. After marrying and starting a farm, Hoham opened his brewery, which was located a mile southwest of Plymouth. It was an underground brewery, with an elevator-type shaft that led to two vaulted rooms, each seventy by twenty feet in size. The large rectangular fermenting vats were handcrafted from locally made brick and then covered with stucco. Local legend has it that the cellar was a station on the Underground Railroad.

Hoham operated the brewery for about ten years before selling it to his brother-in-law, John Klinghammer. Klinghammer's nephew, Jacob Weckerie, also joined the business, until he left the area for Chicago in 1889. Soon after, the *Argos Reflector* reported, "The old Plymouth brewery is lying idle and has been for over a year. The large breweries and brewers trust drive the smaller concerns to the wall." The cellar became an egg-storage facility, then a mushroom cave. In 1958 the *Indianapolis Star* magazine ran an article about the old brewery, indicating that the current owners were going to use the brew vats as a trout-minnow hatchery.

In Michigan City, Phillip Zorn, a Bavarian brewer who had brewed with the Busch and Brandt brewery in Chicago, began his P. H. Zorn Brewing Company in 1871. Using water from a spring-fed well in the building, Zorn brewed about fifteen thousand barrels a year. In 1905 A. J. Lehr, a graduate of Chicago's Zymotechnic school, became Zorn's brewmaster. Circa 1914 Zorn workmen toiled twelve-hour days, the engineers and kettlemen earning eighteen dollars a week, the drivers seventeen, and the bottle-house supervisor fourteen. Zorn's brick building still stands at the corner of York and Ninth streets, as does the brewery stables at West Ninth Street.

F. A. Rettig opened his Wabash Brewing Company in 1854, making ale and beer "thick enough to cut," according to a commentator of the time. Born near Bingen-on-the-Rhine, Rettig came to America in 1848. Starting as a brewer near Philadelphia, Rettig brewed in Cincinnati before establishing his Wabash concern. Also operating under the names Rettig and Adler and Wabash Brewing Company, the firm persisted until 1916.

The sprawling Indiana Brewing Association in Marion began in 1897, a corporation formed by J. N. C. Woelfel, who served as plant superintendent, as well as J. S. Corbett, Thomas Mahaffey, Frederick Seitz, and W. C. Smith. Located at today's 525 Lincoln Boulevard, it was considered one of northern Indiana's best-equipped breweries. The massive plant had an annual capacity of 125,000 barrels, producing about 40,000 barrels by the early twentieth century, primarily Bottled Tiger and Indiana Beer, touted as "The Pride of the State." But the temperance movement did in the Indiana Brewing Association. When Grant County voted to go dry with a "county option" law, so did more than a hundred saloons. Soon after the county option law was repealed, the Prohibitionists quickly instituted "local option" laws, again pushing dry laws through in Marion and most of Grant County in 1913. It was the death knell for the brewers of the Indiana Brewing Association, who turned over their remaining beer to the state revenue agents in June 1913. When the revenue agents poured the remaining barrels down the drain, the *Marion Leader-Tribune* headlined the result: "Drunken Fish Are Captured by 1000s." As the beer washed into the Mississenewa River, the inebriated fish floated to the surface, prompting townspeople to flock to the stream with baskets and barrels. One woman fell in the river trying to fill her bucket from the brewery drain.

The origins of the T. M. Norton Brewing Company in Anderson go back to 1866, when Anderson's first brewery, the Doxey Brewery, burned down. Hard-driving Irishman Thomas Norton teamed up with Patrick Sullivan to establish an ale brewery in a four-story, frame gristmill that had gone bust at Seventh Street and Central Avenue. Born in County Mayo, Ireland, Norton immigrated to America as a young child. He worked as a carpenter before learning to brew in Union City in the early 1860s with Louis Williams in their Norton and Williams Ale Brewery. According to family lore, Norton got control of the gristmill when the owners were unable to pay him for his carpentry work. Norton seemed like a Indiana-Irish version of Tammany Hall's George Washington Plunkitt, who famously claimed, "I seen my opportunities and I took 'em."

At Norton's Anderson brewery in 1882, Michael Crowley briefly replaced Sullivan before Norton went completely on his own. By 1889 forty employees were brewing beer, ale, and porter. In 1900 the new, brick-and-limestone, seven-story T. M. Norton Brewing Company factory opened with great fanfare. At the time, it was the tallest building in Anderson. At its acme, Norton's produced about 250 barrels a day or 55,000 barrels annually of their Old Stock Lager and Norton's Special Beer. They sold through their three-dozen saloons in the Anderson area, as well as for customers in north and central Indiana. "From the standpoint of cleanliness and purity, Norton's beer has no superior," bragged a 1906 city directory advertisement.

An intense, dark-eyed character with a cropped beard, Norton became wealthy through his brewery and other investments. When Norton died in 1907, his obituary stated he was a focused businessman, who had devoted "his time to the development of a business." Though the family was active in Democratic politics, Norton had no interest in public office. When Norton died, his sons, Martin and William, took over the brewery, which garnered some notoriety during Prohibition.

George Rettig began a brewery in Peru in 1859, when it was known as Rettig and Son. In 1860 J. O. Cole, a prospector who had become rich in California's goldfields, bought into the firm, and it became Rettig and Cole. In 1878 it became the James O. Cole Brewery, later known as the Peru Brewery. The Cole family became quite prosperous with its brewery, spring-water company, and famous traveling circus. The family name lives on in the pantheon of Indiana musical history through J. O. Cole's grandson, Cole Porter, who was born in Peru in 1891.

Other German breweries dotted northern Indiana. Wabash had another Rettig brewer, Franz Anton Rettig, who began his brewery with partner Wintz Stanley in 1853. They operated until 1866, when Rettig teamed up with his brother-in-law, Phillipp Alber, a Lichtenstein native, to form Rettig and Alber. In 1900 the firm became the Wabash Brewing Company, which operated until 1909, brewing about twenty thousand barrels a year at its two-and-a-half-acre facility at 225 North Cass Street. The Wabash brewery was another victim of county-option temperance. After Wabash County went dry, a wily businessman who had establishments in both Fort Wayne and Wabash purchased the brewery name and some equipment with the plan of selling beer in the dry county. According to the Byzantine Beardsley law, beer produced in a dry county could be sold there if it looped back from a wet county in a kind of sudsy merry-go-round. However, the Wabash County prosecutor scotched the idea.

Columbia City had the Eagle and Gabriel Moser breweries, along with the Walter-Raupfer Brewing Company, which brewed from 1879 to 1916 at Whitely and Ellsworth streets, peaking at about six thousand barrels a year. The Huntington Brewery at 145 East Tipton operated from 1860 until 1918 under various owners, including Jacob Boos, Carl Lang, Henry W. Hoch, and William P. Knipp, who ran it for a few years under the name of Hoch and Knipp. Hoch was part of a German family of brewers. One brother ran the Gierow and Hoch Brewery in Chilton, Wisconsin, while the second brother, Reiner, founded Duluth Brewing and Malting in Minnesota. Huntington's brews included Silver Cream, "an ideal workingman's beverage," the medium-dark Golden Drops brand, and High Card: "It is a brain food and makes red blood and builds up the tissues," according to the company claims. Huntington also had J. A. Herrberg's brewery for a decade beginning in 1874. In Crown Point, the Crown Brewing Company operated from the 1870s until 1910, when the drainage of their spent grain into Beaver Dam Ditch created a controversy, prompting them to move to more lenient Hammond. Albert Christian F. Wichmann, a Prussian, ran a brewery in Kendallville from just after the Civil War until the 1880s. Other Kendallville breweries included J. George Kratzer's and Joseph Becker's East Lake Brewing Company that operated on the west side of Bixler Lake until the early 1900s. Logansport had a short-lived brewery owned by Jacob Klein, as well as the Columbia Brewing Company, which August Frost began in 1866. Located at 424 High Street, Columbia operated until Prohibition. An 1850s brick residence in Bremen still houses the storage vaults for the Bauer and Hindersheet Brewery that operated in the early 1870s. Hugo Wolff also ran a brewery in Bremen from 1875 to 1884.

Western Indiana

In Terre Haute, a bevy of brewers made beer beside the Wabash River—thirty before 1918, according to one local history. Marylander George Hager opened the city's first brewery in 1835, along with a dry goods store. Hager announced his brewery with an advertisement offering to purchase barley as well as hops: "We will also purchase hops, and as the time for gathering approaches, would remind those who have, that they now have a market for disposing of them. Any person disposed to give their attention to the cultivation of hops can be furnished with a treatise on the subject by calling the subscriber."

After a fire burned Hager's plant, a group of citizens, which included the local Congregational pastor, advanced Hager and his partner Joseph Graff seven thousand dollars to reestablish the brewery. The brewery at Eighth and Poplar streets went through a number of owners before a sheriff's sale placed it with Demas Deming Sr. and Chauncey Warren, who then sold it to Earnest Bleemel. Mathias Mogger bought the business from Bleemel in 1848. Anton Mayer, a trained brewer from Württemberg, bought it in 1868 with his partner, A. Kaufmann. When Kaufman died the following year, Mayer bought out the family. The annual capacity was about twenty-five hundred barrels. Mayer ran the plant for two decades, nurturing it into a bustling facility that covered an entire city block, bounded by Poplar, Swan, and Ninth streets, and the Evansville and Terre Haute Railroad tracks. An 1891 history described the plant: "The buildings embrace the brewery proper, the malt-house, offices, stables, cooper shops (all of brick from one to four stories high), artificial ice machines, immense and elegant cellars, the whole being furnished with six steam engines. The main building is an imposing structure, and fine and well-ventilated cellars are a prominent feature." Mayer sold the company in a joint stock offering for half a million dollars in 1889, when the company was brewing thirty thousand barrels a year. The new executives, distiller Crawford Fairbanks and John H. Beggs, then merged Mayer's brewery with the Terre Haute Brewing Company, which had been operating at First and Ohio streets since the 1870s under Fred Feyh, Coelstein Kinzle, and Theodore Kriescher. In 1891 the Terre Haute Brewing Company's thirty employees were brewing seventy thousand barrels a year. By 1900 THBC was the seventh largest brewery in the United States, with a herd of fifty Clydesdales and Belgians delivering to the local market.

Other Terre Haute breweries included Albert Hertwig's at Eighth and Poplar streets from 1851 to 1860. Herrman Imbery brewed for a year beginning in 1874; Reinhold Klant also had a one-year wonder in 1875, as did N. S. Wheat, whose brewery operated from 1878 to 1879. The People's Brewing Company brewed the Celtic brand from 1904 to 1918 on the bluff between Water and South First streets.

Terre Haute brewers had some notoriety, as their payments to politicians for saloon protection became a national scandal. With its wide-open bordellos, gambling parlors, and round-the-clock saloons, Terre Haute was long known as Sin City. In 1906 voters impeached Mayor Edwin Bidaman, and five years later authorities arraigned Mayor Louis A. Gerhardt for contempt of court. But the mid-1910s administration of Mayor Donn M. Roberts was so corrupt that one wag claimed the only difference between Terre Haute and hell was that hell did not have any railroads. Roberts was convicted of bribery in 1915 and spent three and a half years in prison.

Out in western Indiana's smaller towns and villages, a number of brewers operated. James and Joseph Miller brewed in Covington for a dozen years beginning in 1884. The Crawfordsville brewery began in 1875 under the name of R. H. Hannan and Company, which later brewed under the names of Jacob Muth and Flaiber and Vance, which closed in 1884. The Bowling Green brewery of Frederick Stucki operated from 1874 to 1884. The Brazil Brewing, Ice and Power Company on Main Street brewed from 1901 to 1906.

Central Indiana

Indianapolis's first brewery began in the summer of 1834, established by National Road bridge contractor William Wernweg and his partner, John L. Young, on the south side of Maryland Street, midway between Missouri and West streets. An early sketch shows a sturdy, two-story, brick I-house with an attached *brauhaus*, shaded by a small orchard. A late-nineteenth-century Indianapolis history decreed Wernweg and Young's brewery to be "a not very extensive or profitable establishment, and appears to have sunk almost entirely out of view as a source of business by 1840." However, a Wernweg two-span covered bridge over the White River that opened in 1834 remained in use until 1872, perhaps evidencing that Wernweg was a better builder than brewer.

Within a few years of its closing, Frenchman Rene Faux revived Wernweg's brewery, swapping his strong beer to the local boys for the frog legs they hunted for him. But Faux's best source of profit was the yeast he sold the local housewives, who used it to whip up the daily provender of raised biscuits. Faux moved the brewery to Noble and Washington streets, where he continued his tripartite trade in frog legs, yeast, and beer. John P. Meikel continued brewing at Faux's old location until he moved the business to the posh Carlisle House on West Street, where Meikel's brewery lasted until about 1848. In 1868 Meikel opened up a brewery at 297 West Washington Street, which he began calling the Indianapolis Brewery about 1869. It lasted until about 1875.

In the days leading up to the Civil War, other breweries began popping up. In 1861 Frank Wright started an alehouse on Blake Street near the thirsty butchers of the Landers pork-packing plant. Wright's place lasted for a dozen years. Saxon C. F. Schmidt began brewing in Indianapolis in 1858, when he founded the Schmidt and Jaeger brewery with Charles Jaeger, though the next year Schmidt bought Jaeger out. Schmidt's brewery was at the head of Alabama Street, where he brewed Indianapolis's first lager beer in his ninety-three-foot by forty-foot, two-story building. The Civil War brought prosperity to the Schmidt brewery as thousands of Union troops quartered in the city downed lakes of Schmidt's lager. Union quartermasters contracted with hundreds of brewers to produce lagers for the troops, as the beer was considered to be healthy and nonintoxicating. A U.S. Sanitary Commission study noting that there was less diarrhea among lager drinkers in the army camps stated that lager "regulates the bowels, prevents constipation, and becoming in this way a valuable substitution for vegetables"—important to the greens-deficient army. Through their camp experiences, many Union soldiers took home a taste for lager that accelerated the beer's popularity after the war.

Schmidt's plant eventually stretched the entire block from McCarthy to Wyoming streets and included a multistory ice-house, stables, malting house, and bottling house. When Schmidt died in 1872, his brother-in-law, William Fieber, ran the business until his death two years later, when Schmidt's widow, Caroline, took over the firm. By 1876 the Schmidt brewery was producing twenty-five thousand barrels of beer annually—the second highest production in the state. When Caroline Schmidt died in 1877, her two sons, John W. and Edward, ran the company. By 1882 the C. F. Schmidt brewers produced almost sixty thousand barrels a year, including thirty barrels a day of bottled beer.

The Gack and Biser brewery began in 1859, but four years later Peter Lieber, the well-connected private secretary to Governor Oliver Morton, bought the firm, renaming it the P. Lieber Brewing Company. By 1868 the brewery was located at 213 South Pennsylvania Street, but Lieber relocated it to 512 Madison Avenue, near Morris Street.

Alsatian Caspar Maus was related to the Schmidt family through his brother's marriage. He began his brewery in 1868 on the Fall Creek race near New York Street. In 1882 the Indianapolis Board of Trade said of the Schmidt, Maus, and Lieber breweries, "In short, it is safe to say that the breweries of Indianapolis have no superiors in the completeness of their appointments and quality of their products; and it is well known that they 'hold their own' in competitions with other cities."

In October 1889 the Schmidt, Lieber, and Maus breweries formalized their already functioning partnership by merging into the illustrious Indianapolis Brewing Company. Owned by an English syndicate, the three breweries continued operations at their facilities, with the combined business office and bottling works at the Schmidt plant. Lieber was the first president of the company, and his son, Albert (the grandfather of novelist Kurt Vonnegut Jr.), the first managing director.

In 1900, when the Indianapolis Brewing Company's Dusseldorfer beer won a gold medal at the Paris Exposition, there was a "grand industrial parade" back home in Indiana to celebrate the accomplishment. The grand prize at Saint Louis's Louisiana Purchase Exposition followed in 1904. Two years later Indianapolis Brewing won another gold medal in Liege, Belgium. By 1914 the company with its five hundred employees was among Indianapolis's largest, using thirty million labels a year to export as far away as Latin America and the West Indies. "It is entirely within the truth to say that no product sent out of our city carried the name of Indianapolis to as many people of this earth as do the labels placed upon the products of this company," a 1914 ad crowed.

> "It is entirely within the truth to say that no product sent out of our city carried the name of Indianapolis to as many people of this earth as do the labels placed upon the products of this company," a 1914 ad crowed.

The Home Brewery began in 1891, founded by William P. Jungclaus and August Hook, a native of Viernhelm, Germany. Hook was the former brewmaster at Cincinnati's Lackmann Brewery and the Indianapolis Brewing Company, as well as being the father of druggist John A. Hook. The Home Brewery was located at Cruse and Daly streets, before occupying a new plant at 38 Shelby Street. The American Brewery started operations in 1897 at the corner of Ohio and Missouri streets. The Capital City Brewing Company brewed from 1905 to 1915, when it became the Citizens Brewing Company. All three breweries lasted until 1918.

In Lafayette, German *braumeister* John H. Newman began brewing in 1843 at Fourth Street between Union and Salem streets, producing about eight barrels a day. Around 1856 Newman bought the rights to a spring on an adjacent property, giving his brewery the local name of the Spring Brewery. Newman also bottled the spring water and later piped it to neighboring residences. Lafayette's first fireplug sat in front of the brewery. In 1858 Newman took on a partner, Dietrich Herbert, and the firm became known as Newman and Herbert. Herbert had been

This elegant illustration highlights the heavenly quality of the Indianapolis Brewing Company's ales. COURTESY OF THE INDIANA HISTORICAL SOCIETY

brewing in Lafayette since 1848, when he had formed the Wagner and Herbert Brewery at Fourth Street near Union Street with John Wagner.

The Newman and Herbert partnership lasted until 1872, when Bavarian George A. Bohrer bought Herbert, the new company being renamed Newman and Bohrer. Born near Zweibrucken, Bohrer had immigrated to Cincinnati, where he engaged variously in shoemaking, a livery, grocery, and hotel. Just prior to buying into the Lafayette brewery, Bohrer ran an undertaking firm in Cincinnati. Whatever the skill sets Bohrer brought to Newman and Bohrer, they must have been beneficial, as the firm prospered—so much so that Newman built a turreted mansion near the plant that was heated with excess brewery steam piped through a fifteen-by-eighteen-foot tunnel, which Newman used on rainy days. In 1888 Bohrer purchased the entire firm from the Newman heirs and renamed it the Geo. A. Bohrer Brewing Company, known locally as Bohrer's. It operated until Prohibition.

Not too many years after Herbert left his partnership with

Wagner, Frederick Thieme bought into the business, which became Thieme and Wagner. The company flourished. When the Thieme and Wagner Brewing Company opened its new five-story brewery at 800–814 North Fourth Street in 1899, it was Lafayette's largest brewery. The brewery sold its seven-dollar barrels of brew as far away as Danville, Illinois, which received a daily railway car of Thieme and Wagner beer. The brand names included Lockweiler, Bohemian, T. & W. Special, and Ye Tavern Beer.

Through the last part of the nineteenth century, Lafayette was considered "the wildest place on the Wabash," a slightly shady town with a booming Fourth Street brewery, *biergarten,* saloon, and bordello scene, and wild Wabash River excursion boats that were little more than floating taverns. As the Prohibition movement became more militant, some of the more flagrant establishments became the target of axe-wielding temperance warriors.

The Rise and Fall of the Indiana Beer Reich

The Germans and their beer culture changed the social habits of Hoosiers. Beginning with the rise of breweries after 1850, German beer began to supplant corn whiskey as lager won over increasing numbers of Indiana palates. By 1860 the sixty-one Indiana breweries outnumbered the thirty-seven distilleries in the state. Until Prohibition, the lager culture of saloons and growlers, beer gardens, and *bierstuben* was a part of daily life in Indiana, along with the massive brick brewing complexes that dotted the state from Evansville to the Michigan border.

But there was a countervailing trend—almost two hundred different breweries operated in Indiana from pioneer days until Prohibition, peaking in the 1870s as German immigration soared and industrialization took hold. But from the 1870s on, the number of Indiana breweries began to decline. In 1876 there were seventy-six breweries operating in the state. By 1890 the number was down to forty-seven Indiana breweries; forty-two by 1912; and thirty-one by 1914 (though there were still 2,207 employees working in the consolidated plants). Indiana's brewery closings and consolidations followed the national pattern. In 1873,

4,131 American breweries produced about nine million barrels, roughly twenty-two hundred barrels per brewery. It was to be the high tide for small brewers.

Technological changes at the turn of the century accelerated the development of large breweries. Two-hundred-barrel motorized mash tuns and immense, steam-jacketed brew kettles replaced the old wooden tuns and forty-barrel kettles. Pasteurization in the 1870s and the crown-cap bottling system in the 1890s allowed the larger breweries to expand into locales where the small local brewery had a near monopoly on the home market. Late in the century the Federal Excise Tax doubled, from a dollar a barrel to two dollars. With beer selling for five to seven dollars a barrel, the tax had an outsized impact on the less efficient and less profitable smaller breweries. The result was clear. By 1900 there were only 1,751 American breweries that produced thirty-nine million barrels, an average of twenty-two thousand barrels per brewery, a tenfold production increase from less than three decades before. The various permutations of the Prohibition movement, such as county and local options, further accelerated the decline, as small and medium-sized concerns had to bow to the will of the temperance people. By 1918 there were only one thousand breweries left nationwide; within two years the number had dropped to five hundred. As increasingly dry Indiana stood on the cusp of total state Prohibition in 1918, there were a handful of surviving Hoosier breweries—most of them operating in a state of denial.

> The Germans and their beer culture changed the social habits of Hoosiers. . . . Until Prohibition, the lager culture of saloons and growlers, beer gardens, and *bierstuben* was a part of daily life in Indiana.

CHAPTER FIVE

That's It: Prohibition
1918–1933

· · · · · · · · · · · ·

PROHIBITION COMMENCED IN INDIANA
at midnight on April 2, 1918, when thirty-one
breweries and 3,520 saloons closed their doors—
547 in Indianapolis alone. A driving rainstorm
swept across Indiana the night before Prohibition, but that
did not keep revelers from enjoying their last legal drinks.

In Indianapolis, the manager of the posh Severin Hotel
had to ask the police to clear the elegant barroom at midnight, as the dancing celebrators refused to go home. The
manager needed to close the cabaret, as it was being transformed into a coffee shop the next day. In the slightly more
downscale Brevort Café, a young man sprayed the crowd
with beer a few minutes before midnight, sparking a melee
that brought out knives.

A thousand people lost their jobs in Terre Haute, as
both the town's breweries and 263 bars closed. In spite of the
bad news, the city's bars and dives were packed with rowdy
patrons until closing. In Evansville the cabarets and cafés were
busy until midnight with "general celebration." Quite a few of
Evansville's citizens staged their own festivities: "The number
of parties in private homes, where the basis of the merriment
was a keg or two of beer, was astounding," a correspondent

reported. With 83 bars and both breweries closing in Lafayette, hordes of people turned out for a last fling. The 65 saloons in Vincennes did "a land-office business" right up to closing time. Anderson's 28 bars did not last that long—the patrons drank up the remaining stock long before midnight. In South Bend, Muessel's brewery was dark, but the city's 215 saloons only shut down after "the busiest day in their history." In more sanguine—or perhaps depressed—Fort Wayne, the city was fairly quiet, though 157 bars and the state's two biggest breweries were closing.

Passage of state Prohibition was the culmination of an enormous offensive the year prior by the "drys," led by the Indiana Anti-Saloon League. In the days leading up to the January 1917 vote on the bill, Indianapolis was swamped with twenty-five thousand Prohibition supporters waving banners and pigeon-holing legislators in statehouse halls. Petitions arrived so heavy that aides had to hoist them on their shoulders. When the vote passed the House, 70 to 28, wild temperance-style celebrations broke out, and the statehouse halls reverberated with "Onward Christian Soldiers."

As the Senate debated the bill, the IASL cried for three hundred thousand advocates to descend on Indianapolis. Petitions with more than one hundred and seventy-five thousand names were delivered to the legislators, and hymn-singing temperance supporters waving signs paraded through the Senate chambers. Buckling under to the overwhelming dry support, the Senate unexpectedly passed the bill in a landslide 38 to 11 vote, uncorking "wild jubilation" in the galleries and around the state. The brewers had until April 1918 to put their affairs in order.

In the interim, the Indiana Brewers Association warned that the state would forfeit a trove of taxes and more than 13,600 workers would lose their jobs. Some German brewers in Evansville told the local paper they would return to Germany; saloon keepers just thought they would move to Kentucky. But soon after April 3, 1918, there was little hullabaloo—with Indiana soldiers already on the front lines in France, media attention shifted to Liberty Bonds and crushing the Hun. But Kin Hubbard, the

Governor James P. Goodrich of Indiana, surrounded by prominent "dry" workers, signing the statewide Prohibition bill to take effect April 2, 1918.
COURTESY OF THE LIBRARY OF CONGRESS

pithy cartoonist who created Abe Martin of Brown County fame, caught the internal dialogue with his cartoon that fateful week:

> Sometimes a woman'll get so hard up
> fer somethin' t' boast of
> that she'll say her husband is goin'
> t' buy a car when the state goes dry.

Arrests began soon enough, though Doc Vanderhook, who ran an Indianapolis chili parlor on Massachusetts Avenue, managed on April 4 to get out of the charge of running a speakeasy. On April 13 police busted Indianapolis saloon keeper H. C. Bloomberg for having nine barrels of whiskey and a substantial supply of beer and wine in the cellar of his "soft-drink parlor" at English and State streets. It was the first of thousands of arrests for Prohibition violations. Blind tigers and speakeasies began to spring up all over Indiana, selling now-forbidden booze and beer. While most imbibing households still had substantial (though illegal) stores, enterprising Hoosiers were already making home brew beer and distilling corn whiskey. In some parts of the state—particularly those with large German and Italian populations—brewing, winemaking, and distilling were destined to become substantial cottage industries.

The passage of Indiana's state prohibition law put additional pressure on Congress to institute national prohibition through a constitutional amendment. In December 1917 the U.S. House passed the Eighteenth Amendment, which Indiana legislators voted to ratify on January 14, 1919. Three days later Nebraska became the thirty-sixth state to ratify, making the Eighteenth Amendment part of the Constitution. America went dry on January 17, 1920, one year after ratification. Billy Sunday, the volcanic evangelist from Winona Lake, Indiana, thundered, "The reign of tears is over. The slums will soon only be a memory. We will turn our prisons into factories and our jails into storehouses and corncribs. Men will walk upright now; women will smile, and the children will laugh. Hell will be forever for rent."

> Indiana's first prohibition proved to be short-lived, as the state supreme court declared the law to be unconstitutional within a few months of its ratification.

A Long Time Coming

The temperance and Prohibition movements had a long history in Indiana. In the years prior to the Civil War there was widespread pressure in various states for Prohibition. Primarily led by women, local temperance groups coalesced across Indiana, determined to rid the state of evil liquor. In one case in the 1850s, a number of Centerville Methodist and Presbyterian women roused themselves to action. Armed with hatchets and hammers, the good sisters invaded John Vonderwight's saloon—known locally as "Dutch Jake's." Stove-in whiskey barrels and smashed hogsheads of beer soon gushed on the floor. Cigars and tobacco flew through the air. A torrent of intoxicants ran down the gutters from broken barrels the women had rolled into the street. Their wilding complete, the ladies marched triumphant from the shattered saloon, brandishing Vonderwight's commandeered account books. But an account book held a surprise. Unbeknownst to one of the temperance warriors, her son was one of Dutch Jake's best customers.

Fourteen states eventually passed pre-Civil War Prohibition laws, including Indiana, which in 1855 passed a law that prohibited the manufacture or sale of any intoxicating liquor, save cider and wine made from domestic fruits. But Indiana's first prohibition proved to be short-lived, as the state supreme court declared the law to be unconstitutional within a few months of its ratification.

In the years following Appomattox, the temperance movement continued to pick up steam, spearheaded by evangelicals and politicians virulently opposed to "Rum, Romanism, and Rebellion"—the Romanism referring to the terror that the foreign-born Papists represented, particularly the Irish with their propensity for whiskey and the German Catholics for their love of beer. Pushed by temperance advocates, an 1883 Prohibition bill came within four votes of being passed by the Indiana General Assembly. The prohibitionists marched on after the 1883 vote. Each Sunday the walls of evangelical churches trembled with temperance songs, such as:

Oh, the Brewer's Big Horses coming down the road
Toting all around old Lucifer's load,
They step so high, and step so free,
But the Brewer's Big Horses can't run over me.

Temperance lobbyists made sure Prohibition bills were introduced in every session of the general assembly after 1883, though the vote was never as close until 1918.

But the 1883 prohibition vote must have been the last straw for many Hoosier brewers: an extraordinary number closed in 1884, when more than three dozen breweries changed hands or drained their vats for the last time. Beyond the growing prohibition movement, Indiana brewers had been suffering from wild economic panics, tight credit, and erratic crops for ten years. Many of the closings were small breweries that were now competing with larger brewers equipped with newer and more productive equipment. It all came to a head in 1884 when Bremen, Bowling Green, Cannelton, Huntington, Jasper, Kendallville, Lawrenceville, New Albany, Richmond, Saint Peter's, Seymour, and Tell City all lost their breweries, as did Troy and Valparaiso.

In 1895 the prohibitionists pushed through a law governing taverns, which legislated the establishment had to be on the first or basement floor, as well as banning food, music, partitions, and booths. The strictures helped form the iconography of the turn-of-the-century saloon: free (albeit salty) lunches to accompany libations, which were downed behind the swinging doors and gauzy curtains that shielded the patrons from busybody eyes. With booths prohibited, the brass foot rail at the bar served as a convivial substitute.

The continued growth of the Women's Christian Temperance League and the founding of the IASL in 1898 brought together impassioned foot soldiers and highly skilled organizers, embodied in the IASL's firebrand executive Reverend Edward S. Schumaker. The IASL soon began using the Nicholson remonstrance law to its full extent. Named after the Quaker minister who wrote the law, the measure permitted communities to vote on the establishment and continuation of individual saloons. Through the statute, petitions could be circulated, and if there were enough signatures, a special election could be called to determine the saloon's destiny. It was a contentious system, as towns wrangled over the petitions. In the southeastern Indiana town of Waldron, there was even a pitched battle between gun-slinging wets and drys.

As the twentieth century dawned, prohibitionists turned to a deadlier weapon: local and county options that allowed localities to vote in prohibition. The drys got a boost when Indiana governor Frank Hanly took office in 1905. Hanly championed prohibition (as well as Indiana's infamous Compulsory Sterilization Law, a eugenics statute that mandated sterilization of individuals in state custody). In his last year in office, Hanly waged a "bitter and relentless war" against the brewers and spirits industry—that "unholy traffic," as he called it. By the time Hanly left office in 1909, seventy of Indiana's ninety-two counties were dry. But counties with large German populations stayed wet, including Allen, Vigo, Wayne, Tippecanoe, Marion, Floyd, Knox, Franklin, Dubois, Lake, and La Porte. (Rendered dry by local option, Broad Ripple tipplers made an effort to merge their village with wet Indianapolis so they could drink again.)

In a period when breweries owned 70 percent of Indiana's saloons, the statewide impact was major: 10 percent of the state's 3,681 saloons in 1908 went out of business within a year. In the face of local and county options, some taverns adapted. The telltale swinging doors came down, and "hop ale" replaced beer. Patrons got their whiskey in genteel china cups and saucers. "Literary" and "Educational" Clubs abounded, as did fraternal orders. But as county options took their toll, breweries closed across the state.

There was some reprieve in 1911, when Governor Thomas Marshall told legislators that local and county options enforcement "breeds perjury, discontent, bitterness of feeling and local anarchy." Marshall's law, called the Proctor bill, ended county options, instead controlling saloons through county commissioners and high license fees and bonds. But the new law offered brewers only a short respite before the dry forces, deciding that statewide prohibition was their best alternative, attacked again. By 1917 the Hoosier drys had accomplished their great mission—prohibition in Indiana.

After Hanly's term in office ended in 1909, he took up the cudgel of temperance full time. He was the keynote speaker of the Anti-Saloon League's Jubilee Convention in Columbus, Ohio, on December 10, 1913, rousing the crowd into "a roar as wild as the storm outside," as they rallied for passage of the Eighteenth Amendment. Hanly then formed the "Flying Squadron" of prohibition speakers, who barnstormed the forty-eight states, lecturing to more than a million people in less than a year. Emboldened by the response, Hanly ran for president on the Prohibition Party ticket in 1916, though he only garnered 221,030 votes, about 1.2 percent of the total. In January 1918 Hanly wrote in the conservative *Literary Digest* that Hoosier brewers had "the arrogance of a Hun." Hanly railed, "In all the history of the political and civic life of the American people there has been no combination or organization of power so brutal, so domineering, so corrupt, or so dead to every sense of civic interest or concern as the brewers of America." In his final jeremiad, Hanly said, "The legislatures of the States will be organized into firing squads, and the beer trade will be compelled to meet its fate."

Breweries during Prohibition

The thirty-one Indiana breweries that survived up to Prohibition included two each in Evansville, Fort Wayne, Lafayette, Terre Haute, South Bend, and New Albany, as well as six in Indianapolis. The smallest of the group was the Tell City Brewing Company. After April 2, 1918, several, such as Thieme and Wagner in Lafayette, Muessel in South Bend, Terre Haute Brewing Company, Madison Brewing Company, Peru Brewery, and Tell City Brewing, just closed their doors—if they had not already in the months prior.

The breweries that remained open struggled along with a variety of strategies. Most brewed near beer, which had to have an alcohol content of less than half of 1 percent. The Indianapolis Brewing Company manufactured soft drinks and cereal until 1930, while C. F. Schmidt made Ozotonic and malt extract until closing in 1920. Hack and Simon stumbled along for a while brewing a near beer it called Elite, after their best-selling pre-Prohibition brew. The Evansville Brewing Company, under the name Sterling Products Company, started selling soft drinks and a near beer called Sterling Beverage—"that 'foody' drink with all of the golden grains of which it is made." Like many breweries, Sterling also sold a malt extract that *could* be used to home brew and boost near beer up to normal potency. Of course, drugstore alcohol could do the same thing. Zorn in Michigan City made soda pop. In South Bend, Kamm and Schellinger sold soft drinks and distilled water under the name of Arrow Beverages, Inc. South Bend Brewing sold near beer, root beer, and Hoosier Cream Soda. The Huntington Brewery converted to making caffeine, soap, tannin, and other chemicals. Fort Wayne's Berghoff Products Company, as it was renamed, produced Bergo near beer, soda pop, and Berghoff Malt Tonic. Ads running in major Indiana papers around the start of Prohibition pitched their near beer to saloon keepers, soon to become soda jerks: "Bergo, The Quality Drink. Keep your place open by using Bergo." Another ad aimed at patrons showed a winsome Dutch lass bringing Bergo to a happy American family sitting at a soda fountain, while another offered that Bergo was "a snappy drink" that was ideal to drink before retiring. Centlivre Brewing survived by leasing cold storage and selling ice and near beer, called That's It.

> "there has been no combination or organization of power so brutal, so domineering, so corrupt, or so dead to every sense of civic interest or concern as the brewers of America."

Bootlegging

"Prohibition is better than no liquor at all," humorist Will Rogers quipped, which seemed to sum up the Volstead era. During Prohibition, an ocean of bootleg hooch flowed through the porous U.S. borders. Bootleggers hid moonshine stills in haystacks, concocted gin in bathtubs, and fermented Dago Red in closets and cellars. Crippling Jamaican-ginger Jake ravaged the lower classes. Basement-brewed beer was ubiquitous. One thing was clear—America sure was not going beerless: The Prohibition Bureau estimated that each year Americans consumed several hundred million gallons of homebrew.

Bootlegging was rampant in Indiana, from Dubois County farms to the Calumet region's slick mob-run operations. From the illegal casinos of French Lick all the way up to the speakeasies of Chicago, tipplers particularly respected "Dubois Dew," renowned as a relatively safe and palatable moonshine. Indeed, Al Capone himself repeatedly junketed to rural Dubois County to sample the output of stills concealed on Ferdinand, Dubois, and Haysville farms. Chicago gangsters in their big Chryslers and Packards were a common sight on the county backroads—one folktale of the region tells of a shoot-out with tommy guns on a remote farm, with the local moonshiner farmers burying the loser in the woodlot. Folks from all over the state came to buy, along with policemen from Evansville and other large cities.

The moonshine was not all exported. In Ferdinand, Wilfred Olinger remembered the home brew arrangement that the persnickety owner of the Covered Bridge establishment had: "This family, they were all making beer for him. And he knew which was capped, and aged, you know, to be served. And we went and got the batches that he sent us to and brought them up there. And he had the home brew and like horse troughs with ice, you know, we had no refrigeration, not yet. Oh ja, and moonshine, the Dubois Dew, you know, whisky, that was made out in the county, with stills, you know." In overwhelmingly German Dubois County, moonshining was not only culturally acceptable, but economically critical. During the Great Depression, Ferdinand Township had the lowest number of people on welfare in the entire state.

During Prohibition, northwest Indiana was also a hotbed of illegal brewing under the Johnny Torrio and Capone organizations. In June 1923 Prohibition officers seized the West Hammond Brewing Company for brewing real beer. Near the state line and Chicago, the brewery had started in 1909. By 1923 it was sold and disappeared from view. In La Porte, police raided Guenther's Brewery, where workers were brewing real beer for "known gangsters" from Chicago, as well as their Atlasta near beer. A local history reported, "In a flourish of righteous indignation, Police Chief Alfred Norris led a posse into the brewery and smashed the kegs with axes, thus saving the citizens from the evils of drink."

The Southern Indiana Brewing Company in New Albany brewed Hop-O, its near beer—and quite a bit that was not. Federal Prohibition officers busted the company for bottling beer at a 6 to 7 percent alcohol level to send to southern states. Michael Schrick, president of the brewery, was arrested, and the brewery license was revoked.

During Prohibition, Virgil Hosier was the bottle-shop foreman for Ackerman Brewery, part of the Southern Indiana Brewing Company. In 1993 eighty-three-year-old Hosier reminisced with the Fermenters of Special Southern Indiana Libations Society: "And at one time, when they got to making beer up to 5, 6, and 7 %, we had trucks coming from Louisiana and Alabama. We didn't have a bit of trouble selling beer—we just didn't have enough of it." Hosier remembered a friend of his, Fred LaDuke, was operating a bottling machine when a man walked in and told him to shut it down. "He [LaDuke] said, 'who the hell are you to tell me to shut it down. I'm not shutting it down.' The man just pulled his coat open 'I says shut it down' and they shut it down. Internal Revenue," Hosier recalled.

The Anderson papers began headlining the T. M. Norton brewery on June 17, 1923, the day after Prohibition officers searched the plant. "Two Truck Loads of Beer Is Seized," the *Herald* ungrammatically blared, also noting that "Bert Morgan Also Here." Morgan was Indiana's Prohibition director, a rare "Untouchable" in the midst of raging corruption. At one point, Morgan reportedly declined a $250,000 offer to turn a blind eye. At Norton's, the officers arrested the two Ohio truck drivers, incarcerating them at the county jail along with the forty-nine kegs of 5 percent beer found in the trucks. Morgan also found another ninety barrels of beer in the brewery vats. Police had raided the brewery two years prior, when they confiscated a large quantity of bottled beer. On June 19, 1923, authorities charged brewery executive William J. Norton with conspiracy to violate federal Prohibition laws and padlocked the plant. Norton was at the plant when the raid began, but ran as the police descended, leaving the hapless drivers to take the heat. By the end of the month, a deal had been struck: authorities closed the Norton brewery for a year, but did not confiscate the property, as they could have under the Volstead Act. After his conviction for liquor-law violations, Norton served time at the federal prison in Atlanta.

Repeal!

As the 1920s wore on, Hoosier prohibitionists attracted some unsavory allies—the Ku Klux Klan. At the peak of their power in Indiana, the Klansmen shared many of the drys' conservative views and took to Prohibition enforcement with zeal. Using the previously existing Horse Thief Detective Association, the Klan formed an unfettered civilian legion to uphold the dry laws, sometimes abusing their power to harass wet proponents.

In the mid-1920s the national Prohibition laws got even more draconian. Indiana's Wright Bone Dry law that the legislature passed in 1925 tightened enforcement. Considered one of the most repressive laws ever passed in Indiana, the statute offered financial inducements for successful prosecutions, which not surprisingly fueled an arrest and prosecution binge. The tide turned by 1927. Concerned with enforcement excesses, Indiana attorney general Arthur Gilliom decided to soften the Wright law. Much to the chagrin of the prohibitionists, Gilliom instructed the state's prosecutors to no longer prosecute for possession of "medicinal" whiskey prescribed by doctors, as it did not violate the "spirit" of the law.

With a growing revulsion against mob-controlled bootlegging and widespread corruption, public opinion began to lean toward repeal. The board of directors of the Indiana chapter of the Association Against the Prohibition Amendment included Hoosier literary luminaries George Ade and Meredith Nicholson, as well as a pantheon of executives, bankers, attorneys, and politicians.

But it was the 1929 stock market crash and the depression that followed it that ultimately did in Prohibition. In the austere new era, beer meant jobs and tax revenues. And perhaps there

With the repeal of Prohibition in 1933 there were again smiles at Hoosier bars.
COURTESY OF THE INDIANA HISTORICAL SOCIETY

was a biblical element. As the Book of Proverbs rejoined, "Give strong drink to unto him that is ready to perish, and wine unto those that be of heavy heart. Let him drink, and forget his poverty, and remember his misery no more." As public and political sentiment shifted, visions of beer kegs began to dance in brewers' heads. In April 1932 the *Evansville Courier* reported, "Evansville brewers are ready to begin manufacture practically on short notice," though they were not "especially optimistic about the legalization of beer in the near future." By November of that year, the paper trilled, "Evansville sees brighter prospect of Brewing Jobs," anticipating two hundred men would be hired at Evansville Brewing, whose executives promised to start brewing within thirty days of repeal.

By 1932 both national political parties added repeal planks to their platforms, as did Indiana's Democratic and Republican parties. After Franklin D. Roosevelt's inauguration in March 1933, Congress permitted the sale of 3.2 beer. The Twenty-first Amendment repealing Prohibition was right behind it. Governor Paul McNutt used the momentum to call for the end of the

Wright Bone Dry law and pushed through the Alcohol Beverage Act. On April 7, 1933, legal beer returned to Indiana.

At the beginning of April 1933, Indiana newspapers made the imminent arrival of beer their front-page story. "Beer Trucks Will Race Beer to City Friday," the *Indianapolis Star* headlined on Monday, April 3. With only a few Indiana breweries up and running, most of Indianapolis's Prohibition-relief beer was coming from Cincinnati, Saint Louis, and Milwaukee. Kamm and Schellinger in Mishawaka and Berghoff Brewing in Fort Wayne were going to have beer ready for the first day, but Evansville Brewing could only promise June at the earliest. Centlivre and Cook both applied for licenses. The city was in a tizzy, with speculation about availability, price, and quality. Seven hundred applicants flooded the state office for retail beer licenses. It seemed like Friday was never going to come.

> The White House got the nation's first shipment of 3.2 beer at 12:05 p.m. on April 7, trucked in under U.S. Marine guard. Roosevelt sagely sent it to the press corps.

The White House got the nation's first shipment of 3.2 beer at 12:05 p.m. on April 7, trucked in under U.S. Marine guard. Roosevelt sagely sent it to the press corps. Around mid-morning on the seventh, beer trucks began to trickle into Indianapolis, just in time for the promised lunch-hour debut. But it was far too little, a drop in a beer-thirsty desert. Some trucks had gotten trapped in Milwaukee and Saint Louis traffic jams that were "miles long." There were rumors of beer-truck hijackings in Lake County. In spite of the Indiana State Police reporting that thirty-five of the forty-six trucks checking in at the Seymour weighing station were loaded with beer, Indianapolis failed to receive all the beer it wanted. "Early Rush Exhausts Beer Supply," the *Star* headline read. Cheery crowds had jammed the cafés that had beer—"packed after the manner of a delegation of sardines in a can." Anderson drank up its allocation of Berghoff beer in two hours. Evansville and New Albany got some Falls City from Louisville. Poor Teutonic Batesville did not get any at all. By Sunday, April 9, the *Star* ominously headlined, "Beer Famine Threatens, as Demand for Brewery Supply Exceeds Supply." The paper figured that locals had consumed six hundred thousand pints in the first few days that beer was legal.

There were some changes in the fifteen beer-less years. There were no more "saloons"—bars, taverns, and cafés were now the preferred monikers. And women were right there, drinking out of bottles and slender little glasses, a long way from their older sisters' homebound growlers. But in terms of the beer, the *Star* said it best, "Those who knew the real article in pre-Prohibition days pronounced the 3.2 as 'genuine.'"

Indiana Sunday Sales Laws

"We're just trying to get parity with Indiana wineries," says Brewers of Indiana Guild former president Blaine Stuckey, speaking of his organization's attempt to help liberalize Indiana's alcohol laws. A holdover from Indiana's temperance past, the archaic laws prohibit sales on the Lord's Day, except for restaurants and Indiana wineries, which have been permitted Sunday retail sales since 1986. Spearheaded by a netroots group, Hoosiers for Beverage Choices, the coalition hopes to convince legislators to allow Sunday carryout sales of alcoholic beverages and cold beer sales at drug, grocery, and convenience stores. Indiana is one of only fifteen states that prohibit Sunday sales, and the only one that limits cold beer sales to liquor stores.

BIG's general counsel and lobbyist, Mark Webb, indicates that legislators are realizing that Sunday sales can increase tourism, while boosting state income from excise taxes. "Tourists won't come to Indiana breweries on Sunday if they can't buy product. We don't have anything to sell them. They can taste it, but they can't take it away," said Webb. With the groundswell of citizen support for the alcohol law reform (ten thousand Hoosiers have signed petitions for the measure), the Indiana Blue Law opponents are getting optimistic. "The odds get better all the time," said Webb.

Rebirth and Reprise

1933–1997

HOOSIER BREWERS WERE SOON in furious ferment. Berghoff, Kamm and Schellinger, the Indianapolis Brewing Company, F. W. Cook, Sterling Brewers, Inc., and South Bend Beverage and Ice were brewing in April 1933, with Zorn, Centlivre, and Southern Indiana Beverage and Ice close behind. By November 1934 Indiana had also issued brewery licenses to Lieber Brewing in Indianapolis; Muessel Brewing Company, T. M. Norton, and K. G. Schmidt in Logansport; Kiley Brewing Company, Inc., in Marion; Lafayette Brewing Company; and Fort Wayne's Berghoff Brothers Brewing Company, a new Berghoff family enterprise that was quickly renamed Hoff-Brau Brewing Company.

At the end of 1934, the first full year of repeal, sixteen Indiana breweries produced 741,312 barrels of beer, 652,007 of which Hoosiers consumed in the state, the balance being sold out of state. Another 203,994 barrels came into Indiana from out-of-state brewers. The total 1934 Indiana consumption of 856,001 barrels of beer meant that Hoosiers drank 8.2 gallons per person that year.

Indiana authorities issued eighteen brewery permits in the first four years after repeal, though only seventeen actually went into operation. It was a sharp decline from the thirty-one breweries operating at the onset of Prohibition, but in line with the national trend. Across the country, less than half of the nation's 1,568 breweries reopened after repeal.

When Falstaff Brewing Company of Saint Louis negotiated a lease with Omaha's Krug Brewing Company in 1935, the subsequent consolidation boom further pressured smaller firms. Already stumbling in the rough economy, several Indiana breweries collapsed in the increased competition. Southern Indiana Ice and Beverage in New Albany closed in 1935. That year, P. H. Zorn Brewing Company in Michigan City became the Dunes Brewery, but three years later Dunes brewing was also gone. The T. M. Norton company barely got open in 1933 when it closed again, the victim of poor management and inadequate capitalization. After being closed for a number of years, the company reopened with new equipment as the T. M. Norton and Sons Brewing Company. But the reorganized company only lasted eighteen months, gone by 1940. In the glow of repeal, the William J. Wittekindt Brewing Company, Inc., opened in 1937 at 11 South Kentucky Avenue in Evansville, determined to be the Pocket City's third great brewer. Though Wittekindt's son trained in Germany to brew the firm's Hi Hop and Wittekindt Muenchener brands, the growing demand for bland, nationally marketed beers torpedoed the company, which closed in 1940. In Indianapolis, the Lieber Brewing Company started up in April 1935, but quickly failed. It was reborn in July 1937 as the Phoenix Brewing Company, which proved to be a short-lived species, as within six months it became Ajax Brewing. Ajax was a little more robust, lasting until early 1941. The owner of the Indianapolis Brewing Company, Lawrence P. Bardin, went to jail in the 1940s for short-filling his beer bottles. Hobbled by the scandal, the company closed in September 1948.

By 1950 there were only 407 American breweries. The next year the opening of Anheuser-Busch's ultra-modern brewery in Newark, New Jersey, kicked the competition up another notch. Between 1949 and 1958, another 185 breweries closed across the country.

The surviving Indiana breweries were caught in the same crossfire. The Kiley Brewing Company in Marion opened in 1934 with equipment bought at auction from the long-defunct Marion Brewing Association. In 1941 Kiley consolidated into the Fox Deluxe Brewing Company, which also had plants in Chicago, Grand Rapids, and Oklahoma City. After moving most of the brewed stock to Grand Rapids in mid-1949, Fox shuttered the Marion brewery with no warning in December 1949. Fox dissolved its Indiana subsidiary the next year. In Logansport, the K. G. Schmidt Brewing Company, which was a division of the Chicago firm of the same name, closed in 1950. So did the South Bend Brewing Company (which had changed its name in 1936 from the South Bend Beverage and Ice Association), claiming it was the victim of "big business." A *South Bend Tribune* article about the closing noted that in 1934 725 U.S. breweries produced more than thirty-seven million barrels. By the end of 1949, the number of breweries had dwindled to 405, but the output was almost ninety million barrels. An attorney for the brewery stockholders stated that the "monopoly in the brewing business is unavoidably plain to the naked eye." He also cited the eight-dollar-per-barrel excise tax that had been passed in 1944, claiming it placed an unfair burden on smaller brewers. According to the attorney, the tax snabbed about 45 percent of the small brewer's price, but only constituted one-third of the mega-brewers'.

Kamm and Schellinger suffered an enormous explosion in 1949 that killed two men. The company had brewed fifty thousand barrels the first year it opened after Prohibition, but was producing less than half that amount by 1950. On November 15, 1951, Kamm and Schellinger closed down their brewery, which had began in 1853. Lafayette Brewery, Inc., gave it up in February 1953.

In Evansville, F. W. Cook Company, Inc., started distributing its Goldblume in June 1933—four thousand cases the first day. Evansville residents could get the beer for $2.20 a case, including delivery. At one point during the Great Depression, Cook claimed to be America's largest producer of bottled beer. The company also did contract brewing, including the first Drewrys produced in the United States (the first case of which was shipped to the White House). But in the competitive frenzy of the postwar era, the company battled to stay open. In 1949 Cook commenced a two-million-dollar modernization program, financed in part by Tony Hulman, known for his Indianapolis Motor Speedway. Hulman had bought controlling interest in the brewery the year

An Evansville man ponders the heyday of Pocket City beer.
COURTESY OF THE UNIVERSITY OF SOUTHERN INDIANA

prior, also having a 10 percent stake in the Terre Haute Brewing Company. Scion of the Clabber Girl baking powder company, married to the heiress of the La Fendrich Cigar Company, Hulman was financially well off. But brewing did not work out so well for Hulman. Governor Roger Branigin once famously introduced him: "Tony Hulman, he's in the baking powder business by inheritance; he's in the cigar business by marriage, he's in the brewing business by mistake." In the 1950s the Cook company started a precipitous decline when company principal Adolph Schmidt, who had been a mainstay at the company for sixty-five years, died in his eighties. A couple of weeks later the brewmaster died. Longtime newspaperman and Indiana brewery association executive Harold Feightner remembered, "They tell me he did not leave a formula, he did everything by heart and they got a new one in and he couldn't follow it and their beer went bad. It went wild and then they made another mistake. They didn't go around and gather it up and, of course, they never made another sale in those places. I know. I had some of them down here. It exploded in the kitchen. It was like home brew." A rancorous strike in the summer of 1955 over an expired contract was the final straw, prompting Hulman to abruptly close the 102-year-old brewery.

> In the 1950s the Cook company started a precipitous decline when company principal Adolph Schmidt, who had been a mainstay at the company for sixty-five years, died in his eighties. A couple of weeks later the brewmaster died.

About ten years later, trustees announced that the Cook brewing equipment had been sold. It was headed to Barranquilla, Colombia, where the I. M. Santo Domingo Company was going to install it in its brewery. The Evansville Civic Center now occupies the F. W. Cook site.

The Terre Haute Brewing Company reopened in March 1934, with a Terre Haute native, Oscar Baur, as president. He revived its famous Champagne Velvet lager with a new "Million Dollar Flavor" motto (the recipe was insured for a million dollars) and distribution in nineteen states. Advertising heavily, the company claimed in a 1954 ad that Champagne Velvet had a flavor that was "keener, brighter, more satisfying," as well as "calorie free as any beer can be." Though the company's 950 workers eventually distributed its 1.5 million-barrel production in all forty-eight states, it was not enough to withstand the consolidation imperative. In May 1958 the Atlantic Brewing Company bought the Terre Haute Brewing Company assets. By November the new owners had closed the plant.

Beginning in January 1934, Centlivre Brewing Company in Fort Wayne bounded out of Prohibition with a $650,000 modernization program, again brewing Nickel Plate Special, as well as new brands such as Old Crown Ale. By 1939 Centlivre was brewing one hundred thousand barrels a year. With a 1.5-million-dollar expansion in 1950, the company was producing two hundred thousand barrels a year. In 1957 the company rolled out Alps Brau beer to celebrate the brewery's ninety-fifth birthday and was up to two hundred and fifty thousand barrels the year after. But in the postwar era, the consolidated national brands were overwhelming the regional brewers such as Centlivre with advertising. Centlivre struggled to cope, finally merging with the Chris-Craft corporation in 1961. Renamed the Old Crown Brewing Corporation, the reorganized company became the world's first employee-owned brewery. General Manager Marjorie Aubrey led the company for fourteen years. With the "Lazy Aged" slogan, the brewery's beers through the years included Centlivre, Bohemia, Special Export, Muenchener Export, Old Reliable, Old German, Alps Brau, Nickel Plate, Old Crown, and Van Merritt.

> The Hoff-Brau Brewing Company, which began in May 1934, was housed in a former washing-machine soap factory.... Locals claim you could discern the brewery's soapy past in Hoff-Brau— "The Beer without a Headache," as the company motto contended.

A reconstituted Berghoff Brewing Corporation opened in April 1933 under non-family ownership. The company advertised its Berghoff and International Club brews as "The beer that made itself famous." In June 1954 the Saint Louis-based Falstaff Brewing Company completed the takeover of the Berghoff Brewing Corporation, which was annually brewing more than a million barrels. The former Berghoff facility became the tenth brewing plant in Falstaff's conglomerated lineup. But the final brewing of Fort Wayne Berghoff beer had already shipped out in April 1954, headed for Chicago. A small part of the Berghoff complex remains at 2020 East Washington Street. The brick building with grand brick arches housed the immense boilers. Today, it is an office complex named Bergstaff Place.

Over the next few decades under Falstaff, the Fort Wayne plant produced Falstaff, Ballantine, Haffenreffer, and Narragansett beers. In the 1950s and 1960s, Falstaff got a little grisly fame: singer Hank Williams and beat writer Jack Kerouac both died after drinking cans of Falstaff—albeit respectively accompanied by morphine and whiskey.

The Hoff-Brau Brewing Company, which began in May 1934, was housed in a former washing-machine soap factory that was owned by one of the Berghoff brothers. Rub-No-More soap was so successful that Proctor and Gamble bought them out. Sitting with a now-empty building and a thirsty market for beer, the Berghoffs reverted to what they knew best, starting the new brewery in the old soap factory, perhaps hoping for a clean taste. Locals claim you could discern the brewery's soapy past in Hoff-Brau—"The Beer without a Headache," as the company motto contended. Hoff-Brau was the exclusive beer of the Indiana State Fair. The company operated until late 1951.

Muessel Brewing Company in South Bend had its Silver Edge out in the market in October 1933. By the end of the year, the firm had brewed 250,000 barrels. Its Bohemian brewmaster, Zdenck Sobotka, utilized Minnesota barley and hops from Oregon and Bohemia to brew a high-quality beer that had the "flavor of yesteryear," according to the *South Bend Tribune*. But it was not enough. On May 25, 1936, Muessel's had to reorganize in bankruptcy court, and six months later Drewrys Limited, USA, Inc., acquired the company assets. It was the Canadian brewer's first U.S. plant and became the subsidiary's headquarters. Drewrys had to weather a 1938 Michigan ban on the importation of Hoosier beer (later overturned), then a 1946 strike over higher wages and a government-dictated 30 percent production cut so grain could be redirected to "Europe's starving millions." In 1958 Drewrys produced 1,520,774 barrels of ale and lager, making it the largest brewery in the state. In the course of its production, Drewrys brewed close to an alphabet of beers: All American, Atlas Prager, Bull Dog, Champagne Velvet, Cold Brau, Dorf, Drewrys Extra Dry, Eastern, Edelweiss, F & G Supreme, Friars Club, G. E. S., Gold Coast, Golden Stein, Great Lakes, Heritage, Home, K & J, Katz, Leisy's, Nine Star, Pfeiffer, Prager, Prost, Red Top, Regal, Salzburg, SGA, Silver Edge, Skol, Trophy, Twenty Grand, 9-0-5, and Volks Brau.

And Then There Were None

As the buttoned-down 1950s slurred into the go-go 1960s, the consolidation of American breweries continued apace. There were only 230 breweries remaining in the country in 1961, and only 140 of those were independently run. By 1964, though Hoosiers drank fifteen-and-a-half gallons of beer per capita, Indiana was down to four functioning breweries: Drewrys in South Bend, Old Crown and Falstaff in Fort Wayne, and Sterling in Evansville. One by one, they began to go flat.

Drewrys was the first to go. After joining Associated Brewing Company of Detroit in 1965, Drewrys found itself sold to G. Heileman on August 1, 1972. Two weeks later Heileman announced that Drewrys would close in November 1972, throwing 350 brewery workers out of work. The old Drewrys plant is still standing at 1408 Elwood Avenue in South Bend, a ghostly sixteen-acre site with proud but decaying brick buildings. A few businesses inhabit parts of the complex, but most are empty.

The Old Crown Brewing Corporation was next, brewing its

last batch in late 1973. When Old Crown closed, it was the oldest operating business in Fort Wayne. It was also the demise of the only 100 percent employee-owned and operated brewery in the United States. The new plant that had cost so much just a few decades before now stood unoccupied, open to vandals. After a number of fires in the 1970s, the last of the derelict brewery was demolished in 1989. Though Charles Centlivre died in 1911, his memory lives on in Fort Wayne. The statue of Centlivre astride a beer barrel that once graced the top of the Centlivre brewery now perches on the roof of Hall's Gas House Restaurant.

In 1973 Falstaff invested two million dollars in the Fort Wayne plant so it could take over the brewing previously done in Saint Louis. A year before, Falstaff had also acquired Ballantine. The expansion did not work out. With cash draining rapidly, the company turned to the brewing wolf, Paul Kalmanovitz, who ran his S & P brewing conglomerate, General Brewing, out of San Francisco. By 1975 Kalmanovitz was in control of Falstaff and proceeded with the same strategy that he used to gut Pearl, Stroh's, National Bohemian,

> There were only 230 breweries remaining in the country in 1961, and only 140 of those were independently run. By 1964, though Hoosiers drank fifteen-and-a-half gallons of beer per capita, Indiana was down to four functioning breweries.

Olympia, and Pabst: drastically cut personnel, advertising, maintenance, and quality control. Sell off all possible equipment and real estate. Damn the brewery, full speed ahead. Though it was producing 1.2 million barrels a year, the century-old Berghoff brewery was doomed.

Sales started sliding—by 1976 production was down to nine hundred thousand barrels. S & P moved Ballantine and Narragansett beers to Fort Wayne to fill excess capacity. With Falstaff's marketing budget cut to near zero in the mid-1980s, sales plummeted. On January 7, 1990, the Fort Wayne Falstaff brewery closed. Three years later cranes arrived to rip gaping holes in the brick walls so riggers could yank the giant kettles out of the old building. The equipment was bound for a Pabst plant in China.

Sterling Brewers, Inc., of Evansville was the last big industrial brewing company in Indiana. The firm did all it could to survive. Months before Prohibition ended, workers were in the plant replacing the old wooden vats and fermenters with new steel ones. Newly renovated, Sterling was brewing in April 1933. By 1937 Sterling had enough demand to purchase a second plant in Freeport, Illinois. With Freeport's fifty thousand barrels, Sterling produced five hundred and fifty thousand barrels a year. In the early days of repeal, the company marketed Sterling and Lug o' Ale throughout the Midwest and South, even outselling Falls City in its hometown of Louisville (though at the time, Falls City was outselling Sterling in Evansville—a no-honor-in-your-hometown kind of thing). Sterling also contract-brewed Drewrys from 1933 to 1936, the year that the Canadian firm bought Muessels. In 1938 Sterling began canning its beer. Despite its informal slogan, "if nature won't, Sterling will" (a backhanded reference to the beer's "health" aspect), Sterling remained a big seller throughout the region into the 1950s.

In 1964 Sterling affiliated with Detroit's Associated Brewing Company, which gobbled the company up four years later. Four years after that, Associated dealt the Evansville brewery to G. Heileman, which used the plant to also brew some of the conglomerate's other brands, including Champagne Velvet, Drewrys, Falls City, Weideman, Rheingold, Pfeiffer, Drummond Brothers, 9-0-5, Lederbrau, Katz, Bavarian, Prager Bohemian, and Tropical Ale.

Plagued by overcapacity by the late 1980s, G. Heileman shut the 125-year-old brewery down. A group of Evansville-area investors stepped in, determined to reinvigorate the brewery, which they reopened with great hoopla on September 21, 1988. The new/old name was the Evansville Brewing Company, a throwback to the plant's nineteenth-century title. Under brewer Ken Griffiths, the EBC's ninety employees produced many of the previously brewed brands, as well as Evansville, Gerst, and Lemp, which was inspired by one of America's first lagers. The EBC's contract brews included the first organic beer in the United States, Frontier, White Ridge Wheat, beers for Chicago's State Street Brewing, as well as kinky 1990s beers, such as Bicycle Beer's Veri Berry and Misty Lime, Gringo Light, Hey Mon, Jackaroo, and Joe's Freakin. The EBC also brewed Birell beer under license from Hürlimann Brewery in Zürich. In 1993 the EBC's Drummond Brothers won a gold medal at the Great American Beer Festival in Denver.

By the mid-1990s the Evansville Brewing Company shipped almost 40 percent of its 1.2 million-barrel production overseas. But the company was whipsawed between the highly efficient, heavily marketed national brands and the rise of boutique breweries that catered to a discerning market. It was too much. On October 1, 1997, the Evansville Brewing Company declared bankruptcy and closed—the last industrial brewery in Indiana. In time, only the sadly derelict brick brewery stable and repurposed business office remained at the corner of Fulton Avenue and the Lloyd Expressway. An era had ended. But even as the late-1990s media intoned their eulogies for large-scale brewing in the state, another chapter of Indiana beer was already frothing up.

CHAPTER SEVEN

New Brewing
1989–2009

THE INDIANA MICROBREWING revolution exploded in the 1990s.

By the time Evansville Brewing Company, the last Hoosier industrial brewer, shut down in 1997, nineteen microbrewers had opened across Indiana. The microbreweries were scattered from one end of the state to the other, from Three Floyds up in Hammond down to Main Street in Evansville. There were eight in Indianapolis alone: the Indianapolis Brewing Company, Broad Ripple Brewing, Alcatraz, Circle V, Ram, Rock Bottom, Wildcat, and Glacier's End. There was Oaken Barrel in Greenwood, Duneland in Michigan City, Bloomington Brewing, Lafayette Brewing, Mishawaka Brewing, Just Do It (also in Mishawaka), Back Road in La Porte, and Tucker in Salem. Hometown brewing had returned to Indiana with a vengeance.

The Beginnings

The Indianapolis Brewing Company was the first, opening in 1989. "Our permit took a year," former IBC brewmaster Tom Peters recalled. "I think it was the first new permit to be issued in forty years, so the state didn't have much practice." Operating out of an industrial park at 3250 North Post

Road, the IBC brewers used a twenty-barrel system with forty-barrel fermenters to produce between 2,000 to 3,000 barrels a year. "It was a learning curve," Peters laughed. The bottling line came from the old Hudepohl plant. "Took us two years to slow it down to a speed we could handle," he noted.

Indianapolis native and brewing consultant Jamie Emmerson (now executive brewmaster at Full Sail) helped the rookie IBC brewers with training and recipes out at his Hood River, Oregon, brewery. "I think our first brew—a hoppy golden ale—was a little too much for Indiana," Emmerson remembered. So IBC initially focused on lagers, but soon added ales. Named in honor of the original Indianapolis Brewing Company's award-winning brews, the IBC brands included Indianapolis Dusseldorfer Amber Ale, Pale Ale, and Oktoberfest, as well as a Stout in barrels. Beyond contract beers for Pikes Place in Oregon and the Fort Wayne Brewing Company, the IBC also produced its own Main Street lager and Indianapolis Brick Yard Bock, which garnered a long-lasting regard. "It was pretty yummy," Peters said. "It kind of became jet fuel after a few months."

When the IBC began brewing, Indiana still had the old temperance-era laws on the books that prevented brewers from selling on site. So a brewpub was out. The IBC sold to downtown retailers, package stores, some groceries, and restaurants that included Saint Elmo's and Palamino's. The RCA Dome had a booth that hawked IBC beer. But the IBC found it hard going. "It was a struggle in the middle of light-beer country," Peters said. "We were stuck in no-man's land—too big to be low-cost and too small for economies of scale." Beyond the problem of finding vendors who would supply a small brewer, the IBC dependence on wholesale slowly strangled the company. Retail looked like the way to go. By 1997 the company had run its course, selling its entire operation. But IBC's legacy remains. "It opened some eyes—made people more adventuresome," Peters said. "It was a fun way to make a living for a while."

A transplanted Yorkshireman, John Hill, was the next one to plunge into Indiana microbrewing. In 1990 Hill opened his

Indiana's Microbrewing Mentor

Jamie Emmerson is the executive brewmaster for Full Sail Brewing in Hood River, Oregon, responsible for its 150,000-barrel annual production. Though he signed on with Full Sail in April 1988 when the firm only had four employees, Emmerson served a critical role in the birth of Indiana's microbrewing industry.

A native of Indianapolis, Emmerson was an organic chemistry and German major at Butler University in the mid-1980s. Recognizing the latent potential of his knowledge, his law-school roommates urged him to homebrew for the guys. By 1986 he was brewing some pretty good beer. After visiting some of the "big, old breweries," as Emmerson put it, he enrolled in brewing courses at Chicago's Siebel Institute of Technology, the Massachusetts Institute of Technology of American brewing.

When he finished his training, a number of firms offered him jobs, including Sterling in Evansville, the nascent Full Sail, and the Indianapolis Brewing Company, which was still in the planning phase. Emmerson initially was drawn to IBC as he could return to his hometown, but they weren't quite ready for him. Realizing that Full Sail had the same brewing system IBC was planning to install, Emmerson headed west to work a bit on the system before returning to Indiana. But things did not go as planned.

When Emmerson came back four months later, IBC was still not operational. So instead of brewing in Indiana, the IBC folks came out to Full Sail to train on the equipment. A year or so later, Emmerson helped train another Hoosier microbrewing pioneer, Broad Ripple Brewery's John Hill, solidifying his role as mentor to Indiana's brewing renaissance.

Two decades later, Emmerson's still with Full Sail—indeed, is almost wedded to the place: "I married the boss," Emmerson laughed, referring to his marriage to Irene Firmat, brewery founder and CEO.

Broad Ripple Brewing Company, along with his Broad Ripple Brewpub. Hill had a number of advantages. He already knew the pub business, having run for a number of years the Wellington Wine Bar in Broad Ripple, where he introduced then exotic imported beers and Indianapolis's first wheat beer. Hill was also an electrical engineer and contractor, so the mechanical side of brewing held few fears for him. But most importantly, Hill knew good beer. "Yorkshire has the strongest beer in England," Hill said with his Middlesbrough accent in full thunder, "I was weaned on the stuff," going on to wax lyric about the Old Peculiars and Sam Smiths of his youth.

> By the early 1990s the brewpub scene across the country was bubbling. Not only did microbreweries resonate a warm and fuzzy small-business vibe, they were generating some nice taxes for the states where legislators had allowed them to prosper.

Though both the brewhouse and pub were in the same building, the former Broad Ripple Auto Parts store at Sixty-fifth Street and the Monon Trail, Indiana beer laws that prohibited beer sales at the brewery forced Hill to open the two at separate addresses. So the brewery was listed at 840 East Sixty-fifth and the same-building brewpub was 842 East Sixty-fifth. Pub-goers could down their ESBs and porters while looking through the leaded-glass windows into the brewery, but they couldn't enter one from the other without going outside. The letter of the law was upheld.

Ironically, Hill also did his homework with Emmerson. "We didn't know anything," Hill laughed. "We took pictures of everything on the workbench. We thought everything was important." Whatever brewing wisdom Hill gleaned must have gone to good use, because the Broad Ripple Brewery and Brewpub both prospered. It appeared that full-flavored beer and retail margins would work in Indiana—light-beer land or not.

Legislation: A Successful Model

But the brewing dance of the seven veils was about to end. By the early 1990s the brewpub scene across the country was bubbling. Not only did microbreweries resonate a warm and fuzzy small-business vibe, they were generating some nice taxes for the states where legislators had allowed them to prosper. Nudged by aspiring brewpub entrepreneur Jeff Mease of Bloomington Brewing Company, State Representative Mark Kruzan introduced House Bill 1502 into the Indiana legislature in 1993. Cosponsored by Jerry Bales in the House and Vi Simpson and Joe Harrison in the Senate, the bill liberalized Indiana's brewery laws to allow on-site beer sales for breweries. Kruzan, now mayor of Bloomington, remembered the bill: "There was no brewers association, no lobbyists for it. It was just a small businessman with an idea." Kruzan recalled that many of his colleagues were dismissive, unable to imagine small brewers having the ability to even produce much beer. "Maybe not being taken seriously was an advantage," he said. Kruzan cannily marketed his bill as a small-business matter and sent it to the appropriate committee. "Then it became more about small business, rather than alcohol," he noted.

With virtually no opposition, the bill passed with lightning speed. (Though a big-brewery lobbyist demanded a cap of sixty thousand barrels for microbrewers initially be put in the bill, that demand was ratcheted down to a twenty thousand-barrel limit.) Amended over time, Indiana Statute IC 7.1-3-2-6 permitted microbrewers to "Sell the brewery's beer by the glass for consumption on the premises," as well as allowing brewers to "Install a doorway or other opening between the brewery and an adjacent restaurant that provides the public and the permittee with access to both premises." These seemingly innocuous clauses uncorked a froth of new breweries through the 1990s. As the old saying goes, "Make a law; make a business." When Kruzan assessed his legislative work through the lens of fifteen years of microbrewing, he's impressed by the astounding growth of breweries in the state: "One, it has proven it was a successful model. And two, that it's more about enterprise than alcohol."

Taking the Waters

Given that water comprises more than 90 percent of beer, it's not surprising that brewers focus a lot of attention on this vital component, which impacts harshness, bitterness, taste, clarity, color, and malt extraction. Famous brewing towns often gained their reputations from beer that was crafted to match their particular water. Burton-on-Trent's celebrated pale ales owe much to the deep wells along the Trent and Burton rivers that provide water with high calcium, sulphate, and bicarbonate levels. Calcium is essential for proper enzyme reactions in mashing and yeast development. The high levels in Burton-on-Trent give the ale a firm body and long finish. Sulfates, which encourages bitter resin extraction from the hops, lends their ales its characteristic dryness. Pilsen has very soft water, ideal for its pale, hoppy lagers. While Pilsen has a total dissolved salts of only 30.8 per million in its water, Burton-on-Trent has a near-stony 1,226. Chloride is another critical element, providing enhanced sweetness and a full texture. Porter and stout originated in London and Dublin, in part, due to the high chloride levels in their water.

Indiana was little different, as early brewers tried to locate the best water source they could. Madison brewers hunkered by a clear, sweet spring that gushed from the bluff beside the Ohio River. In Lafayette, the Spring Brewery leased the best spring in town and later became a neighborhood water department. A bounteous spring supplied the Peru Brewery with fine water (which now is the source for Cole Brothers Water Company's natural spring water). Mishawaka's Kamm-Schellinger built beside the Saint Joseph River, from which the company drew its brewing water. In South Bend, Muessel's brewery used deep artesian wells for its beers. Centlivre in Fort Wayne was inordinately proud of its deep "rock water" wells. But once water was secured, the Hoosier brewers made do like all their predecessors, concocting a beer that fit their water.

Today, brewers can determine the mineral composition of water scientifically, and then adjust it to a broad range of beer styles. Depending on the brewery, the water treatment includes pH reduction, mineral salt adjustment, dechlorination, particulate removal, and microbiological control.

Water varies across the state. Upland Brewing's head brewer, Caleb Staton, noted, "Bloomington water quality is very excellent for brewing as is," mentioning that when they brew ales, they add a little hardness to mimic classic Burton-on-Trent water, and when brewing lagers they soften the water by boiling it overnight. In Indianapolis, Alcatraz's Omar Castrellon talks about the extremely hard city water that comes from both reservoirs and wells. In dry periods, Indianapolis water gets even harder. "We either have to live with it, or treat it," he said. Broad Ripple's brewmaster Kevin Matalucci indicates the hard Indianapolis water is conducive to his English ales. Terre Haute sits on a giant aquifer, which Vigo Brewing uses to produce Brugge's fine Belgian ales. Before its demise, Warbird charcoal filtered the Fort Wayne city water to remove aberrant elements such as run-off farm fertilizers and monitored iron content that could have impeded yeast performance. Like many brewers, Warbird former owner Dave Holmes

Today, brewers can determine the mineral composition of water scientifically, and then adjust it to a broad range of beer styles. Depending on the brewery, the water treatment includes pH reduction, mineral salt adjustment, dechlorination, particulate removal, and microbiological control.

dreamed of a reverse-osmosis water treatment system: "Some day we'll R/O our water and re-build it, but not yet."

Chuck Krcilek at Back Road Brewery in La Porte takes a more personal approach to his water. Krcilek's brewery is across the street from the city water department run by a customer of his, Todd Taylor. "We have really good water here, from seven deep wells," Krcilek said. "Todd makes the water right, then I take it from there and work my magic." Krcilek charcoal filters the water and preheats it overnight to drive off whatever unwanted chemicals that remain. Occasionally, Taylor drops by to sample Krcilek's alchemy. "He gets a pint and I get water. We're both happy," Krcilek said.

Winners and Losers

By the end of 1999 twenty-three breweries had begun in Indiana, most of them brewpubs, which included new companies that opened from 1998 to 1999: Mad Anthony in Fort Wayne, Upland Brewing in Bloomington, Barley Island in Noblesville, and Hops Grill Brewery in Indianapolis. But there were also casualties in the 1990s, both in Indiana and across the nation. Beer's low material cost and potential for profit seduced a number of entrepreneurs, several of whom failed to understand that they also had to brew a good product. Some home brewers who thought they could make the jump to being professionals found that it was a steep step. Undercapitalized, ignorant, poorly managed, or just plain hapless breweries fell to the wayside. Evansville's Firkin Brewpub tossed in the towel in 1998. In Indianapolis, Wildcat, an extract brewer, also closed in 1998; Hops Grill Brewing barely lasted a year, closing in 1999, the same year Glacier's End Brewing at Castleton Square Mall ended.

As the new millennium dawned, the pace continued: Terre Haute Brewing, Aberdeen Brewing in Valparaiso, and the Oyster Bar in Fort Wayne began brewing in 2000, but all stopped brewing within six years. Just Brew It stopped it in 2000. The next year Circle V Brewing in Indianapolis closed its doors, as did the Tucker Brewing/Silver Creek Brewing in southern Indiana. A psychiatrist-aviator opened Warbird Brewing in Fort Wayne in 2004 with a beer-canning system. Brugge Brasserie in Broad Ripple also started brewing its Belgian-inspired beers in 2004, the same year Duneland Brewhouse in Michigan City closed. Another aviator team launched Nine G Brewing in South Bend in 2005, but closed the next year when Evansville's Little Cheers, the successor to Firkin's, also ended. Michigan City's Shoreline Brewery started in 2005, as did Rock Bottom's College Park brewpub in Indianapolis. In 2006 Terre Haute Brewing stopped production. The next year, Half Moon Restaurant in Kokomo began brewing, as did Powerhouse Brewing in Columbus and Vigo Brewing Company in Terre Haute, which took over the defunct Terre Haute Brewing system. In 2008 two veterans of the Three Floyds operation began Crown Brewing in Crown Point. That same year, a Kokomo elementary schoolteacher utilized his home-brewing rig to start Indiana's smallest brewery, Brass Monkey, which proved to be one of the best, winning a gold and silver medal at the Indiana State Fair Brewers Cup competition. In Aurora, a husband and wife named their brewery to honor their hometown pride, the Great Crescent Brewery, which was one of Indiana's largest in the nineteenth century.

Well over forty microbreweries have opened in Indiana since 1989, with more popping up each year. There are more breweries in Indiana than any time since Prohibition.

> **Well over forty microbreweries have opened in Indiana since 1989, with more popping up each year. There are more breweries in Indiana than any time since Prohibition.**

But they've not all been hits—fifteen of the microbreweries have closed. And among those brewers who've prospered, there's been no small amount of heartache and toil as they struggled to master their craft and express their creativity. But in the process, they've enlivened their communities, providing both a hand-crafted brew that is redolent of home and a welcoming place to socialize among friends. Now that we know what's come before, let's explore who's brewing what out there in the Hoosier State, and get to know Indiana a little better in the process.

ELKHART
LA PORTE   MISHAWAKA
MICHIGAN CITY
VALPARAISO
HOBART   FORT WAYNE
CROWN POINT
MUNSTER

KOKOMO
LAFAYETTE

NOBLESVILLE
INDIANAPOLIS

BRAZIL   GREENWOOD
TERRE HAUTE
BATESVILLE
COLUMBUS
BLOOMINGTON
NASHVILLE
AURORA

NEW ALBANY
EVANSVILLE

CHAPTER EIGHT

CRAFT BREWING
Central Indiana

C ENTRAL INDIANA IS IN THE HEART of Hoosier brewing country. In spite of its tabletop
topography, it is a region that ranges from downtown Indianapolis's pulsing sports, shopping,
and entertainment district to Broad Ripple's artsy environs
to the bustling suburbs of Hamilton County and Southport
to the former temperance stronghold of Kokomo to charm-
ing college-town Lafayette. In each one of these communities
there are unique breweries that cater to their residents—and
equally important, welcome those from outside.

Some of the state's largest breweries are here, as well as
some of the country's leading brewpubs. There are hometown places that glory in their connection to the past. There
are über-modern brewers who are looking to the far zymurgic
horizon. There are British-style brewpubs and Belgian-style
brewpubs, sports-bar brewpubs, yuppie sipping-and-chat-
ting brewpubs, and old-style family-oriented brewpubs. The
brewers come in different sizes and sometimes have different
dreams. Their backstories reflect the idiosyncratic paths that

PHOTOGRAPHY BY RICHARD SPAHR

many of them followed. But the brewers all share the same goal: brewing excellent beer and sharing it with those who find the way to their doors.

Broad Ripple Brewery and Brewpub

840–842 East Sixty-fifth Street
Indianapolis, IN 46220
(317) 253–2739
www.broadripplebrewpub.com

THE BROAD RIPPLE BREWPUB is a piece of Yorkshire transplanted to the heart of Indianapolis. With its small paneled rooms replete with pub snuggery, fireplace, ticking grandfather clock, Staffordshire pots, and pressed-tin ceiling, it is Britannia on the Monon. Its imperial pints of English-style ale further bespeak the origins of the owner, John Hill, a curmudgeon of a Yorkshireman known for his fair and open ways. "I knew what an English pub looked like," Hill said. "It's like an extension of your living room."

Indiana clearly appreciates Hill's work, as crowds have flocked to his warm and intimate place since it opened in 1990. Located near the core of Broad Ripple's trendy entertainment district, just adjacent to the Monon Trail, the Broad Ripple Brewpub has extensive outdoor seating to complement its cozy interior. For more than ten years, *NUVO* and *Indianapolis Monthly* have honored the Brewpub with the Best Brewpub award. And Broad Ripple's beer has also garnered accolades: the Extra Special Bitter won a gold medal at the 1991 Great American Beer Festival and took Best of Show at the 1999 Indiana State Fair Brewers Cup competition. The Redbird Mild, an English Dark Mild Ale, won at the Brewers Cup in 2002 and

John Hill and head brewer, Kevin Matalucci, the Yorkshireman and the Hoosier.

a gold medal in 2008. The hard-nosed reviewers at beeradvocate.com gave Broad Ripple Brewpub an overall A- rating.

Broad Ripple was Indiana's first brewpub. "I'm unique," said Hill. "I never home brewed—I just knew what good beer tasted like." Accordingly, Hill did a lot of research before he started in 1990. A California brewing equipment dealer had tried to foist a $280,000 system on the newbie, but with the canny purchase of his seven-barrel Century system and tight control on his construction costs, Hill started up with a manageable overhead. To economize, Hill bought a large surplus commercial refrigerator from

Beers Brewed:
Broad Ripple's draught beers include a golden Pilsner, India Pale Ale, Extra Special Bitter, Lawn Mower Pale Ale, Herr Kevin's Alt Bier, and the American-style, unfiltered Wheat. Broad Ripple typically has one or two English-style cask ales on tap, served through traditional British beer engines. The cask ales include Diving Duck American Brown, Wobbly Bob's American Pale Ale, Best Bitter, ESB, Monon Porter, and Finneen's Auld Sod Stout. Broad Ripple brews thirty to forty seasonals each year.

the Boys School state prison. "It was made with solid-steel panels, so the convicts couldn't escape," Hill noted. "It was *heavy.*" The first year Broad Ripple brewed seven hundred barrels of beer. "We were in the black from the first day," Hill fondly remembered.

An Indiana University environmental science graduate, head brewer Kevin Matalucci was Broad Ripple's fourth brewer when he began in 1994. Matalucci got his start at the Brewpub as a waiter and bartender. In his off time, he would hang around the brewery with then-brewer Ted Miller (now the owner-brewer at nearby Brugge Brasserie). When Miller took off on a round-the-world brewing adventure, Matalucci was ready to step in—and he has been the brewer ever since. A solid, tousle-haired guy with ruddy cheeks and a ready smile, Matalucci is at one with his equipment, dancing an intricate jitterbug among the hoses, pipes, tanks, and valves. He scoffed at the automated brewhouses used by larger breweries. "That's all run by computer. I'm more an erector-set kind of guy," he said as he bolted to fine-tune the temperature. When asked, Matalucci declined to name his favorite brew: "I like them all. It's kind of like asking a polygamist who's his favorite wife."

Hot-Dog Brown Ale

Hoosier brewers tell the story about a colleague who was brewing during the Indiana State Fair. Unable to go, he asked his buddies to bring him a hot dog. When they returned, he was stirring the mash tun. "Toss it up here," he said. But the toss went a bit awry and ended up in the mash. Reportedly, it was a beer with some body and a whiff of the old dog.

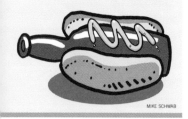

MIKE SCHWAB

Opened: November 1990 • Owner: John Hill • Brewer: Kevin Matalucci • Brewing System: 7-barrel Century Manufacturing System • Annual Production: 1,000 barrels • Tours: No • Hours: Monday through Thursday 11:00 a.m. to midnight; Friday and Saturday 11:00 a.m. to 1:00 a.m.; Sunday 3:00 p.m. to 10:00 p.m. • Beer to go: Growlers are available for purchase. • Food: The brewpub offers a full menu, including several Yorkshire specialties such as Fish and Chips, Bangers and Mash, and Shepherd's Pie.

Brugge Brasserie
1011a East Westfield Boulevard
Indianapolis, IN 46220
(317) 255–0978
www.brugebrasserie.com

Ted Miller, on top of his operation.

BRUGGE BREWMASTER TED MILLER is an intense guy, a nimble-minded Gen-Xer whose quick-footed, up-and-gone moves belie his previous life as an international soccer player. After a stint as head brewer at the Broad Ripple Brewpub in the early 1990s, Miller took off on a global beer adventure, brewing in Seattle with part of Pyramid, in the Caribbean's Turks and Caicos, and in Hong Kong with the South China Brewing Company. In Chengdu, the capital of China's chili-loving Sichuan province, Miller set up a brewery, where he experimented brewing with *hua jiao,* the benumbing Sichuan flower pepper.

But Miller's 1990 trip through Europe, where he delved into Belgium's more that 450 different kinds of beer, inspired him on his current course. "The Germans, they're very stubborn with their lagers," Miller said. "The English are arrogant about their real ales. Then you have the Belgians—they brew it all." With almost endless brewing possibilities, Belgian beer seemed a perfect fit for Miller's restless, creative mind. "Belgian ales have a certain

'Je ne sais quoi'—maybe it's the no-rules thing—maybe it's the monks. Who knows? But I love it!" he said.

So after many years of peripatetic brewing, Miller returned to his hometown with his wife, Shannon, and their three children, determined to bring Belgian-style craft beer to Indiana. The result was Brugge Brasserie, which opened in April 2005. Located right next to the Monon Trail in Broad Ripple, it is a chic gastro-pub, with an edgy neo-industrial esthetic. Brewed with classic hops and exotica that include rosewater, pickled plums, chamomile, orange peel, coriander, chocolate, coffee, and grains of paradise, Brugge's full-flavored Belgian-style White and Black beers found almost immediate acceptance, as did his Tripel de Ripple, a va- nilla- and pear-tinged blond ale with a heady 9.85 percent alcohol level. Miller's Diamond Kings of Heaven is what he calls his "wild beer." Fermented with persimmons and Brettanomyces, the wild yeast strain of lambic fame, the beer is barrel-aged for a year.

Miller's beers have won big

Beers Brewed:
Brugge White, a lively witbier; Brugge Black, an ancient style of chocolaty dark beer; Brugge Sacre Fleur Saison, a slightly sour beer with a floral hint of rosewater; Brugge Dubbel; and Tripel de Ripple.

Brugge specializes in beer-enhanced Belgiun cuisine including *moules frites* (mussels and French fries.)

awards: his Irish Red took a Gold Medal in the 1996 World Beer Cup, and he also won a Silver at the 2005 Great American Beer Festival. In 2007 the Indiana State Fair Brewers Cup judges awarded Brugge a Gold in the Belgian Specialty category and gave the Diamond Kings of Heaven a Silver in 2008. Beeradvocate.com gave Brugge Brasserie a "Very Good" B+ grade, and ratebeer.com visitors sent in high marks: "Very quaffable and very enjoyable brew. Nicely done!" one drinker gushed about his Quad.

In 2007 Miller embarked on a major expansion, purchasing the Terre Haute Brewing Company under his new company, the Vigo Brewing Group. By 2008 Miller and his brewmaster Micah Weichert were brewing most of the brasserie's beer, along with bottled Brugge beers. In the fourteen thousand-square-foot facility, Miller's group can produce up to twenty-five thousand barrels a year.

Opened: April 2005 • Owners: Ted and Shannon Miller, Shannon Stone, actor Abraham Benrubi • Brewer: Ted Miller • Brewing System: A system made of miscellaneous "bits and pieces from all over," as Miller said. "We do things the smart way—CHEAP OR FREE!!!" Brugge can brew ten barrels in the rig. • Annual Production: 400 barrels at the small Brasserie brewhouse. Primary brewing is done at Miller's Vigo Brewing Group in Terre Haute. • Tours: No. • Hours: Monday through Thursday 11:30 a.m. to 12:30 a.m.; Friday and Saturday 11:30 a.m. to 1:30 a.m.; Sunday Noon to 9:00 p.m. • Beer to go: Not at Brugge Brasserie, though bottled Brugge beer is widely available in Indiana's better beer outlets. • Food: Brugge Brasserie specializes in beer-enhanced Belgian cuisine, including *moules frites* (mussels and French fries), carbonade flambé (beef stew made with beer), and *waterzooi* (fish stew). The café features regionally produced ingredients, including Indiana duck and locally grown produce.

Barley Island Brewing Company

639 Conner Street
(Indiana 32, just east of White River Bridge)
Noblesville, IN 46060
(317) 770–5280
www.barleyisland.com

BARLEY ISLAND is the seventeenth-century name for the alehouse room where patrons downed their beer. With its dark paneling, stained glass, and womb-like bar, the Barley Island brewpub fits its name. But the pool tables, big-screen televisions, video games, and live-music stage bring it right into the modern world, as do the broad range of people enjoying Barley Island's award-winning brews and handcrafted food: workmen and professionals, families and singles. It is booming Hamilton County's only brewery.

Beers Brewed:
BarFly IPA, an American-style India Pale Ale with a Summit-hops tropical-fruit flavor; Dirty Helen Brown Ale; a light and lemony Flat Top Wheat Ale; Sheet Metal Blonde Ale; Blind Tiger Pale Ale; coffee-enhanced Black Majic Java Stout; complex Brass Knuckles Oatmeal Stout.

Barley Island had an academic genesis. A Wabash College biology graduate who is now a global marketing manager for Roche Diagnostics, Barley Island's founder Jeffrey Eaton used his microbrewing dream as a planning project for part of his Butler University masters of business administration education. In December 1999 Eaton opened the doors to his dream, beginning to produce beers that reflected his building's history as a reputed prohibition-era brewery. His Blind Tiger Pale Ale celebrates the name for illicit speakeasies, where they would put a stuffed tiger in the window when hooch was available. Dirty Helen Brown Ale commemorates an earthy local bartender. Brass Knuckles Oatmeal Stout explains itself. The company now distributes its bottled beer in Indiana, Kentucky, and Illinois outside of Chicago.

The Barley Island brewhouse is a bright, airy place, light pouring in the plateglass windows. Head brewer Jon Lang inauspiciously started brewing there on September 11, 2001. "It was actually a relief," Lang said, "just to come in and get away from the TV and brew." Lang was a Minnesota hydraulic engineer and home brewer when his wife was transferred to Indianapolis. "I don't think I ever brewed anything twice," he said about his ten years of home brewing, going on to say how "brewing the same thing over and over again" helped his consistency. Lang has to be running one of the nation's most colorful brewing systems. Barley Island's original ten-barrel Saaz System was purchased used from The Strip brewpub in Pittsburgh. The tall, copper bright tank came out of the Monte Carlo Brewery in Las Vegas. The strip-and-casino system has served them well, producing a number of winners: a Great American Beer Festival Silver Medal in 2006 for Java Stout and a 2007 Brewers Cup Gold Medal for Brass Knuckles Oatmeal Stout and Bourbon Barrel Stout. In 2008 Great American Beer Festival judges awarded Barley Island a coveted Bronze Medal for its Beastie Barrel Stout.

Opened: December 1999 • Owner: Jeffrey and Linda Eaton • Brewer: Jon Lang, Assistant Mike Hess • Brewing System: Ten-barrel Saaz system with three twenty-barrel fermenters • Annual Production: 800 to 1,000 barrels • Tours: Yes, call two days ahead for availability. • Hours: Monday through Thursday 11:00 a.m. to midnight; Friday and Saturday 11:00 a.m. to 1:00 a.m.; Sunday 3:00 p.m. to midnight. • Beer to go: Bottled beer and growlers are available. • Food: A full menu, including popular beer-battered mushrooms, shrimp, and fish and chips, as well as salads, soups, and desserts.

Rock Bottom Brewery, College Park

2801 Lake Circle Drive
Indianapolis, IN 46268
(317) 471–8840
www.rockbottom.com

ROCK BOTTOM BREWERY is an odd kind of microbrewing chain, allowing each brewer to craft the beer they find best. While the twenty-nine Rock Bottom locations across the country may share beer names, as in the Circle City Light that both of Indianapolis's Rock Bottom locations serve, the recipes and brew can vary widely. It gives the Rock Bottom brewers a freedom and creativity typically not found among chain breweries intent on maintaining a strict corporate style. And judging from the award-winning beers made by the chain's two Indiana breweries, the strategy is yielding some big successes.

The College Park location off of Eighty-sixth Street between Township Line and Michigan roads sports that clubby neo-Adirondack look so prevalent in contemporary suburban upscale eateries: soaring ceilings, dark polished woods, shiny brass, and warm earth tones. The brewery also reflects an attention to detail, with its gleaming twenty-four-barrel, stainless-steel JV Northwest brewing system standing proudly in a Trappist-clean environment. Brewster Liz Laughlin presides over the system, one of Indiana's growing number of female brewers. "I have my baby, I keep her clean," Laughlin said. A native of Cape Cod, Massachusetts, who professionally brewed for almost a decade in the craft-beer hotbeds of Eugene and Portland, Oregon, before Rock Bottom transferred her in November 2006, Laughlin's been "pleasantly surprised" by Indianapolis: "Hoosiers want big beers—they want hops. They love Belgians, big IPAs, double IPAs."

With her small, slender frame and short hair, Laughlin looks like a gymnast, albeit oddly attired in brown brewer boots and Carhartt trousers. She's already gathered Indiana kudos for her beer, taking a 2008 Brewers Cup Gold Medal for her Trippel Trouble in the Belgian Strong category, as well as a bronze for her Circle City Light, a Munich Helles lager. Laughlin contends she's a very traditional brewer who

Beers Brewed:

Circle City Light, a flavorful light lager with floral hops; a Seasonal Wheat ranging from Witbier to Hefeweizen; Heartland Red, an extra special bitter; copper-hued Double Barrel Pale Ale with a hop kick (the most popular); Brickway Brown in a brown porter style, and the Hoosier Ma Stout varies in style through the year, including Dry Irish Stout, Milk Stout, and Imperial Stout. Seasonals include a crisp unfiltered Blue Dogz Pale with an upright malt structure, Happy Pils, and the 3 Cs Brown, which uses three kinds of Mexican peppers, chocolate, and cinnamon.

enjoys the challenges of making a great lager. "From when I started, I was just making beer," she said. "When I got here as head
brewer, I've been creating my own."

Opened: May 2005 • Owner: Frank Day • Brewer: Liz Laughlin • Brewing System: Twenty-
four-barrel JV Northwest System • Annual Production: 900 barrels • Tours: Yes. • Hours:
Monday through Wednesday 11:00 a.m. to midnight; Thursday 11:00 a.m. to 1:30 a.m.;
Friday 11:00 a.m. to 1:00 a.m.; Saturday 11:30 a.m. to 1:00 a.m.; Sunday 11:30 a.m.
to 11:30 p.m. • Beer to go: Growlers • Food: Rock Bottom's slogan, "Serious about our
food. Crazy about our beer," gives you a sense of the full menu available. Popular
dishes include the Asian Ahi Tuna Salad, Southwest Chicken and Shrimp Pasta, and
the Texas Fire Steak.

Alcatraz Brewing Company
Circle Centre Mall, 49 West Maryland Street, Suite 104
Indianapolis, IN 46204
(317) 488–1230
www.alcatrazbrewing.com/indianapolis.php

ALCATRAZ BREWING COMPANY was downtown Indianapo-
lis's first brewpub, dating back to 1995 when the city hatched the
Circle Centre Mall as part of its ambitious urban development
project. Conspicuously sited near a mall entrance, the brewery's
tall tanks served as a visible symbol of hip gastronomy. For many
visitors venturing downtown after its decades of decline, Alcatraz
was their first experience with craft beer. Many convention goers
today look forward to Alcatraz's crisp lagers.

Omar Castrellón arrived at Alcatraz as its craft brewer in
2002 after more than a decade of brewing in the South. He started
with the German-owned Heidelberg Brewery in Durham, North
Carolina, learning to make quality lagers from a German brewmaster. Then there were stints at breweries in Greensboro and
Raleigh, North Carolina; Tuscaloosa, Alabama; and Little Rock,
Arkansas, before joining Alcatraz. A compact fellow with hip
designer glasses and an earnest manner, Castrellón's been a mainstay of the Indiana craft-brewing scene since.

Born in Panama, Castrellón came to the United States when

he was fourteen. He maintains a complex approach to brewing. On the one hand, he considers himself a glorified janitor, contending that 85 percent of his time is spent foiling aberrant bacteria that can contaminate his brews. On the other hand, Castrellón takes a cerebral approach to beer, as befits a man who's studied philosophy and biochemistry and did graduate studies in nineteenth-century American and Latin American history. He has a long view. "There's only a small group in the brewing industry who can create new things, and that's the craft brewers," Castrellón said. "But to be creative is very taxing. Philosophy and history helps me understand the industry." As evidence of his inquiring mind, after reading the African novel, *Don't Let's Go to the Dogs Tonight*, Castrellón decided to brew an African-styled sorghum beer, *chibuku*, intrigued by the grain's gluten-free qualities for hyper-allergic people. While it won a Silver Medal at the 2007 Brewers Cup, Castrellón did not declare it a success: "Kind of tasted like cheap wine, a Chardonnay that wasn't right."

Beers Brewed: Searchlight, a light American blond ale; unfiltered Weiss Guy Wheat; an amber Eaglecreek Rouge; an American-style Pelican Pale Ale; a Black Lager with Cascade and Challenger hops; Saxaphone Saison, a complex tart ale; and Sinister Double, a red Belgian dubbel. Castellón's seasonal, Naptown Alt, was a 2007 Brewers Cup winner.

Castrellón seems to embody the extraordinary collegiality among Indiana brewers. He is eternally supportive of his fellow brewers, often talking up their latest beers. In his spare time, he teaches an Indiana University–Purdue University Indianapolis course, "Introduction to Microbrewing," where he presents the complexity of craft brewing to his students. "Not being negative, working with people—it's my whole philosophy of life—not just brewing," he noted.

Opened: 1995 • Owner: Tavistock LLC • Brewer: Omar Castrellón • Brewing System: DME Brewing Services fifteen-barrel system • Annual Production: 500 barrels • Tours: Yes, call to schedule. • Hours: Monday though Thursday 11:00 a.m. to 11:00 p.m.; Friday and Saturday 11:00 a.m. to midnight; Sunday Noon to 9:00 p.m.; Beer to go:

Growlers • Food: Alcatraz serves a full menu, including small plates, soups (the beer cheese soup is flavorful and substantive), salads, burgers and sandwiches (if you're in a homey mood, check out the "Hoosier" hand-breaded pork cutlet), pizzas, pastas, fish, and steaks.

The Ram Restaurant and Brewery

140 South Illinois Street
Indianapolis, IN 46225
(317) 955–9900
www.theram.com/indiana/indianapolis.shtml

THE RAM RESTAURANT AND BREWERY is a booming operation, located in the former Planet Hollywood location in downtown Indianapolis. The place never really stopped being into entertainment, as sports fans and conventioneers flock to their own customized watering hole. When the mammoth convention for fantasy gamers, Gen Con, came to the convention center, the Ram was ready with immense posters of fierce tentacled creatures, ogres, and a voluptuous Amazon with a heroic décolletage. The Ram embraced the gamers when they came to Indy in 2003, with specials such as an 80-shilling Scottish named Apocalypse Ale and an Underdark Stout, along with Terra Khan's Terra-burger and Gorghadra's chicken gorgonzola—"Nothing can satiate Gorghadra's will for devouring entire planets," the menu description reads. "The feast of the worlds begins with a single hearty entrée." Not surprisingly, the gamers appreciate the attention: Gen Con is the Ram's busiest beer week of the year. It's not just the gamers: 1,500 convening agronomists downed a

Beers Brewed:
Ram produces a half-dozen beers that are crafted to company-wide standards: a golden Blond Ale; a Bavarian-style unfiltered Hefeweizen; a malty Buttface Amber ale; Big Red IPA, with an Amarillo-hops citrus flavor; Total Disorder Porter is a brown porter with hints of chocolate and caramel; coppery 71 Pale Ale is brewed with 5 hops and rye. Ram also brews 16 to 24 seasonals per year that are the Indianapolis brewers' prerogative.

Indiana Bourbon-Barrel-Aged Beer

Indiana brewers swept the awards in the Wood- and Barrel-Aged category at the 2008 Great American Beer Festival, an extraordinary achievement in this highly competitive, blind-judged event. The Ram Restaurant and Brewery in Indianapolis took both the Gold and Silver medals. Barley Island Brewing Company in Noblesville walked off with the Bronze.

After winning a Bronze for his Buffalo Bock at the 2007 GABF, Ram brewer Dave Colt harbored some hopes for a repeat. At the awards event, Colt was elated by the Silver medal. But as he walked toward the stage to receive the Silver, they announced his Gold. "I felt like I jumped ten feet in the air. It was a good, numb, three-feet-off-the-ground feeling for the rest of the night," he said. Colt had used a Buffalo Trace whiskey barrel for his Buffalo Bock mai-bock. "The barrel added a hint of bourbon in the nose, and another layer of flavor and complexity—hazelnut and butterscotch," Colt said. For his Gold-medal Old Jack American-style stout, Colt used a Jack Daniel barrel. "It tastes like a coffee-chocolate-whiskey milk-shake—in the best sense," he noted.

Barley Island's Jon Lang was surprised when they announced his name for the Bronze medal. "My dad and I go to GABF together. He smacked me on the back and said, 'That's you!'" said Lang. Lang used a Buffalo Trace barrel to age his oatmeal stout for six months, which brought out a vanilla flavor that enhanced the beer's chocolate character.

Hoosier brewers have been using bourbon barrels to age their beer for a number of years, almost to the point where it is somewhat of an Indiana specialty. Jeff Arnett, the Master Distiller at Jack Daniels, explained some of the characteristics that the whiskey barrels impart to beer. "We view the barrel as pretty important to the making of Jack Daniels," he said. Given that, the distillery maintains quality control by coopering their own oak barrels—three hundred and fifty thousand to four hundred thousand of them a year. The whiskey typically barrel-ages from four to seven years. As the American whiskey distillers only use their barrels once, there is a great trade in used ones. Most go to the Scotch industry, though the used whiskey barrels are also used for rum and tequila, as well as for aging Tabasco sauce. And, for aging beer. When the whiskey barrel moves on to its second life, it is a thoroughly impregnated vessel: it has absorbed three gallons of whiskey into the wood, about twenty pounds of liquor. With the whiskey residue comes the attendant flavors, which in Jack Daniels includes vanilla, caramel, butterscotch, and toasted oak—even cinnamon and banana to some palates. That all gets worked into barrel-aged beer.

"It doesn't surprise me that Indiana brewers won," said Keith Lemcke, vice president of the Siebel Institute of Technology, the nation's foremost brewing school, about the GABF awards.

When the whiskey barrel moves on to its second life, it is a thoroughly impregnated vessel: it has absorbed three gallons of whiskey into the wood, about twenty pounds of liquor. With the whiskey residue comes the attendant flavors ... vanilla, caramel, butterscotch, and toasted oak.... That all gets worked into barrel-aged beer.

KENTUCKY BOURBON Indiana Beer

MIKE SCHWAB

"There's a lot of great brewers down there. They've mastered barrel aging. Because of their proximity to Kentucky, they've got access to the raw material of the bourbon barrels," said Lemcke. Colt conjectured that the closeness of Kentucky distilleries gives Hoosier brewers an edge over brewers further afield: "Maybe the barrels are just fresher for us." Whatever the case, the GABF judges determined Hoosier bourbon-barrel-aged brews deserved international recognition. As Lang said, "To have all three of the winners from Indiana—that's great."

three-week supply of porter in two days. A convention of chemists drained the brewery. "Chemists don't get out much," former head brewer Dave Colt says, "but when they do, they get out all the way." Colt began brewing at the Circle V Brewing Company, where his training under the old guild system gave him a good brewing foundation to succeed as Ram's head brewer.

The Ram's another chain that offers brewers the opportunity for creativity. There is a lineup of six flagship brews that the Ram brewers are required to produce to company standards. Beyond that, the sky is the limit for the rotating seasonals, such as E.S.B.s, dopplebocks, maibocks, Kölsch, wildly popular Scottish ales, Farmhouse Ale made with Indiana shagbark hickory flavoring, a Saison brewed with Tulip Poplar essence, and the highly hopped and malty Old Jack Ale.

Under Colt, Ram Brewery won a 2005 Great American Beer Festival Bronze Medal for the Detonator Dopplebock. In 2007 Ram won a GABF Bronze for bourbon-barrel-aged Buffalo Bock, as well as six Brewers Cup medals, including a gold for Brute brown ale. At the 2008 Brewers Cup, Ram took a Gold for Wisecracker Wheat, Silvers for Single Barrel Stout, Indy Blonde, and Rye Pils, and a Bronze for the Kölsch. The 2008 GABF Wood- and Barrel-Aged judges awarded both the Gold for Old Jack and the Silver for Buffalo Bock to Ram Brewery.

In 2009 Dave Colt's assistant brewer, Jon Simmons, took over. A Virginia native who grew up in Bloomington, Indiana, Simmons apprenticed at Rock Bottom with Jerry Sutherlin. From there he moved over to the Ram, where he worked under Colt.

Or to restate the Ram brewers' linage and training with a little Gen Con lingo: After Colt and Simmons's arduous apprenticeship under their Brew Masters, they embarked on their own heroic journeys of zymurgic discovery, battling demon yeasts and evil bacteria to triumph with champion brews—and the world is a better place for it.

Opened: September 2000 • Owners: Dave and Jeff Iverson • Brewer: Jon Simmons • Brewing Systems: JV Northwest 10-barrel rig • Annual Production: 1,400 barrels • Tours: With appointment • Hours: Sunday through Monday 11:00 a.m. to close • Beer to go: Growlers • Food: The Ram has a full menu, including Buttface Amber Ale Beer Cheese Dip and the Brewers Steak that is marinated in their Total Disorder Porter.

Rock Bottom Restaurant and Brewery

10 West Washington Street
Indianapolis, IN 46204
(317) 681–8180
www.rockbottom.com

ROCK BOTTOM BREWER Jerry Sutherlin has witnessed the evolving tastes of Hoosier beer drinkers: "You can't brew a hoppy enough beer on the West Coast and Colorado, but the East Coast is similar to us. The Midwest likes lighter, less hoppy beers, but they're really coming around. Light lager is dropping, and pale and red ales are coming up," said Sutherlin. He credits Indiana's great brewmasters with providing complex brews that have broadened their patrons' horizons.

Sutherlin credits part of his success to the Rock Bottom philosophy of letting each brewer develop individual recipes. "They give us all the freedom in the world," he noted. At the Brewers Cup, the downtown Rock Bottom brewpub won four Silvers for Sutherlin's Circle City Light, Raccoon Red ale, Olde Number Ten strong ale, and Goat Topper Maibock, as well as a Bronze for his Strong Scottish ale. The beeradvocate.com reviewers

Beers Brewed: Circle City Light is a flavorful balanced lager with floral hops; Seasonal Wheat varies among Witbier, hefeweizen, and dunkelweizen styles; Sugar Creek Pale Ale uses Centennial and Cascade hops for both citrus and piney notes; Raccoon Red is an extra special bitter; Brickway Brown is a porter with toffee and chocolate flavors; and Hoosier Ma Stout rotates among Dry Irish, Milk, Oatmeal, and Imperial stout styles. Rock Bottom typically serves two seasonals that change through the year. The seasonals include a dry-hopped pilsner, a Bourbon-barrel stout, a cask-conditioned porter, and a Saison that's "got that funkiness," as Sutherlin said.

consistently gave A grades to Sutherlin's Rock Bottom stouts.

Sutherlin's a vet, brewing for more than ten years—six of them at the Oaken Barrel in Greenwood. "I was waiting tables at the Oaken Barrel. Had a couple of beers and wanted to see how it happened," he laughed. Sutherlin's been the brewmaster at Rock Bottom since 2005.

Opened: 1996 • Owner: Frank Day • Brewer: Jerry Sutherlin • Brewing System: Twelve-barrel JV Northwest system • Annual Production: 1,200 barrels • Tours: Yes, call to schedule. • Hours: Monday through Thursday 11:00 a.m. to 1:00 a.m. Friday 11:00 a.m. to 2:00 a.m. • Saturday noon to 2:00 a.m. • Sunday noon to midnight. • Beer to go: Growlers • Food: Rock Bottom has a full and complete menu including an onion soup made with house stout.

Sun King Brewing Company
135 North College Avenue
Indianapolis, IN 46202
(317) 602–3702
www.sunkingbrewing.com

TO SHED LIGHT ON SUN KING: Though the brewery only opened in July 2009, the two brewmasters, Dave Colt and Clay Robinson, have a wealth of experience between them. Both are veteran Indianapolis brewers, working together for a number of years at Ram Brewery.

Sun King is their vehicle for innovation. "You live and you learn. I'm into tweaking recipes; trying new and interesting things," said Colt. "Seasonals, that's a big focus of ours. We're going to be doing lots of seasonals and specialty beers." Those include edgy Belgian styles, such as their Saison de Taffy and Firefly Wheat. "It's where the craft market is going," Colt said. "We use local ingredients whenever possible." Sun King's B-Java brew has locally roasted coffee, and the specialty wheat beer is sweetened with Hoosier Tulip Poplar syrup. The company's big hoppy beers are brewed with the beer geeks in mind. "There's a place for people who like the blood sport of beer," Colt laughed.

Now selling kegs in the greater Indianapolis area, Sun King

intends to distribute statewide. There are also plans for a canning operation. The brewery sees cans as a green alternative, which additionally better preserves flavor and freshness compared to bottles.

A graduate of Hanover College, Colt began his career at the Circle V Brewing Company. Robinson brewed at both Rock Bottom and Ram. While at Ram, Colt and Robinson won a 2005 Great American Beer Festival Bronze Medal for their Detonator Dopplebock, and in 2007 a GABF Bronze for Buffalo Bock, a Maibock aged in a Buffalo Trace bourbon barrel. Colt's brews grabbed a fistful of medals at the 2008 Brewers Cup, including a Gold for his Wisecracker Wheat, Silvers for his Single Barrel Stout, Indy Blonde, and Rye Pils, as well as a Bronze for Colt's Kölsch, following up the six Brewers Cup medals he won in 2007, including a gold for his Brute brown ale. In 2008 the Great American Beer Festival judges for the Wood- and Barrel-Aged category arrived at an extraordinary decision: They awarded both the Gold and Silver medals to Colt's Ram Brewery—the Gold for Old Jack and the Silver for Buffalo Bock. "Indiana has started to develop a barrel-aged following," Colt said. "Indiana is making a mark as a place where great beer is brewed."

Beers Brewed:
Sunlight Cream Ale is an accessible biscuit-y beer with a touch of hops. The Bitter Druid ESB is American style, its malt backbone is embellished with a spicy Glacier hop finish. The malty Wee Mac Scottish-style brown ale sports hazelnut, toffee, and cacao flavors. With three assertive hops, Osiris Pale Ale is a citrusy dry-hopped American style. Sun King's seasonals include Saison de Taffy, a sprightly sour beer; Octoberfest—"It's time for lederhosen and brats," Colt says; a big, dry, hop-head IPA with Nugget and Cascade hops, clocking in at 8.8% and 83 IBU; Johan the Barleywine, a soft, English-style brew.

Opened: July 2009 • Owners: Andy Fagg, Dave Colt, Clay Robinson, Omar Robinson; Brewers: Dave Colt and Clay Robinson • Brewing System: 15-barrel JV Northwest with 30-barrel conditioning tank • Annual Production: 600 barrels July-Dec. 2009; 2,500 barrels 2010 (projected) • Tours: With appointment • Hours: Tasting room Thursday 5:00

p.m. to 7:00 p.m., Friday 3:00 p.m. to 7 p.m., Saturday 1:00 p.m. to 4:00 p.m.. • Beer to go: Growlers and kegs • Food: No—tasting room

Granite City Food and Brewery Limited

150 West 96th Street
Indianapolis, IN 46260
(317) 281–7185
www.gcfb.net

THE FAR NORTHSIDE INDY'S GRANITE CITY is the latest Midwestern outpost of this expansion-minded chain. Like the other Granite City restaurants, this location utilizes the sweet (unfermented) wort that is trucked in from the central Iowa worthouse. The wort is fermented in their 12 ½-barrel stainless steel fermenters adjacent to the dining room. Brewer Kendra Travez began with Granite City two years ago in Fort Wayne as a server. When an opportunity arose to be the brewer in Indianapolis, she took advantage of the chain's one-week training program and its extensive Standard Operating Procedures to join the growing ranks of brewsters. "I loved every minute of it," Travez said. Mike Deweese, formerly of the brew emporium J. Gumbo's, is one of the Granite City managers.

Beers Brewed:
Duke of Wellington IPA; Broad Axe Stout; Brother Benedict Bock lager; a light Northern Light Lager; and Two-Pull, a half-and-half of Northern Light and Bock beers. Specialty beers include Oktoberfest, Ostara Spring Ale, Hefeweizen, Belgian Wit, and Scottish Ale.

Opened: February 2009 • Owners: Shawn Kelly, managing partner • Brewer: Kendra Travez • Brewing Systems: 12 ½-barrel Newlands Systems Inc. fermenters at the Indianapolis brewpub; 25-barrel Newlands System Inc. rig at the Granite City central brewery in Iowa. • Annual Production: 700 barrels (projected) • Tours: Yes, inquire about availability. • Hours: Monday through Thursday 11 a.m. to midnight; Friday and Saturday 11 a.m. to 1 a.m.; Sunday 10 a.m. to 10 p.m.. • Beer to go: Growlers • Food: Granite City has a full menu, with fresh made-from-scratch appetizers, salads, sandwiches, flatbread pizzas, and entrées. Ale and cheese soup is a specialty.

The Oaken Barrel Brewing Company

50 North Airport Parkway, Suite L
Greenwood, IN 46143
(317) 887–2287
www.oakenbarrel.com

THE OAKEN BARREL IS PART of Indiana craftbrewing history, as the small brewpub took over the defunct Indianapolis Brewing Company operation in 1997. It was a sudden step for the Oaken Barrel, moving from its compact seven-barrel system in a 650-square-foot brewpub up to the IBC's twenty-five-barrel system, fifty-barrel fermenters, and cantankerous bottling line that was housed in a cavernous eleven thousand square-foot industrial warehouse. After crafting mid-market brews for a number of years, the Oaken Barrel shut down the large system in 2005 and returned to being an award-winning suburban southside brewpub.

Owner Kwang Casey has a background as an electrical engineer and a restaurateur. In the mid-1990s he became intrigued by the brewpubs popping up around the country and determined to start one up. "At first people wanted light lagers," Casey said, "but now people are getting away from that. The same guy who drank ambers ten years ago, now wants pale ales and IPAs."

The Oaken Barrel's current brewmaster, Mark Havens, was a Johnson County jailer with a penchant for craft beers. After a long, wallet-draining exploration of beer styles, Havens's better half decided to economize: "My wife went out and bought me an extract homebrewing kit," he said. Havens started asking Ken Price, then the Oaken Barrel brewer, for advice. One day in 2005 Havens came in the back door of the brewery as Price was having an argument with his keg boy. When the keg boy

Beers Brewed:
Indiana Amber, a malt-forward brew; Razz-Wheat is a balanced American-style Belgian fruit beer that is made with raspberry puree; hoppy Gnaw Bone Pale Ale; Superfly IPA; and malty Snake-Pit Porter. The twenty seasonals each year include Alabaster that is enhanced with coriander, chamomile, and orange-peel; Uberweizen; Java Stout; Summer White; and an autumn apple-cider beer.

Mash Unit

Brewing generates a lot of spent grain, the name for mash drained of liquid. As spent grain is 80 percent wet to 20 percent dry solids, it's not stable and needs to be used ASAP—think rotting. With millions of tons of wet grain, mass-market breweries have big solutions. Miller turns it into a fiber supplement for farmers and bakers called Barley's Best. Anheuser-Busch feeds it to dairy cows, 1.76 million tons to two hundred thousand cows one year. Molson mixes mash with old beer into cattle porridge, which they feed to cows at a rate of twelve beers and forty pounds of grain per day. Mooooo. The Austrian Göss Brewery partnered with the University of Leoben to come up with a way to utilize spent grain for energy. The researchers developed a dewatering technique that reduced the liquid component to 60 percent, allowing cost-efficient incineration. Göss now incinerates two to three tons of wet grain per hour, capturing the energy to help with further production, making more mash, etc.

Microbrewers sometimes dispose of their spent grain in novel ways. A few brewpubs sell it as a menu item, though it reportedly tastes like "wallpaper," as most of the flavor flowed away with the liquid wort. Others give it away as (excellent) compost. Bakers occasionally use it in bread, though more for fiber than flavor. Brewers traditionally partnered with farmers, who converted the mash into eggs, milk, and meat. Great Lakes Brewing Company has arrangements with organic vegetable growers, natural-cattle farmers, and a mushroom operation. One Alaskan brewer sends its spent grain in garbage cans to a reindeer farm, where the dumped frozen mash stands upright on the tundra like so many cereal Popsicles for the Donners' and Blitzens' eating convenience.

Upland Brewing in Bloomington trades its spent grain with a local buffalo farmer, who returns his part of the bargain as buffalo steaks and hamburger. Bloomington Brewing's Jeff Mease is eliminating the middleman. Mease bought a large farm that he is converting into a multiuse facility that will eventually include a new brewery and pastures for his water buffalo herd, which he will feed with—you know. Mease intends to make artisanal mozzarella cheese. Oaken Barrel's Kwang Casey laughed about their mash that a farmer picks up on brewing days: "The farmer says, the pigs know our buckets. When he pulls up in his pick-up and they see the buckets, they come running. It's ninety gallons of fermented mash—the pigs get drunk."

MIKE SCHWAB

snidely asked who was going to help with the rest of the brew, Price spun and pointed to home brewer Havens. A new career was born. "I was not afraid to ask questions," Havens said.

Havens took over the brewhouse in 2007 and has since had a meteoric rise. In 2008 Havens received the Indiana Brewer of the Year award from the Indiana State Fair Brewers Cup competition. His beers took eight medals: four silvers for his Uberweizen, Der Alter Konig, The Beginning Scottish eighty-shilling, and Epiphany Belgian triple, as well as Bronzes for his Indiana Amber, Controversy American barleywine, wood-aged Snake Venom, and Alabaster witbier. A youthful enthusiast with a close-cropped beard and wire rims, Havens excitedly remembered the moment he received the trophy, "Me and my assistant, Andrew Castner, we were like, 'Yeaaaaah!'," punching his fist in the air, Rocky-style.

Awards have long been part of Oaken Barrel's history, including a 1995 GABF Silver Medal for its Razz Wheat, a 1997 GABF Silver for its Meridian Lager, and a 2005 Silver for its Alabaster witbier. Reviewers at beeradvocate.com gave the Oaken Barrel's IPA, stout, and saison A- ratings, and ratebeer.com came up with a high 3.52 rating for the IPA and a 3.46 for the Snake-Pit Porter. But Kwang Casey remembered a couple of craft beer luminaries who delivered the ultimate accolades: "Ken Grossman of Sierra Nevada came in one day when he was doing some work in Indianapolis. After he drank our beer, he said, 'Get rid of these tables, put in big tanks. This beer is fantastic.'" And Casey recalled the visit of beer writer Michael Jackson. "He loved our porters. Had three or four. 'Cancel my appointments,' he said. He stayed here all afternoon," Jackson recalled.

Opened: July 1994 • Owner: Kwang Casey • Brewer: Mark Havens • Brewing System: Fifteen-barrel DME System • Annual Production: 1,500 barrels • Tours: Yes, call for availability. • Hours: Monday through Thursday 11:00 a.m. to midnight; Friday and Saturday 11:00 a.m. to 1:00 a.m.; Sunday 11:00 a.m. to 10:00 p.m. • Beer to go: Growlers and bottled beer are available. • Food: Full menu; the Oaken Barrel "Nouveau American" cuisine includes Shepherd's Pie, mesquite-smoked ribs, and Cajun Jambalaya pasta.

Brass Monkey Brewing Company

115 East Sycamore
Kokomo, IN 46901
www.brassmonkeybrewing.com

INDIANA'S SMALLEST COMMERCIAL brewery is also one of its best. When he started, the Brass Monkey Brewing Company's brewer/owner, Andrew Lewis, produced award-winning craft beers in his Lilliputian ten-gallon homebrewing rig in the basement of an old downtown Kokomo building. Each night in his immaculate underground brewery, Lewis (a third-grade schoolteacher by day) brewed a batch in plastic tubs and glass carboys, using kegs with airlocks as fermenters. His fermenting room was a closet under the stairs

Beers Brewed:

A malty Green Tea Pale Ale with hints of apple, pear, and tea; an elegant See No Evil IPA with Cascade, Columbus, Centennial, and Amarillo hops; Tenacious Apple Tripel, a 10.1 percent ale that's fermented on a bed of apples. Seasonals include the award-winning barleywine that is available in late October.

In spite of his constraints, Lewis gathered kudos at the 2008 Brewers Cup, winning the Gold Medal for his Belligerent in the barleywine division. His See No Evil IPA took a Silver Medal, coming in behind Three Floyds Dreadnaught. Reviewers at www.beeradvocate.com gave the brewery a sterling A rating, with extraordinary grades of A or A+ for every beer tasted. What could Lewis have accomplished if he'd been open for a full year?

"We try to be as adventurous as we can be," Lewis said, brewing "One and Done" seasonals such as White Flag Wit, Double Down Brown, and Silver Back Stout. "I take feedback very seriously," Lewis admitted. When patrons said his brown ales and stouts were too sweet, he quickly adjusted the crystal malts. Inspired by baklava, Lewis judged his attempt at a honey and almond brew a failure: "It did not work out," he ruefully said. But he's undeterred by a few glitches: "The exciting part is putting out something new, and seeing what people say," Lewis added. Judging from the positive response to Brass Monkey's initial offerings, people most likely are going to have a lot of great things to say.

But there was a surprise in December 2008: The Marketplace shopping and dining emporium where Brass Monkey brewed and sold its beer suddenly closed. Brass Monkey's Web site hopefully read: "Plans are in the works for a reemergence in 2009." But as of late 2009, the Brass Monkey is not yet scampering again.

Opened: May 2008; closed December 2009 • Owner: Andrew Lewis • Brewer: Andrew Lewis • Brewing System: 1/3-barrel (10-gallon) homebrewing system • Annual Production: 50 barrels.

Half Moon Restaurant and Brewery
4051 South LaFountain
Kokomo, IN 46902
(765) 455–2739
www.halfmoonbrewery.com

THOUGH TEMPERANCE-MINDED KOKOMO did not have much of a brewing history, it's catching up fast. Famous for the first auto, first stoplight, first howitzer shell, and canned tomato juice, the "City of Firsts" now boasts two craft brewers, including the Half Moon Restaurant and Brewery, located out in the burgeoning suburban edge of Kokomo. The Half Moon brewers playfully claim they are serving "The Great City of Thirsts."

A new structure doctored to look vintage with beer memorabilia, exposed brick, and dark woodwork, it feels like an old brewery gone upscale. Owner Chris Roegner is a Kokomo native, who's been in food service since he graduated from Purdue University with a restaurant management degree. After long service in Florida, Roegner and his wife decided to return home. "Kokomo had a niche open," Roegner said about his decision to dive into brewing. Brewing's low material costs were an allure to

Beers Brewed:
Pre-Prohibition Pilsner, unfiltered Wildcat Wheat, Irish-style Stoplight City Red, Old Ben Brown, Elwood's IPA, and a robust Cole Porter with roasted malts. Half Moon typically also has one to three seasonals on tap.

a manager used to monitoring the numbers.

Head brewer John Templet got his start in Mendocino's Hopland brewery, where he worked for more than eight years. He then brewed in Little Rock's Diamond Bear and at Boscos in Memphis. A quiet, earnest man who opens up, Templet was a great addition to Roegner's team, helping him sort out brewery-specific construction issues. Brewing to its patrons' current tastes, Half Moon is focusing on accessible beers, including its traditional lager and the Wildcat Wheat. Seasonals lean toward offerings such as a blueberry-tinged beer, brewed with all-natural fruit, and its Hazelnut Brown Ale, which won a 2008 Brewers Cup Silver Medal. Half Moon's 7.1 percent Honey Rye was "light and easy to drink," Templet said, "but packed quite a punch," as did the Kokomonster with its 8.1 percent kick. They were both big hits, "Kokomo being the kind of town it is"—which is, evidently, a city of great thirsts.

Opened: May 2007 • Owner: Chris Roegner • Brewer: John Templet • Brewing System: Three and a half-barrel Pub Brewing Company system • Annual Production: 500 barrels • Tours: Yes, ask about availability. • Hours: Sunday through Thursday 11:00 a.m. to 10:00 p.m.; Friday and Saturday 11:00 a.m. to 11:00 p.m. • Beer to go: Growlers • Food: Half Moon has an extensive menu, including a full array of starters, salads, sandwiches, pasta, steaks, chicken, and fish. Smokehouse offerings include ribs, brisket, pulled pork, and chicken.

Lafayette Brewing Company
622 Main Street
Lafayette, IN 47901
(765) 742–2591
www.lafayettebrewingco.com

GREG EMIG, LAFAYETTE BREWING COMPANY'S articulate owner/brewer, was a pioneer Indiana craft brewer. "I was a homebrewer," Emig said, "who was lucky enough to work at the Broad Ripple Brewpub." Emig helped start up the Broad Ripple brewery and served as its first brewer. "I always wanted to be an entrepreneur, and once I got into brewing, I knew that was the career for me," he said. On September 17, 1993, Emig opened his Lafayette Brewing Company in the nineteenth-century Ross, Carnahan, Kaplan Building in Lafayette's declining downtown. Naming his new enterprise after the historic Lafayette Brewing Company, Emig had received Indiana's first small brewers permit just the previous month. The new brewpub emanated a friendly saloon vibe with its high-ceilinged room, long bar, big windows, dark wainscoting, and local beer memorabilia. There must have been a pent-up demand, as a crush of patrons rushed in the doors when they opened.

"People say you brew the beer to your customer base," Emig

Beers Brewed:
Ouiatenon Wit Beer with notes of citrus, banana, and clove; Prophets Rock Pale Ale; Eastside Bitter, a copper-colored ESB; Pipers Pride, a traditional ruby-colored Scottish ale with a tinge of smokiness; the Tippecanoe Common Ale has the grapefruit tang of Amarillo hops; the Eighty-Five is a highly bittered American-style ale; and Black Angus Oatmeal Stout uses five malts to yield a big, chocolaty brew. LBC offers rotating cask-conditioned beers, as well as numerous seasonals, including Big Boris Barley Ale, Hunters Moon Pale Ale, and Phoenix Strong Ale.

Greg Emig and his assistant brew their early American ale at the annual Feast of the Hunters Moon at Fort Ouiatenon in West Lafayette.

mused. "Not really. I brew the beer I like. It's a combination of art and craft." People must like what Emig likes, as the crowds never stopped coming. That first tumultuous year, the LBC brewed 450 barrels of beer. The brewery has won numerous awards, including World Beer Championship medals for its Piper's Pride Scottish Ale, Eighty-Five extreme ale, Eastside Bitter, and Black Angus Oatmeal Stout. The brewery's also taken a slew of Indiana State Fair medals through the years. In both 2007 and 2008 the Brewers Cup judges awarded LBC a Gold Medal for its Tippecanoe Common Ale. Reviewers for beeradvocate.com seconded the judgment, giving A grades to the common ale, along with LBC's Weeping Hog IPA, Piper's Pride Scottish Ale, Smokehouse Porter, and Bill, the strong ale that Greg Emig named in honor of his late friend and local homebrewer, Bill Friday.

Emig is a burly, blond, blue-eyed guy, kind of an idealized German brewer. He's firmly rooted in Indiana's traditions. He's also deeply engaged in the future of both his community and Hoosier craft brewing. With his thoughtfulness and loquacity, he can give voice to beer as a life experience; beer as celebration. Each autumn, Emig hand gathers wild hops near the Wabash River, preparing for the annual Feast of the Hunters Moon, a celebration of Indiana's colonial past at Fort Ouiatenon, a re-creation of an eighteenth-century French trading post. Using a hand-hammered copper pot and old wooden casks and barrels, frontier-costumed Emig and his assistants brew their early American ale. When Emig married his wife, Nancy, he brewed a

Lafayette Brewing Company is located in the nineteenth-century Ross, Carnahan, Kaplan Building in downtown Lafayette.

Bridal Ale. When she gave birth to their first child, Carly, he eased the pain (and celebrated) with a Groaning Ale.

With two bustling floors of brewpub, LBC now sits as a mainstay in a rapidly rejuvenating downtown perking with activity. The Emigs have been a big part of that. There were four downtown restaurants when the Emigs opened their brewpub; there are twenty-two eateries operating now, with more on the way. Renovation and new construction abound. Emig has also long been a stalwart of the Hoosier craft brewers' organization, the Brewers of Indiana Guild. "The cooperative spirit is part of the craft brewery tradition," he said. "Having a sense of community makes a big difference."

Opened: September 1993 • Owner: Greg Emig • Brewer: Greg Emig • Brewing System: Seven-barrel Century system • Annual Production: 800 barrels • Tours: Yes, call for availability. • Hours: Monday through Thursday 11:00 a.m. to midnight; Friday and Saturday 11:00 a.m. to 1:00 a.m. Closed Sunday. • Beer to go: Growlers and bottles. • Food: Lafayette Brewing has a full menu. Starters include Bavarian Beer Nuggets, breaded balls of spicy sausage, sauerkraut, and cream cheese that are deep-fried and served with horseradish sauce. The hearty Cheddar Ale Soup with andouille sausage, potatoes, and vegetables is the house specialty. The Black and Bleu Caesar Salad features a beer-marinated sirloin.

People's Brewing Company

2006 North 9th Street
Lafayette, IN 47904
(765) 413–3072
www.peoplesbrew.com

SCHEDULED TO OPEN in November 2009, the People's Brewing Company was still a thicket of 2 x 4s and hanging electrical wires when I stopped by. The shining brewery tanks were akimbo, waiting for final plumbing; the tasting room needed drywall. But the vision of a bustling brewery was clearly dancing in the heads of owners Chris Johnson and Brett Vander Plaats.

Beers Brewed:
People's plans on brewing four to six regular brews and three seasonals, including Irish Porter, English Imperial Ale, Kolsch, Scottish Wee Heavy Ale and English Barleywine.

The People's brewer is Chris Johnson, who has nearly a decade of brewing experience at the Lafayette Brewing Company. He will craft a variety of beers that the team will market in Tippecanoe County and the Indianapolis area. Johnson says, "We're going to brew beer that appeals to a large section of the market: A light refreshing German-style pilsner that everyone will like. Amber will be middle of the road, a little more malt, with high-alpha-acid hops. Hops-forward stuff is big in the world, not just locally," said Johnson.

With the growing market for craft beers, a strong home brewing community, and "bars popping up everywhere," Johnson and Vander Plaats are confident about the People's future. They will initially sell only kegs and growlers, but have plans for a bottling line. "We'll use bottles as an entrée into new markets," Vander Plaats said.

Opened: November 2009 (projected) • Owners: Chris Johnson and Brett Vander Plaats • Brewer: Chris Johnson • Brewing System: 20-barrel Triple A • Annual Production: 1,000 barrels (projected) • Tours: Yes • Hours: Check Web site • Beer to go: Growlers • Food: No—"We see ourselves more like a winery tasting room."

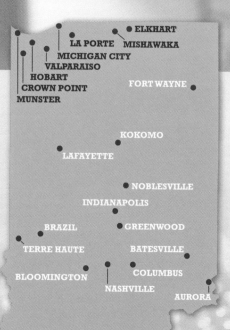

ELKHART
LA PORTE MISHAWAKA
MICHIGAN CITY
VALPARAISO
HOBART
CROWN POINT
MUNSTER

FORT WAYNE

KOKOMO

LAFAYETTE

NOBLESVILLE
INDIANAPOLIS

BRAZIL GREENWOOD

TERRE HAUTE BATESVILLE

BLOOMINGTON COLUMBUS

NASHVILLE
AURORA

NEW ALBANY

EVANSVILLE

CHAPTER NINE

CRAFT BREWING

Northern Indiana

ORTHWESTERN INDIANA is diversity incarnate, from the subtle ecologies of the Lake Michigan dunes to the industrial might of the Gary steel mills. From small, picket-fenced towns to dense suburbs of Chicago. From the rock-ribbed farmers of the flat tablelands to the Calumet Region's polyglot ethnic admixtures. Rural and urban, homogenous and not—all right there in a small, complicated knot.

Northwestern Indiana was a swampy place of sloughs and slow rivers when the French explorers Marquette and Joliet passed through in 1673. For much of the next two-and-a-quarter centuries, the area's challenging geography kept development low. But at the turn of the twentieth century, industrialists realized the sixteen miles of Indiana's basically undeveloped Lake Michigan lakeshore lay strategically in the middle of America's population core between the Mesabi-range iron ore and the endless Appalachian coalfields. They were soon plotting a dramatic transformation. The amazing Calumet Region industrial complex quickly arose on the Indiana lakeshore, a colossus of manufacturing that turned the night alight with eternal flames and dimmed the day with smokestacks belching black soot. It attracted

PHOTOGRAPHY BY RICHARD SPAHR

peoples from across the globe: African Americans from the Deep South, Hispanics from even further south, Greeks, Italians, Baltic nationals, an entire Cyrillic alphabet of eastern European Slavic folk coming together to labor in the mills and refineries that fueled America's relentless growth. It remains an extraordinary part of Indiana.

The Hoosier brewers of the north seem to reflect the region's wild variety. There's small-town brewers and big-city, take-no-prisoners brewers; traditionalist brewers and make-it-up-as-they-go-along brewers. If you want to experience a wide range of beers, this is the place to do it.

Three Floyds Brewing Company
9750 Indiana Parkway
Munster, IN 46321
(219) 922–4425; (219) 922–3565
www.threefloyds.com

AT 5:00 A.M., THE FIRST PEOPLE are queueing up at Three Floyds, intent on securing their six-bottle allotment of the legendary Dark Lord imperial stout. Sold only one day each year at the brewery, Dark Lord was ranked the best beer in the world by the influential Web site, ratebeer.com. As the cold, gray, blustery day in late April dawns, lines of half awake beer lovers

snake down the street of the Calumet Region industrial park where renegade Three Floyds is counterintuitively ensconced. Hoods up, hands in pockets, hunkered against the wind in blankets and flannels, the resolute, red-nosed fans await their moment. Beer traders arrange tables of their bottled wares. A lively swap meet begins. A gust sends hats flying into the air.

"I think people come here for

The Three Floyds Brewpub is an urban boîte in a Calumet Region industrial park.

the great atmosphere," said Clint Puckett, a Rose-Hulman Institute of Technology student standing first in line with his parents, who drove from Nevada. "Of course, the beer is fantastic." His parents laughed. He flushed and admitted, "Oh, then there's the 'cha-ching.'" While Dark Lord sells for fifteen dollars a bottle at the event, gray-marketers can make big money reselling their stash. A little after 8:00 a.m., it's 43 degrees. A posse of tent-rental people try to erect a canopy, but the gale snatches it from their hands. The file of people is already blocks long, though it's still hours from the 11:00 a.m. opening. Up and down the line, liter bottles of squid-oil-dark stouts begin appearing—the breakfast of champions, evidently.

The Three Floyds Brewery started in 1996 in an old brick building at Field Street and Calumet Avenue in Hammond. The shriek of departing sirens accompanied the early brewing, as the brewery stood across the street from a fire station. The first Three Floyds brewhouse was basic, a five-barrel system made up of used Swiss-cheese tanks with a wok-burner under the mash tun. "It was really, really austere," Three Floyds brewer and minister of culture Barnaby Struve remembered.

A cerebral South African with shaved head and a Maoriwarrior number of tattoos, Struve marvels at the rise of Three Floyds into cult status: "None of us got into this to conquer the world." Instead, the anarchistic dream of staying small to produce excellent, unfiltered, un-pasteurized beers sustained him and his craft-beer brethren. "We're all pretty like-minded here, I'm not going anywhere. I work with my friends," he said. Indeed, tattoos, a shaven head, and a Wild-Bunch attitude seem almost obligatory for Three Floyds' brewers. They're a band of merry buccaneers, rampaging the Midwestern Main with their flavorful, often idio-syncratically extreme brews. "We do things in a technically sound manner," Struve said, "but we want to do it our way."

In 2000 Three Floyds purchased a warehouse building in a

**The Three Floyds' bottles fly down the line
as one of the Merry Buccaneer brewers cleans a kettle**

Munster industrial park. The brewery's neighbors include a large litho house, wholesale distributors, and the local school corpo-ration's service building, where yellow school buses sometimes park. After five years in the warehouse, the Floyds decided to put in a brewpub—again doing it their way. With its stained con-crete floors and exposed ducts, the Three Floyds brewhouse is the ultimate urban hipster destination, decorated with Japanese horror-film posters, as well as European soccer and craft-beer mementos. A surreal cartoon mural by Chicago artist Chris Berg fills one wall. Big-screen televisions play soccer and Yul Brynner in *Westworld*. It's a cross between a Boho coffee shop and an edgy bôite, incongruously tucked into a Calumet Region industrial zone. But like the other Floyd do-it-our-way enterprises, the brewpub has been wildly successful.

"Doc" Floyd—Doctor Michael Floyd—is Three Floyds' progenitor and pirate captain. A retired nephrologist who famously transplanted a kidney into Philippine dictator Fernando Marcos, Floyd is a trim, raffish Englishman with a graying ponytail. Shambling around the Three Floyds brewpub in his dirt-dusted t-shirt, khaki shorts, and brewers boots, Floyd introduces himself: "I'm the gardener." Out back, his 2,500-square-foot, raised-bed organic garden is a pocket-sized paradise of herbs, flowers, heirloom tomatoes, and ten-foot-high raspberry plants. Floyd is from

Beers Brewed:
The flagship Alpha King pale ale, a big hoppy brew; Robert the Bruce Scottish-style ale; Pride and Joy, a lower-alcohol, less bitter American pale ale; Gumballhead wheat beer with citrusy Amarillo hops; and the formidable Dreadnaught IPA, with 9.5 percent alcohol and ninety-nine IBUs. Seasonals include wintertime Behemoth barleywine; Brian Boru Irish red ale; spicy Rabbid Rabbit, a Belgian Saison-style farmhouse ale; Blackheart English-style IPA; Fantabulous Resplendence, an anniversary ale clocking in at 11 percent alcohol and 100 IBU; Gorch Fock Munich-style helles; Moloko milk stout; Munster Fest Octoberfest beer; apricot-hued Broo Doo, made with fresh hops straight off the vine; Alpha Klaus Christmas porter; Black Sun stout; Topless Wytch Baltic porter; and Picklehaub Pilsner. Dark Lord is a massive 13 percent alcohol Russian imperial stout. Three Floyds also brews an array of small-batch beers that are sold only in the brewpub.

Northumberland, where his father was an intense industrial chemist who imparted a deep scientific connection into the family. Floyd's mother was a supertaster, one of the individuals who have a heightened taste capacity thanks to having up to twice the normal number of fungiform papillae (the projections on human tongues where tastebuds are located).

"She knew when a meal was just perfect," he said. "I grew up on the best tastes." So science and fine taste were part of the Floyd family heritage from the start.

Floyd's student days were in Swinging England—"It was England in the '60s—anything goes," he fondly recalled. It appears to have engendered a multigenerational iconoclasm. Floyd's medical work then took him to the Pacific Northwest and Houston, where Tex-Mex and good barbeque expanded the family palate. In 1980 Floyd settled his family in northwestern Indiana, where he joined a large kidney practice. Diverse foods continued to abound in the Floyd house, including Indian dishes with their complex balance of intense flavors. And there was also good beer. "Nick started secretly brewing in high school, I think," Floyd said proudly, speaking of his celebrated brewer son.

Doctor Michael "Doc" Floyd and his organic garden. The brewery's sculpture stands at the entrance to the facility.

Dark Lord Day

The Three Floyds Dark Lord Day is the only time the Russian imperial stout is sold at the brewery. Originally brewed by nineteenth-century British industrial brewers for the Russian and Baltic markets, the imperial stouts carried extremely high alcohol levels to help them survive the rough Baltic passage. Rich and porridge thick, the imperial stouts became favorites in the frigid northern climes, including among the Russian aristocracy. The famously wanton Catherine the Great was a fan of Russian imperial stouts, adding to its reputation as an aphrodisiac.

Typically held in the spring (April 26 in 2008), Dark Lord Day is often a source of great conjecture (and misinformation) on the Web. Check out www.threefloyds.com for the real skinny. Beyond Dark Lord, there are a number of offerings from guest breweries, along with tasty grub, bands, and Three Floyds merchandise for your friends (if you are not sharing your precious Dark Lord).

Nick Floyd, the brewer behind Three Floyds fame, is a linebacker-sized guy with a cue-ball head and laconic manner—until you get him talking about beer. Beyond the family predilections, Nick's inspiration comes from "traveling and trying other people's stuff," as well as his creative heroes, moviemaker Stanley Kubrick, Dungeons and Dragons creator Gary Gygax, and Genghis Khan. "Those are the big three," Nick laughed. Part of his beer education came during his wanderings in Europe, visiting England, Belgium, and Germany. There were stints at the Weinkeller in Chicago and with the Florida Brewery in Auburndale, Florida, where he brewed on a rattletrap three hundred-barrel system for the U.S., Caribbean, and Central American markets. Training at the Seibel Institute formalized some of his on-the-job experience.

"We just keep trying to get the best and newest ingredients," Nick said, using high-alpha-acid Bravo hops as an example. "I think they're amazing, but hard to get." The Three Floyds grape-fruity Gumballhead uses scarce Amarillo hops. The wheat beer's popularity has contributed to a boom for the relatively new hybrid hop. The Floyds seek out the best malts, Simpsons from the northern English borderlands and Weyermann from Bamberg, Germany. "We try to pitch the best and most viable yeast we can find," Nick noted.

The result is eye opening—swashbuckling brews that expand zymurgic horizons. Packaged with a quirky D&D-meets-mad-cartoonist style, the Three Floyds' bottled beers are visual magnets for a trendy clientele. In 2010 ratebeer.com ranked Three Floyds the best brewery in the world. Out of 110,000 rated beers, Three Floyds had three of the top ten beers. In 2008 the reviewers at ratebeer.com ranked Three Floyds Oak-aged Dark Lord as the best beer in the world, with regular Dark Lord thirteenth best, Dreadnaught forty-third, Alpha King sixty-fifth, Behemoth barleywine eighty-first, and Alpha Klaus ninety-third. That's *six* of the planet's top hundred beers. That year the ratebeer.com's judges ranked Three Floyds among the world's five best breweries. With its intuitive creativity, Three Floyds beer often leaps over the rigid style categories that guide brewing competitions. "Usually our stuff is thrown out right away," Nick chuckled. "Everything about it's not normal." But the 2008 World Beer Cup judges still saw fit to honor the Behemoth with a Gold Medal, and the Dreadnaught with a Bronze. At the 2007 Great American Beer Festival, the Gorch Fock helles won a Silver, and in 2008 their Munsterfest German-style Märzen took a Bronze. Three Floyds is now Indiana's largest brewery.

By 10:45 a.m. on Dark Lord Day, the five thousand beer fanciers facing the Three Floyds Brewery are restive. The line is nearly half-a-mile long and the latecomers feared the Dark Lord might sell out before they get theirs. The streets around the brewery are jammed with cars from dozens of states—Indiana, Illinois, Michigan, Ohio, Minnesota, Pennsylvania, Wisconsin, Iowa, Kentucky, Missouri, Alabama, Maryland, Louisiana, Washington, New York, and California plates among them. Coveys of bicyclists are still pedaling in. Already hundreds of bikes are locked together like

Three Floyds Brewery is located in a Munster industrial park warehouse building.

vivid kinetic sculptures. The traders are bleary and fading.

As the Three Floyds crew steady themselves for the crush, thumps and electronic screeches from Viper, the heavy-metal band warming up begin leaking out of the brewery warehouse. At 11:00 a.m., the burly bouncer opens the overhead door and grizzle-bearded Nick stoically welcomes the throng streaming in. With a shriek of guitars, Viper kicks in with a scream-heavy, hair-flailing rendition of "Dark Lord." Eager buyers snatch their precious six bottles. Across the way, queues form for draughts of espresso-black Dark Lord. The viscosity of used forty-weight motor oil, the Russian Imperial Stout is pungent and complex from the gumbo of roasted malts, Intelligensia coffee, Mexican vanilla, and Indian sugar. Happy folks toast one another, savoring ephemera of dried cherries and caramel, wafts of licorice, fleeting memories of port. All agree, this is a brew worth the wait.

Opened: 1996 • Owner: Dr. Michael Floyd • Brewer: Nick Floyd • Brewing System: Forty-barrel Chinese system • Annual Production: 10,000 barrels • Tours: Most Saturdays at 3:00 p.m. • Hours: Tuesday through Friday 11:00 a.m. to 12:00 p.m.; Saturday noon to midnight; Sunday noon to 10:00 p.m. • Beer to go: Bottles and growlers • Food: The Three Floyds brewpub serves pub fare, including a fine Scotch Egg with Scottish-ale sausage, chili made with Three Floyds's seasonals, soup, salads, sandwiches, and pizzas. Doc Floyd's back-of-brewery organic vegetable garden provides some of the seasonal provender.

Back Road Brewery
308 Perry Street
LaPorte, IN 46350
(219) 362–7623
www.backroadbrewery.com

BACK ROAD BREWERY'S president, Chuck Krcilek, stands at the door of his 1885 brick brewery like a figure from an earlier time. Just across the street from the site of the Crystal Spring Brewery, famous in the early twentieth century for its Excelsior beer, Back Road is at the locus of LaPorte brewing history.

A redheaded, blue-eyed Czech, Krcilek started home brewing in 1990, right after graduation from Purdue University as a civilian pilot. "I was always kind of fascinated with brewing," he said, sharing happy memories of his father and grandfather. "Drinking beer at picnics or a party, that's what you did." Krcilek realized that there was an opening for a microbrewery in the area: "There was nothing really around here." One thing led to another, and by 1996 he was commercially brewing under the name of Brick Road Brewery. But there was soon a crisis, when the Canadian Brick Brewery threatened legal action over the name. In 1998 Krcilek

Chuck Krcilek of Back Roads is a civilian pilot. Aviation memorabilia hangs in the brewery.

deftly changed the company name to Back Road, with his witty slogan, "Take a Back Road Home."

His beer is a LaPorte favorite. The night before, a waitress at an upscale restaurant had exclaimed, "We've got Back Road, our local brewery!" Each year Back Road hosts a popular Fall Festival at the brewery that includes neighboring northern-Indiana brewers Three Floyds and Shoreline, as well as a twenty-five-piece German oom-pah band, Ein Prosit.

Through the years, Krcilek has brewed forty-one different beers, including what he calls his "train-ing wheels" beer, Back Road Ale, which won 2006 and 2008 Brewers Cup Gold Medals. His Belle Gun-ness Stout commemorates a local legend, Belle Gunness, who mur-dered four people in 1908 before feeding the bodies to her hogs. "It definitely would not kill you to dig some up," the brew's sardonic ad copy reads. Belle Gunness Stout won a 2008 Brewers Cup Bronze. The 2008 Brewers Cup judges also awarded the Back Road Millenium Lager a Gold Medal. "We've really educated people in the region—now they want hoppy, now they want seasonals," Krcilek said. Aviator Doppelbock won a 2007 Brewers Cup Gold, as did Krcilek's Baltic porter Christmas Ale in 2006. The brewery's best-known beer, the Back Road Blue-berry Ale, also won a 2008 Brewers Cup Gold Medal. "There's a hint of blueberry that dances around in your mouth a little bit," he noted.

Beers Brewed:
Back Road Ale is a copper-hued dry-hopped brew, American Pale Ale is made with two-row malted barley and Cascade hops, Belle Gunness Stout is an Irish style, and Belgian-style Wit has the classic cloudy canary color and citrus notes. Seasonals include early spring Aviator Dopplebock with a 9 percent ABV, nut-brown Autumn Ale and the Christmas Ale imperial schwarzbier.

Krcilek episodically acts as the Back Road brewmaster for seasonals and the "crazy small-batch stuff." Siebel graduate Matt Peterson, now at Schafly in Saint Louis, was Back Road's first brewer. Current brewmaster Sean McKinley began brewing with Back Road in 1998. Krcilek laughed, "I give them a lot of freedom—kind of let them fly their freak flag."

Opened: 1996 under the name Brick Road Brewery, the name changing to Back Road Brewery in 1998. • Owners: Chuck Krcilek and Jim Hannon • Brewers: Sean McKinley and Chuck Krcilek • Brewing System: A seven-barrel Cross Distribution Company kettle, with four fourteen-barrel fermenters. • Annual Production: Approximately 500 barrels • Tours: Saturday 1:00 p.m. to 4:00 p.m. • Hours: As a production brewery, Back Road has variable hours, though is often open 9:00 a.m. to 5:00 p.m. Monday through Friday. • Beer to go: Bottles and growlers • Food: Back Road is a production brewery only.

Shoreline Brewery
208 Wabash Street
Michigan City, IN 46360
(219) 879–4677
www.shorelinebrewery.com

THE SHORELINE BREWERY IN MICHIGAN CITY is near the Lake Michigan waterfront in a tall, brick salmon-colored building that was originally built in 1857 for the Alaska Lumberyard. Inside, the exposed brick walls, high ceilings, and battered old wooden bar out of a Southside Chicago speakeasy tell the tales of an earlier time. With a logo based on the famous Shoreline Railroad insignia, the Shoreline Brewery is clearly attached to local history. Regional lore informs some of Shoreline's names, such as Curse the Goat Doppleboch. The brewery's beers further reflect a respect for brewing traditions. "We're style-specific," Shoreline brewer and owner Sam Strupek said, going on to explain his adherence to the time-honored techniques and materials to brew fine Scottish and English ales, as well as Belgian- and German-style beers.

Judges have liked what Strupek has wrought. Strupek's Beltaine Scottish-style ale took a 2006 World Cup Silver Medal.

Sam Strupek runs a tight ship at Shoreline.

Reviewers at beeradvocate.com give the brewpub a solid B+ ranking, rating all of his beers with As or Bs. Stewartofgondor, a rater at ratebeer.com, completely lost his composure over Shoreline's Big Bourbon Series Curse the Goat Dopplebock: "Transparent and magnifying amber copper in color with a casual grey head. Aroma glistens with caramel cookies, bourbon, hazelnuts and jojoba butter. A hint of forest greenery peers through the toffee atmospheric pressure. Flavor is fully bourbonous at every bend. Jim Beam teams with caramel, butterscotch and toffee to dominate the bock's lager traits. Great serving temperature, but the barrel is the beer. Full bodied and slickly butterscotch, finishing with a pool of caramel, caramelized butterscotch candies and bourbon in the end."

Strupek was focused on biology in college, eventually determining that a career in landscape architecture was for him. "It was art and science combined," Strupek said. But a brewing position opened up in the (now-defunct) Aberdeen Brewery in Valparaiso, sending Strupek's art and science off on a zymurgic tangent.

When Shoreline opened in August 2005, Strupek faced a great challenge of too much business. "We were down to two beers," he remembered with a shudder. But production and demand are balanced now. With award-winning beers, live music, and a sprightly atmosphere, the brewpub has a loyal following. More than a hundred and fifty handblown glass mugs glimmering with bright spirals of molten color sparkle in the brewery window. They are artful evidence of Shoreline's popular Mug Club that allows regulars to experience Strupek's fine beers at bargain prices—and experience more challenging brews in the process. "Our beers are hoppier up here. All of our original recipes have been tweaked," Strupek reported. "They're bigger beers. That has to do with how our customers have evolved. It blows me away sometimes."

Beers Brewed:
Don't Panic English Pale Ale; a hoppier American-style Leaper Pale Ale; Cluster Phuch IPA, the popular Sum Nug India Pale Ale; One Hit "One-Da" with nine different malts and nine different hops; Region Rat Red Ale; best-selling Beltaine Scottish Ale; Curse the Goat Dopplebock; the intense Discombobulation Celebration Ale; Chester Brown Ale; Big Bella Heavy Scotch Ale; Singing Sands Oatmeal Stout; and Lost Sailor Imperial Stout, made with locally brewed Lakeshore coffee. Shoreline brews approximately thirty different beers each year.

Opened: August 2005 • Owners: Sam Strupek, Dave Strupek • Brewer: Sam Strupek • Brewing System: Ten-barrel Specific Mechanical system with nine fermenters • Annual Production: 600 barrels in 2008; estimate 1,000 barrels in 2009 • Tours: Yes, call for availability. • Hours: Sunday through Thursday 11:00 a.m. to 11:00 p.m.; Friday and Saturday 11:00 a.m. to 2:00 p.m. • Beer to go: Growlers • Food: Shoreline serves a full menu, including starters (with a daily sushi offering), sandwiches that include a Brew Burger served on pretzel bread with beer-caramelized onions, salads, pastas, fish, and steaks. It's an all-fresh menu—no walk-in freezers here.

Mishawaka Brewing Company

2414 Lowell Street
Elkhart, IN 46516
(574) 295–5348
www.mishawakabrewingco.com

TOM SCHMIDT GOES BACK to the first days of microbrewing. While working in the food division at Miles Laboratory in 1986, Schmidt had an opportunity to attend the inaugural national meeting of microbrewers. As he hobnobbed with the two hundred craft brewers (who included Fritz Maytag and Jim Koch), he drank some life-changing beers. "I was intrigued," Schmidt said. "I just fell in love with the whole idea." He came back with two and a half notebooks stuffed with data. "It had nothing to do with my job," he laughed.

But Schmidt had seen his destiny and persevered. It took from 1986 to 1992 to get Mishawaka Brewing Company going. "We thought people knew more about brewpubs than they did," Schmidt said. It was before the 1993 microbrewery law change,

Rick and Tom Schmidt amidst the hops. Prior to closing Mishawaka, Tom Schmidt was Indiana's longest operating brewer.

so like the Broad Ripple Brewery, Schmidt and his partners had to set up separate premises for the brewpub and brewery, though they were both in the same building, which was located at 3703 North Main Street. They installed an eight and a half-barrel Specific Mechanical system. The Mishawaka brewpub that opened in 1992 was a nine thousand-square-foot former fitness center in a suburban retail area. It had a sports-bar feel, with pool tables, table soccer, and televisions tuned to Chicago White Sox games. Vintage photos of northern Indiana breweries lined the hunter-green walls. It served as a local hangout for regular folks looking for a good meal with a beer, along with hophead "Nuevo hippies," as Tom Schmidt called them.

Beers Brewed:
The bestselling copper-red Four Horsemen Irish Ale is brewed with six malts and three hop varieties; Lake Effect Pale Ale; the moderately hopped INDIAana Pale Ale; golden Mishawaka Kolsch; Raspberry Wheat Ale made with two-row Pilsner malt, white wheat malt, and Sterling hops; Wall Street Wheat Beer; and Irish-style Founder's Classic Dry Stout with roasted coffee undertones. Seasonals include Seven Mules Kick Ass Ale, Hop Head Ale, and Jibber Jabber Java Stout.

Critical success came pretty quick. Schmidt's Four Horsemen Irish Ale was a Silver Medal winner at the 1994 Great American Beer Festival. The Lake Effect Pale Ale took a Silver Medal at the 1995 World Beer Championships, and the next year, the Founder's Stout won the World Beer Cup's Gold Cup, as well as a 1998 World Beer Cup Silver Cup and the 1995 Silver Medal Winner at the Great American Beer Festival. Today, Tom Schmidt, with his white hair and intense blue eyes, is the grand old man of Hoosier craft beer, having professionally brewed longer than anyone active in Indiana.

In 2005 the Schmidts started a production brewery in Elkhart with a fifteen-barrel system purchased from the defunct Duneland Brewery. With an eventual capacity of three thousand barrels a year, the system and bottling line produced about five hundred barrels in 2008. Mishawaka brewery previously self distributed, but with the addition of a Michigan distributor and plans in the works for an Indiana distributor, the company is poised to rapidly increase production. Mishawaka Brewing has also built a bustling business with soft drinks, including orange and cream sodas and Lazy Dog root beer.

In December 2008 the Schmidts announced that the Mishawaka brewpub was closing after sixteen years. But the Mishawaka Brewing Company is carrying on with its production brewery in Elkhart, as well as The Pub, located at 408 West Cleveland in Mishawaka.

Opened: 1992, closed December 2008 • Owner: Tom Schmidt • Brewers: Tom Schmidt, Rick Schmidt • Brewing System: Fifteen-barrel Specific Mechanical at Elkhart production brewery. • Annual Production: 1,800 barrels in 2008 • Tours: No • Hours: It is a production brewery. • Beer to go: No • Food: No

Granite City Food and Brewery Limited
University Park Mall, 6501 Grape Road
Mishawaka, IN 45645
(574) 243–0900
www.gcfb.net

GRANITE CITY LAUDS its *fermentus interruptus,* a patented process that utilizes unfermented wort trucked from its central brewery in Iowa to each restaurant in the chain for on-site fermentation, maturation, and filtering. Tim Cary, Granite City's chief operating officer, commented in a company press release, "We have great beer products that compliment our menu and we get consumer credit for freshly brewed proprietary products even though we have eliminated much of the labor and operational complexity through our 'par-brewing' process. From an operational standpoint we refer to this as 'beverage leverage,' and we are the only operator in the restaurant business that has it."

Many patrons find the concept appealing. They flock to the upscale suburban Granite City brewpubs that are styled like Martha Stewart's own northwoods cabin, all fieldstone and polished wood. The stainless steel fermenting tanks gleam behind spotless glass windows as the crack kitchen cranks out embellished comfort food. From its beginnings in Saint Cloud, Minnesota, in 2000, the NASDAQ-listed firm has expanded to twenty-five locations in twelve states, all served from the central "worthouse" in Elsworth, Iowa.

Beers Brewed:
A copper-colored IPA, Duke of Wellington; Broad Axe Stout, a dry Irish style; a German-style Brother Benedict Bock lager; a light golden Northern Light Lager; and Two-Pull, a half-and-half of Northern Light and Mai Bock beers. Specialty beers include Ostara Spring Ale, Hefeweizen, Belgian Wit, Oktoberfest, Scottish Ale, and Burning Barn Irish Red.

Larry Crane runs the central brewery in Iowa. He's been with Granite City for eight years, after three years working in microbreweries. "We've got a twenty-five-barrel system here. After we produce the wort, we knock the temperature down to under 40 degrees," Crane said. "We've got custom-built tanker trucks that can hold six pods of twelve-and-a-half barrels each. We then truck the wort to the restaurant, where we pump it into the fermenters, where they raise the temperature, pitch the yeast, and finish the beer." The stainless-steel tanker trucks, which deliver to the Granite Citys within a 500-mile radius of the worthouse, look somewhat like small, old-style gasoline tankers. "The trucks are well-insulated, so temperature rise is not much of an issue for us, in terms of contamination," Crane said. The Granite City chain typically trains restaurant managers to handle the beer finishing as part of their responsibilities. Strict standard operating procedures and a professional brewer who travels between the locations help keep the product consistent. "We're a national chain, so consistency and quality are important," Crane said. "That's what chains are all about."

JToad, a reviewer on beeradvocate.com, gave the brewpub a B+ rating, noting that it was definitely a restaurant first. But it is a very friendly, service-oriented restaurant that is enthusiastic about its brews. Granite City's Mug Club is well-liked, delivering discounted beers and point rewards to its regulars. "We're a little bit limited on the number of beers we can produce," Crane noted, though customers appear to be more than satisfied by Granite City's offerings.

Opened: July 2008 • Owner: Managing Partner Tony Pepe • Brewer: Steve Kotsianis • Brewing System: Twelve and a half-barrel Newlands Systems Inc. fermenters at the Mishawaka brewpub and twenty-five-barrel Newlands System Inc. rig at the Granite City central brewery in Iowa. • Annual Production: Approximately 750 barrels fermented at each restaurant location • Tours: Yes, inquire about availability. • Hours: Monday through Thursday 11:00 a.m. to midnight; Friday and Saturday 11:00 a.m. to 1:00 a.m.; Sunday 10:00 a.m. to 10:00 p.m. • Beer to go: Growlers • Food: Granite City is a full-service restaurant, with appetizers, salads, sandwiches, flatbread pizzas, and entrées, including Granite City meatloaf. The flavorful walleye dinners belie Granite City's northern lake origins. The ale and cheese soup is touted. All of the food is made from scratch.

Crown Brewing LLC
211 South East Street
Crown Point, IN 46307
(219) 663–4545
www.crownbrewing.com

CROWN BREWING WAS NO ORDINARY microbrewery start-up. As Crown Brewing came up to its June 2008 opening, beer sites were atwitter with anticipation. Beer geeks considered brewer Jim Cibak to be one of the fellows to follow. He studied at Chicago's Siebel Institute of Technology and worked with Chicago's renowned Goose Island before serving as brewmaster at Three Floyds. Beginning in 2006, Cibak brewed at California's refined Firestone Walker brewery, when both the Great American

Beer Festival and World Beer Cup awarded the brewery Mid-sized Brewery of the Year. Small wonder there was jubilation in Hoosier beer circles when Cibak decided to return home to open Crown Brewing.

Beers Brewed:
English Mild Ale; Octoberfest with German yeasts and Vienna and CaraMunich malts; clove- and banana-scented Weizenheimer hefeweizen; dry-hopped Hop Fix American pale ale with CTZ, Centennial, and Summit hops; Sarah, an American blond ale; Bodacious Brown Ale; and a lightly bittered Powderhorn porter.

With a tall brick smokestack looming overhead, Crown Brewing is housed in a small brick building at the rear of a local favorite, Carriage Court Pizza. The structure is the former boiler house for the Lake County jail, infamous as the site of John Dillinger's daring carved-wooden-gun escape. The brewery has a small intimate bar area, fittingly lit by a beer-bottle light fixture. With a window into the brewhouse, it's a homey spot to sample Crown beers. The brewery is equipped with a seven-barrel Bavarian Brewing System, which has a combination mash-tun and water-tun, as well as a combination brew-kettle and whirlpool, allowing the brewhouse footprint to fit into a relatively compact space. Early reviews of the Crown Brewing beers by beeradvocate.com came in with all A+ and A grades.

But in December 2008 the brewery hit a bump in the road: Cibak decided to move on. The beeradvocate.com folks were distraught. "Jesus," one wrote, "That is flat out heartbreaking news." But brewing goes on.

Chicago native Steve Mazylewski soon stepped up. A twenty-year brewing vet, Mazylewski has brewed award winners at the Wild Onion brewpub in Illinois and the Hog Haus in Arkansas.

Opened: June 2008 • Owners: Dave Bryan and Tim Walsh • Brewer: Steve Mazylewski • Brewing System: 7-barrel Bavarian Brewing System • Annual Production: 300 barrels • Tours: Yes, ask about availability. • Hours: Monday through Wednesday noon to 11:00 p.m.; Thursday through Saturday noon until late; Sunday noon to 11:00 p.m. • Beer to go: Growlers • Food: Diners can eat Carriage House Pizza in the brewery bar or drink Crown beer with their pizza in the pizzaria.

Brickworks Brewing Company

327 Main Street
Hobart, IN 46342
(219) 942–2337
www.brickworksbrewing.com

BRICKS MADE HOBART, and Brickworks Brewing Company's owner and brewer, Tom Coster, is determined to celebrate it. From the mid-nineteenth century until well into the twentieth century, brickyards catering to the Chicago market were the industrial engine of Hobart. Hoping to bond Brickies (Hobart folks' nickname) to his new brewery, Coster has made bricks his theme, starting with the name. Antique bricks plucked by divers from the bottom of Hidden Lake, where an old brickyard used to stand, now decorate the brewery's dining room wall and bar. Pictures of old brickhouses line the walls. Some of the beers are even named after bricks.

The brewery's soft opening in early September 2009 was a rout, with so much business the brewery reportedly ran out of register tape. Coster told the local paper, "I knew it was going to be a crazy opening, but I didn't know it was going to be this crazy." The Brickworks Brewery is a place of ambient lighting and warm earth tones, with the staff serving a variety of pub food. The brewhouse's stainless-steel tanks are beacons of beer that are eye-catchers from both the dining room and the street. It's been a hit: One fan gushed on yelp.com, "This place is awesome!!!!"

Beers Brewed:
The Brickworks's beers include a porter, an IPA, a Dunkelweizen, and an amber.

Opened: September 2009 • Owner: Tom Coster • Brewer: Tom Coster • Brewing System: Premier 7-barrel system • Annual Production: 1,000 barrels (Projected) • Tours: With appointment • Hours: Monday through Thursday 11:00 a.m. to midnight; Friday and Saturday 11:00 a.m. to 1:00 a.m.; Sunday 11:00 a.m. to 10:00 p.m. • Beer to go: Growlers. • Food: Pub food, including pizza, beer-battered fish and chips, burgers, and other sandwiches.

Figure Eight Brewing LLC

1555 West Lincolnway, Suite 105
Valparaiso, IN 46385
(219) 477–2000
www.figure8brewing.com

THE FIGURE EIGHT, the essential rock climber's knot, inspired Tom and Lynne Uban to name their new Valparaiso brewery. Both passionate rock climbers, the two saw the knot's resemblance to the symbol for infinity. As they wrote on their Web site, "So sticking with our passions, we hope to take Figure Eight Brewing to infinity and beyond! (Or at least to the point where we are producing some very tasty and satisfying brews.)"

Tom Uban is a Purdue-grad software engineer originally from Valparaiso. A home brewer since 1983, Uban saw a hole in the market and decided to go pro. "Now was the time," he said. The Ubans handcrafted their brewery in a 1,400-square-foot facility in a new strip mall. Uban touted his beer to the local paper, "It will have flavor, and you can put your nose to it and it will have different scents."

Beers Brewed:
Five to six "tasty beers," as Tom Uban terms them, will be on tap.

Opened: December 2009 (projected) • Owners: Tom and Lynne Uban • Brewer: Tom Uban • Brewing Systems: A 7-barrel Premier • Annual Production: 1,000 barrels (projected) • Tours: Yes • Hours: To be determined • Beer to go: Kegs, growlers, bottles • Food: No

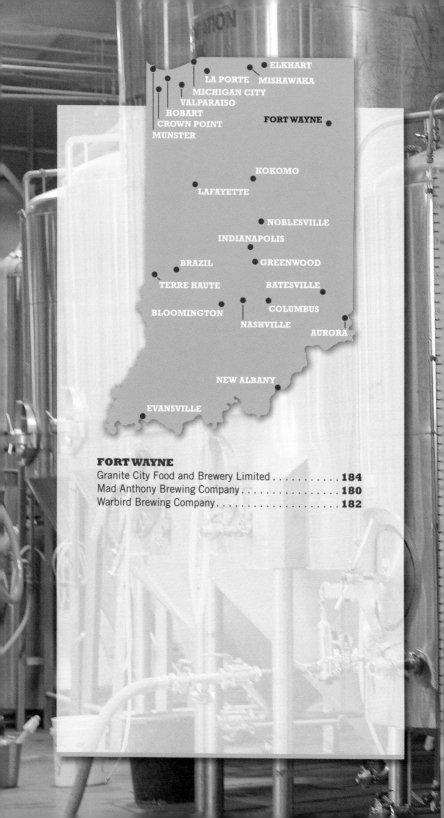

ELKHART
MISHAWAKA
LA PORTE
MICHIGAN CITY
VALPARAISO
HOBART
CROWN POINT
MUNSTER

FORT WAYNE

KOKOMO
LAFAYETTE

NOBLESVILLE
INDIANAPOLIS
BRAZIL GREENWOOD
TERRE HAUTE
BATESVILLE
BLOOMINGTON COLUMBUS
NASHVILLE AURORA

NEW ALBANY

EVANSVILLE

FORT WAYNE

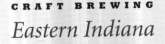

CHAPTER TEN

CRAFT BREWING

Eastern Indiana

. . . .

ASTERN INDIANA HAS HISTORY. The early nineteenth-century settlements along the Whitewater River were among the state's earliest developed areas. The Wayne County Quakers formed the nation's second-largest enclave, trailing only Philadelphia in numbers of Friends, a distinction it still holds today. It's the final resting place of Johnny Appleseed, that early American mystic who traipsed a hundred thousand miles across the Midwest, leaving swaths of blooming apple trees (and barrels of hard cider) in his wake.

Fort Wayne goes back even earlier, to its early-eighteenth-century origins as a French trading post at Kekionga, the Miami tribal capital. Located at the crucial portage between the Great Lakes and Mississippi watersheds, the area was known as the Glorious Gate.

Traversed by thousands of voyageurs from Quebec questing rich Midwestern beaver pelts, the portage was a strategic pinch point. By 1722 the French had established Fort Miami, which became an important staging ground during the French and Indian War. After the American Revolution, the young American government under General Mad Anthony Wayne conquered the region's Native American tribes. In

1794 the American army erected Fort Wayne on the portage.

The early-nineteenth-century Wabash and Erie Canal brought prosperity to the little town, which became known as the Summit City with its position on the high point of the canal route. Soon hundreds of mercantilists flooded the town, their brick warehouses rising beside the canal. When the chuff of locomotives replaced the bray of canal-boat mules in the 1860s and 1870s, Fort Wayne deftly became a railroad town, home to foundries and switching yards galore. Attracted by the economic possibilities, central European immigrants thronged to Fort Wayne, helping to make it a great industrial city. And where there is industry, there is beer. The thousands of immigrants included a coterie of brewers who created a tradition that persists. As we gallop into the twenty-first century, Fort Wayne is still a brewing town.

Mad Anthony Brewing Company

2002 Broadway Avenue
Fort Wayne, IN 46802
(260) 426–2537
www.madbrew.com

MAD ANTHONY BREWING COMPANY is continuing Fort Wayne's long and colorful brewing tradition. Since the brewery opened in April 1996, it has been a stalwart of the Hoosier brewing scene. Located in the colorful Broadway Corridor, the brewpub is housed in Fort Wayne's original Kroger's, which has also been a deli, drugstore, furniture store, and video shop. A five-cent hamburger stand used to operate in one part of the building. With its checkerboard floors, encrustations of old advertising art, vintage bikes and sleds, jungles of plants, open mike, and friendly waitresses, it is that local place you've always wanted.

That makes the folks at Mad Anthony very happy. They call it "Our Place," endeavoring to keep it informal and welcoming, a spot where families can gather and friends can tip a few. And there's quite a few brews to tip, with a constantly evolving lineup of beers that emerge from the creativity of brewmaster Todd Grantham, who began home brewing in 1992. "It's just like cooking," Grantham noted. "You can look at the recipes and you can look at the guidelines, but you just have to work it to your tastes. If it doesn't quite suit me this time, I can always adjust a little the next time. Very few beers are exactly the same." It seems to work. The wall above the bar is filled with numerous ribbons and awards. In 1999 the Great American Beer Festival judges awarded Mad Anthony a Silver Medal for its Auburn Lager,

Beers Brewed:
An amber, American-style Auburn Lager; crisp Gabby Blonde Lager; American-styled Ol' Woody Pale Ale with Cascade hops; IPA; Big Daddy Brown; Old Fort Porter; Ruby Raspberry Wheat dosed with Oregon raspberries; Black Lager; Cream Stout; Crystal Lager; American Red; a black, creamy Harry Baals Irish Stout pushed with nitrogen; Pre-prohibition Pilsner; Summer Daze Wheat; and Barr Street Bock.

with a World Beer Cup Bronze the following year. The brewery's Anniversary Ale, an 11 percent imperial IPA that Mad Anthony produced to celebrate its tenth anniversary, received an A- rating from beeradvocate.com, with ratebeer.com grading the ale in the ninety-fifth percentile. The 2008 Brewers Cup judges awarded the ale a Bronze Medal. "We find the darker and hoppier beers sell better," said partner Jeff Neels. "Kölschs and ESBs don't move so well. People want the full-flavored, hoppier beers."

Named after the illustrious war hero, Mad Anthony Wayne, the company was founded by Grantham and Blaine Stuckey. (Stuckey has served as the Brewers of Indiana Guild president for three terms and leads the current lobbying efforts to reform Sunday sales laws.) The two partners initially started business with their seven-barrel brewing system in a five hundred-square-foot brewery located in the popular Munchies restaurant. Mad Anthony eventually bought out Munchies, adding college friend Neels as a partner. With its base secure at the corner of Broadway and Taylor, Mad Anthony launched itself on another expedition in 2001, establishing a production brewery in a neighboring 2,500-square-foot pole building on Taylor Street. With an additional fifteen-barrel Bavarian Brewing System, the company was poised to move some suds. The next year it opened the Auburn Taproom in that car-crazy town, where *those* hometown folks began enjoying Indiana craft beer. In 2006 Mad Anthony embarked on its third location, the Lake City Tap House in Warsaw. And in 2008 the company began a fourth taproom in downtown Elkhart.

Opened: April 1998 • Owners: Blaine Stuckey, Todd Grantham, Jeff Neels • Brewer: Todd Grantham • Brewing Systems: Seven-barrel Cross Distributing System and 15-barrel Monoblock system • Annual Production: 1,800 barrels • Tours: Yes, call for availability. • Hours: Monday through Sunday 11:00 a.m. to midnight. • Beer to go: Bottles and growlers • Food: Mad Anthony serves some serious pub grub, including "almost famous" Chicago-style pizza, "Unwraps," which are large tortilla shells stuffed with a variety of fillings, sandwiches, salads, and Cajun-style red beans and rice.

Warbird Brewing Company
10515 Majic Port Lane
Fort Wayne, IN 46819
www.warbirdbrewing.com

IN BREWER DAVE HOLMES'S VIEW, Warbird beer is patriotism in a bottle. A veteran of the Persian Gulf War and aficionado of vintage warplanes, founder and brewer Holmes uses his brews to glorify America's military aviation history. As he writes on the company's Web site, "Warbird is a brand with distinctive military character." He later stated, "The Warbird brand is unique, patriotic and respectful. If you appreciate airplanes, our military, and our history, this is your beer."

Warbird's packaging features illustrations of famous World War II fighter planes, including the Thunderbolt, T-6, and Mustang, highlighted with 1940s-era typography. A production brewery, Warbird primarily sells bottled beer. Though the brewery initially canned its beer, the machinery has now been sold. "I'm brewing approachable beers," Holmes said. His Web site trumpets his beer as "The World's Most Drinkable Craft Beer." Jaded beer-site raters, in spite of their bias toward the brewing extremes, award Warbird beer solid B grades, with an A- for the P-47 Warbird Wheat beer, a hefeweizen. But Warbird's real targeted market is the armed forces: "You know somebody who likes airplanes, or who served in the military? Buy them a six-pack of Warbird and see what they say. I promise you. They'll appreciate it," the Web site reads. Yet it's more than military personnel who approve the beer. The 2008 Brewers Cup judges awarded a Gold Medal to Warbird for its Shanty Irish in the Scottish and Irish category, as well as a Gold Medal in 2005 for the T-6 Red Ale.

Beers Brewed:
Mustang Gold Ale, an entry beer; the light, malty T-6 Red Ale; Thunderbolt Wheat, a hefeweizen; the American-style Warhawk Pale Ale made with Amarillo hops; and the sweetish Shanty Irish red Irish ale.

In September 2008 respected brewing historian Maureen Ogle wrote an article for the *Washington Post* on the sale of Anheuser-Busch to InBev, the Brazilian-Belgian corporation. At the conclusion of the article, she places Warbird in some pretty storied company: "On this 232nd anniversary of our founding (try saying that after you've hoisted a few), this Bud—or this Yuengling, Saranac, Russian River, Abita, Anchor, Magic Hat, Summit, Warbird, or New Glarus—is for us." Holmes e-mailed the friends of the brewery: "When I started making beer in my kitchen, I did not imagine that one day I would have a beer company mentioned among the best in the country by a major publication such as the *Washington Post*."

Holmes is a psychiatrist, drawn to commercial brewing after developing his skills as a home brewer. He's a burly, shaven-headed fellow, with the assured intensity of a doctor. "There is no better training for brewing than medical school," he said. In his medical specialty, he considers himself a "brain chemistry technician," which prepares him for the mechanical and organic complexities of brewing. "We are yeast ranchers," he declared. You can see his hospital training in his twenty-barrel brewery, which is meticulously organized and surgery clean—a far cry from some of the more rustic breweries that dot the state. Noting the challenges of working with the sometimes helter-skelter craft-brewing industry, Holmes concluded, "Brewing has been a great spiritual journey."

But Holmes's great spiritual journey took another route in October 2009, when he announced the brewery was closing. "We have no choice but to face reality that we did our best but we did not achieve financial success," he wrote. "The beer business is a very tough business. I'm sorry to say it. It's game over for Warbird."

Opened: December 2004; closed October 2009 • Owner: Doctor Dave Holmes • Brewer: Holmes • Brewing Systems: Twenty-barrel Heavy Duty Products system • Annual Production: 800 barrels • Tours: Yes, call for availability. • Hours: No • Beer to go: No • Food: No

Granite City Food and Brewery Limited
3809 Coldwater Road
Fort Wayne, IN 46805
(260) 471–3030
www.gcfb.com

THE GRANITE CITY BREWERY IN FORT WAYNE was the chain's first location in Indiana. Located just off Spy Run Avenue near the location of the old Centlivre Brewery, Granite City is Fort Wayne's latest microbrewery. Like other restaurants in the twenty-six-location chain, the Fort Wayne restaurant takes the sweet (unfermented) wort that is trucked in from the central worthouse in Iowa and finishes the brewing in its twelve-and-a-half-barrel stainless steel fermenters adjacent to the dining room. (See Granite City, Mishawaka.)

Beers Brewed:
Duke of Wellington IPA; Broad Axe Stout; Brother Benedict Bock lager; a light Northern Light Lager; and Two-Pull, a half-and-half of Northern Light and Mai Bock beers. Specialty beers include Ostara Spring Ale, Hefeweizen, Belgian Wit, Oktoberfest, Scottish Ale, and Burning Barn Irish Red.

Fort Wayne native Justin Dirig is the brewer-manager. A Wabash

College graduate, Dirig home brewed for more than two years before taking his position. In his off hours, he hangs out at Mad Anthony's. "I'd love to do the whole process," Dirig said, speaking of the wort production done in Iowa. But his Granite City customers are enthusiastic about the two-stage brewing. There are more than 4,200 Fort Wayne members of the brewery's Mug Club, and most nights the place is booming.

Opened: January 2008 • Owner: Brenda Deskins • Brewer: Justin Dirig • Brewing System: Twelve and a half-barrel Newlands Systems Inc. fermenters at the Fort Wayne brewpub and a twenty-five-barrel Newlands System Inc. rig at the Granite City central brewery in Iowa. • Annual Production: Approximately 750 barrels fermented at each restaurant location • Tours: Yes, inquire about availability. • Hours: Monday through Thursday 11:00 a.m. to midnight; Friday and Saturday 11:00 a.m. to 1:00 a.m.; Sunday 10:00 a.m. to 10:00 p.m. • Beer to go: Growlers • Food: Granite City is a full-service restaurant with appetizers, salads, sandwiches, flatbread pizzas, and entrées that are made from scratch. Reviewers praise the ale and cheese soup.

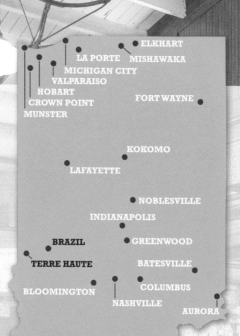

ELKHART
LA PORTE MISHAWAKA
MICHIGAN CITY
VALPARAISO
HOBART FORT WAYNE
CROWN POINT
MUNSTER

KOKOMO
LAFAYETTE

NOBLESVILLE
INDIANAPOLIS
BRAZIL GREENWOOD
TERRE HAUTE BATESVILLE
COLUMBUS
BLOOMINGTON AURORA
NASHVILLE

NEW ALBANY

EVANSVILLE

CHAPTER ELEVEN

CRAFT BREWING
Western Indiana

TERRE HAUTE WAS ONE OF INDIANA'S early industrial epicenters. A canal town, railroad town, burly, brawling, wide-open city, it has been part of our rough-and-tumble history from the beginning. Thanks to being the northernmost navigable spot on the Wabash River in the steamboat era, the city was first an agricultural entrepôt for the region's salt pork and whiskey producers. The mid-nineteenth-century arrival of the Wabash and Erie Canal and the National Road added to Terre Haute's bustle. Even before the Civil War, plentiful Wabash Valley coal fueled the city's many foundries, rolling mills, and iron works. Hometown of working-class hero Eugene V. Debs, the famous Socialist presidential candidate and labor organizer, Terre Haute hosted an 1881 craft labor conference that eventually spawned the American Federation of Labor.

Terre Haute has also long been an industrial brewing center. From its origins in 1835, the Terre Haute Brewing Company was producing seventy thousand barrels a year by the 1890s. By 1900 it had grown to be the seventh-largest brewery in the United States. Terre Haute breweries were also the primary owners of the city's hundreds of round-the-clock saloons. To keep things lubricated, Terre Haute brewers greased the palms of generations of local politicians. With the saloon corruption, the infamous red-light district centered on Cherry Street, and dozens of boisterous gambling parlors, Terre Haute became known around the country as Sin City, a moniker that lasted well into the mid-twentieth century. The vice scene that Hoosier author Theodore Dreiser witnessed as a boy from his window at the edge of the bordello district inspired his great novels of dissolution, *Sister Carrie* and *Jennie Gerhardt.* But when yet another series of corruption scandals hit later in the twentieth century, Terre Haute began to shed its bad-boy image. Today it's a fairly staid Midwestern manufacturing town, proud of Larry Bird, its universities and hospitals, and its reborn brewing scene.

Vigo Brewing Group
401–03 South Ninth Street
Terre Haute, IN 47807
(812) 235–6758

VIGO BREWING GROUP is the phoenix of Terre Haute, rising in the heart of the city's historic beer-manufacturing district. Vigo is located in the original Terre Haute Brewing Company carpenter shop, where workmen crafted the elaborate wooden bars that symbolized saloons of an earlier era. A powerhouse of early twentieth-century Indiana brewing, Terre Haute Brewing Company closed in 1958.

Vigo Brewing goes back to 2000, when Terre Haute history buff and entrepreneur Mike Rowe revived the Terre Haute Brewing Company name with a three-and-a-half-barrel system that he housed in an 1837 brewery building. A longtime collector of local beer memorabilia, Rowe had located the original 1901 recipes for the famous Champagne Velvet line of beers. "A guy came into my office one day with a handwritten book, asked me if I'd give him twenty bucks for it. Never even got his name," said Rowe. It was the journal of Terre Haute Brewing's assistant brewer, Walter Braun. The recipes included the company's Ger-

Memorabilia from the Terre Haute Brewing Company, which closed in 1958.

man-style pilsner, an amber, and a bock. After spending a year knocking down the gargantuan recipes to a microbrew size with the help of microbiologist/home brewer Ted Herrera, Rowe commenced brewing Champagne Velvet. It was a success. Soon he found himself unable to keep up with demand with his small system.

In the chaos following 9/11, Rowe located a used 20-barrel DME brew system that was languishing in a New Jersey scrap yard. The beautiful copper brewing rig was originally in Manhattan's Commonwealth Brewing Company, a vaunted brewpub located in Rockefeller Center. Install-

Beers Brewed:
Vigo Brewing Group brews all of the Brugge beers (except the seasonals that are brewed at the Indianapolis brewpub), though primarily focus on Brugge Black and Tripel de Ripple.

While you're in the area visit Mogger's, a vintage bar.

ing the equipment in the old brick carpenter shop, Rowe expanded his production. In one corner of the cavernous building, Rowe installed a speakeasy, replete with vintage grain-painted bar and Champagne Velvet advertising art. It became a cherished local gathering place.

But by 2006 he was ready for other challenges. In early 2008 Ted Miller of Brugge in Indianapolis took over the brewery and renamed it the Vigo Brewing Company. Micah Weichert was Vigo's first brewermaster. A blue-eyed Kansan with blond dreadlocks, Weichert brewed award-winning beers for a number of years in Kansas and Hawaii, including two years on the island of Kauai at Waimea, "the world's most westernmost brewpub," before relaunching the Terre Haute operation. Primarily brew-

The Lost Speakeasy

There's an urban legend among brewers that a Prohibition-era speakeasy is hidden in the catacombs under the old Terre Haute Brewing Company complex. According to the oral history, a gas company man stumbled upon the completely intact bar while spelunking under the old complex. When he shined his light into the long-abandoned room, he saw glasses still sitting on the tables, bottles still behind the bar, the dusty mirrors reflecting a scene that looked abruptly interrupted in the 1920s, perhaps by a police raid.

Mike Rowe, Terre Haute beer historian and reviver of the Terre Haute Brewing Company, knows more about it than anyone. "There's always been talk that the Chicago gangsters used to come to Terre Haute, but people didn't know why," he said. "Over in Peoria, Illinois, there was an illegal speakeasy under the Joseph Huber brewery that the Al Capone people ran." Rowe talked about the massive cellars deep under the old Terre Haute brewery, with a shallow perimeter tunnel that ran at the edge of the complex. In the early 1990s, a gas company crew was installing a new line in the curb strip adjacent to the brewery when the drill suddenly broke through. The crew called for a backhoe, which dug out an entry. They had hit the perimeter tunnel. A volunteer dropped into the tunnel with a light. He proceeded north on Ninth Street, and then east, under what is now the CVS parking lot. "He found a Quonset hut down there, with French doors," Rowe said. But no speakeasy. The Lost Speakeasy yet awaits other explorers.

MIKE SCHWAB

ing and bottling for Brugge, Vigo also contract-brewed for the Wabash Valley Malt Beverage Company for a period before the marketing company ceased operations.

When Vigo stepped up production in 2008, the *Terre Haute Tribune Star* celebrated, quoting Wabash Valley's Bob Mack: "We look at Terre Haute as being the beer mecca of Indiana, just as it used to be. The feeling there is just palpable. You can just feel it." But it turned out to be a rocky road to Mecca. After a strong start in 2008, the brewery hit a patch of equipment problems, eventually having to replace the boiler. Unable to produce in Terre Haute, Brugge kept up with their brewpub demand by brewing at the pub, but put bottling on hold.

With the new boiler almost functional, Weichert returned to Kansas in summer 2009, when the assistant brewer, John Kopta, took over. A biochemistry graduate of Colorado State, Kopta put his homebrewing experience and Vigo apprenticeship to good use. As of the fall of 2009, the brewery has risen again. "I've had people call me from all over the state," Kopta said. "Where's my Tripel. Everybody's just missing our beer."

Opened: January 2008 • Owners: Ted Miller and Shannon Stone; Abraham Benrubi • Brewer: John Kopta • Brewing Systems: 20-barrel DME system • Annual Production: 1,200 barrels 2008; 1,000 2009 (projected) • Tours: No • Hours: No • Beer to go: No • Food: No

Bee Creek Brewing Company

P. O. Box 515
Brazil, IN 47834
(812) 446–2833
www.beecreekbrewing.com

BEE CREEK BREWING IS COLLABORATION between a former submariner and a geriatric psychologist. Doctor Frank Forster has a two-hundred-acre Waco-Texas-style spread out in Clay County, where he and his brother-in-law Mark Snelling like to roam on the trails. "We get liquored up and drive around the property," Forster laughed. "We wanted high-alcohol stuff, so we brewed it." The result is Hoosier Honey Wheat, which weighs in at 7.5 to 8 percent alcohol ABV. "Real smooth, real sweet, got a kick," Forster said. "We like to say, 'It's strong enough for a man, and sweet enough for a woman.'"

It took three years of experimentation at their cattle-ranch brewery until they got the beer to their satisfaction. Snelling, who's been brewing for twenty-five years since his San Francisco navy days, uses ninety pounds of honey from Martinsville's Hunter Honey Farm in each batch of beer. Indianabeer.com's Bob Ostrander described Hoosier Honey Wheat as "a German Hefeweizen brewed with copious honey to give a bold 7.0 percent ABV. Lots of banana and honey sweetness takes out some of the traditional clove notes and leaves a long, sweet finish." Bee Creek Brewing will initially distribute bottled beer in western Indiana and Indianapolis.

Beers Brewed:
Hoosier Honey Wheat Beer and the Clay County Coffee Stout, which uses coffee roasted in Greencastle.

Opened: February 2009 • Owners: Doctor Frank Forster, Julie Forster, Mark Snelling • Brewer: Mark Snelling • Brewing Systems: A 7-barrel "American Hybrid," as Frank Forster laughingly calls this hodgepodge system. • Annual Production: 1,000 barrels (projected) • Tours: No • Hours: Production brewery only • Beer to go: No • Food: No

Hops

The tall, climbing hop plant is almost exclusively cultivated for beer. Hops preserve beer, help maintain a frothy head, and impart the flavors and aromas that often make a beer a beer. Hops had a shaky eighth-century beginning, as medieval brewers feared it caused "melancholy and tormenting disease." Despite the rap, hops usage spread through Germany, France, and the Low Countries during the Middle Ages. In the early 1400s, Flemish traders introduced hops to Britain, whose colonists toted it to Massachusetts in 1629.

Today about 75 percent of the hops harvested in America are grown in Washington State's Yakima Valley, where ample irrigation water, deep, sandy soil, and dry desert conditions are ideal for the persnickety crop. Washington, Oregon, and Idaho are the main hop-producing states, with small amounts grown in the upper Midwest. The total U.S. production was 79 million pounds in 2008, a big jump from the bleak harvest of 2007, when the annual production was only 59 million pounds. Trailing only Germany, the United States is the second largest hops producer in the world.

The hop plants' shoots, or bines, corkscrew up towering trellises eighteen to twenty-five feet into the air. When mature, the pale, green female cones develop sticky, resinous glands that contain lupilin, brewings' essential flavor- and aroma-producing resins and oils. Vital for bittering, alpha acids typically constitute about 4.5 to 7 percent of the cones' dried weight in U.S. varieties; up to 8 percent to 12 percent in British varieties. With cones ranging from taut little buds to blowsy, loose forms, the hops grown in the United States include European varieties and associated American hybrids. Some hop varieties are noted for their aroma-imparting characteristics, with relatively low 4 percent to 8 percent alpha-acid contents. These varieties include Cascade, Fuggle, Columbia, and Willamette, as well as German cultivars such as Hallentauer and Tettnanger. Aroma descriptions range from floral, citrusy, and piney to delicate, mild, and strong. The American hybrid of the Czech Saaz, for example, is revered for its earthy spiciness.

The increasingly popular Extract or High-Alpha varieties include such workhorses as Bullion and Brewer's Gold, which were introduced in the 1930s. More recent hybrids produce up to 17 percent alpha acids, giving the kick that craft brewers seek for the high-hopped beers of today's market. These varieties include Galena, Olympic, Amarillo, Simcoe, and Columbus. Some dual-purpose hops that contribute both aroma and higher bittering acids are Perle, Glacier, and Cluster.

It takes about eight to thirteen ounces of hops for each barrel of beer. Rather than using dried whole-hop cones, most brewers use hop pellets, which are hops that have been ground in a hammer mill and then pressed into pellets. But purists remain. A few major breweries, such as Sierra Nevada, still use whole hops, though Anheuser-Busch only recently switched to pellets. At the Yakima Fresh Hop Ale Festival, a dozen craft breweries brew with hops gathered less than a day before.

In 2008 there was a perfect storm in the hops world. Prices leapt up to six times what they'd been the year before—from six to eight dollars a pound to forty and even sixty dollars a pound. In some cases, craft brewers scrambled to even find hops. In hindsight, an October 2006 warehouse fire in Yakima, Washington, was the signal flare for the upcoming crisis. When the S. S. Steiner, Inc., hops warehouse went up in flames, two million pounds of hops went with it—4 percent of the U.S. total. The following growing season, Europe had a spate of bad weather, causing the hop harvest to plummet. The hop situation was already dicey. Over the previous decade, the combination of encroaching urban development and an ethanol-fueled corn boom had closed hop farms across the Northwest. Worldwide, hop acreage had dropped from 234,000 acres in 1994 down to 118,000 acres by 2007. With the growth of the international beer market in Latin America and China, exacerbated by the popularity of highly bittered brews, demand for hops was skyrocketing. Supply and demand collided, resulting in the explosive price increases. (Hops remain a relatively small percentage of beer's total material costs. Hops purveyors used to say hops cost about the same as the bottle cap's plastic liner. With the price increases, they bumped the comparison up to the whole cap.)

But after a year of shortages, price hikes, and general nervousness among craft brewers, the hops situation is starting to sort itself out. Ralph Olson is a partner at Hopunion, a Washington State hops distributor that caters to craft brewers. He spoke in the winter of 2008 about the improvement in the hops market: "This year is night and day from last year. It's great." He noted an almost 25 percent increase in hops acreage in the U.S., up to 41,000 acres—most of the new acreage coming in the prime Washington State hop-growing regions. "Prices are coming down significantly from its high. Next year will come down some more. It will be back to normal within a few years," said Olson.

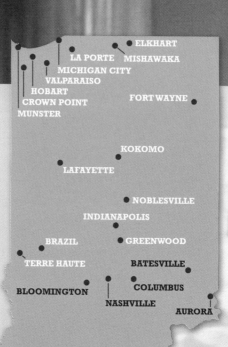

ELKHART
LA PORTE   MISHAWAKA
MICHIGAN CITY
VALPARAISO
HOBART   FORT WAYNE
CROWN POINT
MUNSTER

KOKOMO
LAFAYETTE

NOBLESVILLE
INDIANAPOLIS
BRAZIL   GREENWOOD
TERRE HAUTE   BATESVILLE
                COLUMBUS
BLOOMINGTON
        NASHVILLE   AURORA

NEW ALBANY

EVANSVILLE

CHAPTER TWELVE

CRAFT BREWING

Southern Indiana

. . . .

SOUTHERN INDIANA is almost iconically Hoosier: bucolic farms tucked among rolling hills and lazy rivers, rustic characters proffering witty epigrams over fencerows, and small towns with a James Whitcomb Riley charm. But it's also a place of big-shouldered industrial cities and university towns that commingle tweedy eggheads with raffish bohos: spots where the nineteenth century can speak to the twenty-first in a seamless conversation.

The rivers were the first highways here, and early history hugs the Ohio and Wabash rivers, where the first people built their mounds and French fur traders decided to hang around for a while. Many of the state's first towns are strung along the southern waterways, including Angel Mounds, Vincennes, the Falls Cities of New Albany, Clarksville, and Jeffersonville, Troy, Madison, and the brewing utopia of New Harmony.

The brewers down in the Hoosier south are an independent lot, pursuing their own dreams with a verve and vigor. While traditional brewing styles seem to hold, creativity burbles eternal. Check out the southern heartland's fine brewers and their many flavorful offerings.

PHOTOGRAPHY BY RICHARD SPAHR

Bloomington Brewing Company

1795 East Tenth Street
Bloomington, IN 47408
(812) 323–2112
bbc.bloomington.com

"I'M A LITTLE IN CRUNCH TIME," Bloomington Brewing Company founder Jeff Mease said in September 2008. "I've got eleven water buffalo coming next week." As evidenced by his unusual herd and wide-ranging curiosity, Mease is not your average brewer. A former Indiana University student who settled in Bloomington, Mease is as likely to be at Burning Man, the Telluride Mushroom Festival, the hot spots of south Florida, Italy's Slow Food Festival, or in the Bolivian mountains as he is to be managing his culinary micro-empire of Bloomington Brewing, a Pizza Express chain, Lennie's restaurant, and his agri-tourism farm where his artisanal mozzarella-cheese herd was headed. (All of which he co-owns with partner and former wife, Lennie Busch). He's a numbers guy with a distinct tropism toward quality, cooperation, and green consciousness. It's an intriguing combination.

Beers Brewed:
FreeStone Blond Ale, a crisp entry beer; dry-hopped Quarrymen Pale Ale; malty Ruby Bloom Amber; and full-bodied Big Stone Stout. Seasonals include spicy Vision Weiss, B-Town Brown Ale that is made with chocolate malt, and coffee-spiked Java Porter.

"I liked the idea of unique local brands," Mease said. "It got me interested in craft brewing in the early 1990s. I went to a craft-brewing conference and got inculcated with ideas." As he planned his craft brewery, Mease became instrumental in the 1994 Indiana state brewery law revision that permitted on-site sales of micro-brewed beer. He'd seen how craft breweries in California, Oregon, and Washington had proliferated once state laws were amended to allow brewpubs. Working with state legislators and other interested parties, Mease spearheaded the new brewing law. The legislation opened the door for the extraordinary growth of brewpubs across Indiana. With other Hoosier microbrewers, he then helped organize the Brewers of

Owner Jeff Mease and Floyd Rosenbaum, brewer.

Indiana Guild, a mutual-aid society to increase the quality and awareness of Indiana craft beer.

Floyd Rosenbaum is Bloomington Brewing Company's brewer, master of the seven hundred-square-foot, near-campus brewery that's crammed with a fifteen-barrel Specific Mechanical system. A Stinesville native, Rosenbaum got started home brewing in the 1970s. Formerly a pipefitter and machine technician, his background ideally prepared him to tackle the challenges of the brewery's pumps and valves. A stint in Alaska exposed him to homesteaders brewing and baking with the same ingredients, triggering some

Freestone Blond Ale and Big Stone Stout.

thoughts about self-sufficiency. "Hey Jude" blares as Rosenbaum deftly dances amongst the stainless-steel tanks and webs of hoses, adjusting a valve here, twisting a knob there. A slender, sweat-shirted man with a gravelly southern Indiana accent, Rosenbaum monitors the mash. "You got to push the button, you got to pull the lever," he said about the semi-automatic system. "You got to do the work. I like it. It's still really exciting to me to be working on a small traditional scale—it's fun." The scent of cooking grain fills the air—like being in a celestial granola factory. A tang of yeast wafts by. "You put it on, set it up," Rosenbaum said as he boogies by, "then you rock."

And rock they have. Drawn by Rosenbaum's flavorful brews, regulars throng the BBC's chic brewpub near the IU campus.

Bloomington Brewing has received a cluster of Indiana State Fair ribbons for its FreeStone Blonde, Pale Ale, and Big Stone Stout. In 2008 Brewers Cup judges awarded a Silver for the brewery's B-Town Brown ale. The World Beer Cup competition has awarded Bloomington Brewing Company medals for its Vision Weiss, Quarrymen Pale Ale, Java Porter, and Big Stone Stout.

Out on Bloomington's rural fringe, Mease strides his sixty-nine-acre farm, burbling with ideas for his new brewery as his coddled water buffalo browse. The long-range plans include a thirty to fifty-barrel production brewery and bottling line, with a particular emphasis on green solutions to the packaging conundrum. He raves about his emission-free electric vehicle he uses to whiz around town. In the meantime, Rosenbaum continues his jitterbug back at the original BBC brewery. He laughed, "Run out of Ruby? There'd be people who'd be throwing a temper tantrum like kids at Christmas."

Opened: 1994 • Owners: Jeff Mease and Lennie Busch • Brewer: Floyd Rosenbaum • Brewing System: Fifteen-barrel Specific Mechanical System • Annual Production: 900 barrels • Tours: Yes, ask about availability • Hours: Sunday through Thursday 11:00 a.m. to midnight; Friday and Saturday 11:00 a.m. to 1:00 a.m. • Beer to go: Growlers • Food: The brewpub offers an array of pub grub, salads, and Lennie's pizza, a Bloomington favorite.

Upland Brewing Company
350 West Eleventh Street
Bloomington, IN 47404
(812) 336–2337
www.uplandbeer.com

UPLAND BREWING COMPANY is southern Indiana's largest brewer. The giant silver grain bins looming over the rambling former icehouse and print shop telegraphs that this is a serious place. At the back door, the large silage spreader filled with spent grain is a clue that this is also a resourceful brewery. Traded to Buffalo Nickel farm, the ten tons of spent grain toted off each week comes back as Indiana bison burgers and chops for the brewpub. It's just one of the things that makes Upland a special Indiana brewery.

Upland celebrates its southern Indiana roots. Its very name honors the rumpled Hoosier hills of home, Bad Elmer Porter speaks of hill-country characters, and Valley Weizen brings to mind the verdant rural vales around Bloomington. Even Upland's buffalo connection reflects the Indiana state seal's nimble, fence-leaping bison. It's not surprising that the Upland staff is heavy with Hoosiers. Owner Doug Dayhoff is a Shelbyville native and longtime Bloomingtonian, who earned an Indiana University philosophy degree, along with a masters of business administration from Dartmouth. Dayhoff purchased the brewery in 2006 and soon embarked on a major expansion, including two sixty-barrel fermenters. Brewmaster Caleb Staton is also a Hoosier and a graduate of Hanover College with degrees in communications and chemistry. Long a home brewer, Staton enrolled in the Master Brewer Program at the University of California, Davis, the nation's premier brewing program. "Home brewing—that's how we all get into it," he chuckled. Starting as a cellarman at Upland, Staton took over the brewing responsibilities in 2005.

Beers Brewed:
Upland Wheat, a tart, citrusy wit beer; the nutty Amber ale; American-style Pale Ale; malty Bad Elmer's Porter; hoppy DragonFly IPA; and crisp Preservation Pilsner. Beginning with their mid-winter offerings, the seasonals include Chocolate Stout brewed with chocolate; the malty 9 percent ABV Ard Ri Irish-style Imperial Red Ale, Maibock lager, Valley Weizen hefeweizen, Belgian farmhouse-style Bumblebee Saison, Oktoberfest, Schwarz black lager, and Winter Warmer barley wine.

Upland had started in 1998 with a thirty-barrel system, large for a craft beer start-up, and a cantankerous bottling line. The first head brewer was Russ Levitt, who had also started the Bloomington Brewing Company operation. Ed Herrmann replaced Levitt as head brewer in late 1999. Trained in Germany for almost three years at Zwolf Aposteln (Twelve Apostles) brewpub and the

Eileen Martin, assistant brewer, and Caleb Staton, head brewer.

Henniger brewery, Herrmann organized the operation, brewing some award-winning beers and dramatically increasing production in the process. By 2004 Upland was Indiana's largest brewery, producing about three thousand barrels annually (second largest in 2008, behind Three Floyds). When he began as head brewer, Staton inherited a generally debugged system. "I was lucky enough to not have to pay that fool's tax," he smiled. Assistant brewer Eileen Martin ("Ale-leen" as she's known in the trade) is a pioneer female brewer who's been part of Upland's team. She started at The Silo in Louisville in 1992 and was the brewmaster at Browning's Pub.

"We brew crisp, clean, balanced beer," Dayhoff said. "It's well-disciplined beer." Beer competitions have seconded his assessment. In 2002 the Great American Beer Festival awarded the Upland Wheat a Gold Medal. Upland Wheat soon became the best-selling beer made in Indiana, its fresh citrusy taste particularly appreciated by distaff drinkers. In 2006 the Wheat won Best of the Midwest at the U.S. Beer Tasting Championship. The Upland Pale Ale walked away with a GABF Silver in 2003, and in 2004 Bad Elmer's Porter garnered a Bronze. In 2005 all eleven of Upland's entries in the Indiana State Fair won medals, including Gold for the Upland Wheat. The Winter Warmer took a 2007 Brewers Cup Silver Medal. In 2008 the Brewer Cup judges gave Gold medals to Upland's Nut Hugger Brown American ale and the Valley Weizen, along with a Silver for the porter and Bronzes for the Maibock and Amber. At the prestigious World Beer Cup in 2008, the Winter Warmer won a Silver Medal. The beeradvocate.com summary gave the brewpub and its beers a solid B+.

A sampler of Upland brews out on the patio. The Brewpub hops with a convivial crowd.

Both beeradvocate.com and ratebeer.com reviewers raved about Upland's lambics.

Through arrangements with three distributors, Upland is sold in all ninety-two Indiana counties—"Indiana's beer," it brags. The brewery puts on events around the year, many designed to help Indiana nonprofits. Their Schwatz beer rollout, for example, supported the Exotic Feline Rescue Center, which brought a mountain lion to the event. Upland donates 10 percent of the profits from the sale of its Preservation Pilsner to environmental organizations laboring to preserve natural areas and family farms.

After some tumultuous years, Upland Brewing is rolling along with ambitious plans. But brewing a lot of beer is not just the whole story at Upland. "For a lot of us, it's not the money," Staton said. "It comes down to the pint at the end of the day of your own beer."

Opened: April 1998 • Owner: Doug Dayhoff • Brewer: Caleb Staton head brewer; Eileen Martin, assistant brewer • Brewing System: Thirty-seven-barrel J. V. Northwest brew kettle and other vessels, along with Northern Brew components • Annual Production: 5,600 barrels • Tours: Yes, ask about availability. • Hours: Monday through Thursday 11:00 a.m. to midnight; Friday and Saturday 11:00 a.m. to 1:00 a.m.; Sunday noon to midnight. • Beer to go: Bottles and growlers • Food: With a focus on local ingredients, Upland serves a full menu, including starters, salads, soups, sandwiches, and entrées that include seafood and vegetarian dishes, as well as buffalo burgers made from Indiana bison fattened on Upland's spent mash.

Power House Brewing Company
322 Fourth Street
Columbus, IN 47201
(812) 375–8800
www.powerhousebrewingco.com

POWER HOUSE BREWING COMPANY is a little dynamo. With its Lilliputian twenty-gallon brewing system that sits in the front window of the old Columbus Bar, Power House has produced some electrifying beers. In 2007, the first year it was brewing, Power House's Working Wheat beer won a Brewer Cup Silver Medal in the weizen category, and its White River Brown Ale took a Bronze. At the 2007 Indianapolis Brewer Fest, its Diesel Stout was featured. Named in honor of Columbus's Cummins Engine and their workhorse diesels, the stout is Power House's best-selling beer. "It's got a dirty brown head," brewmaster Jon Myers said, "so it looks the part."

Myers is a Ball State University philosophy major who moved from ethereal abstraction to zymurgic reality. He and his partner, Doug Memering, were aimed toward a brewing operation when they learned the 1930s-era Columbus Bar, with its unique art-deco streetcar bar, was for sale. They decided it could be the perfect spot for the pub side of their brewing business. Soon they were bar owners deep in a renovation process. Wanting to keep moving with their brewing dreams, they yanked out the round booth that had sat in the front window for generations and installed their brewing rig. "We thought it was a good way to get started, to get our feet wet in brewing," Myers said. (One older Columbus couple was heartbroken by the booth removal, as they had their first date there. But with the help of Power House brews, they coped with their loss.)

Beers Brewed:
A golden, malty Columbus Common beer; Workingman Wheat Ale hefeweizen with hints of banana and clove flavors; hoppy White River Brown Ale; an American-style Two Dave's IPA; a sweetish Ancient Amber beer with a light hop character; a malty Blackhole Porter; smoky Wee Heavy Scotch Ale; and Diesel Oil Stout, a milk stout brewed with dark roasted malts and distinct hops profile.

Myers began home brewing back in 2002, furthering his beer education by working with Indiana beer cheerleader Mike Deweese at BW3 (now J. Gumbo's) in Indianapolis. Like many Indiana craft brewers, Power House finds home brewers among their most stalwart fans. "We've got a big connection with home brewers," Myers said. "They're some of our best and most loyal customers." But even his best patrons are occasionally disappointed when they ask for one of Power House's craft brews—they are sold out. "Yeah," Myers laughed, "it's a three-week process to make the beer, and we sell out in three days."

Opened: 2007 • Owners: Jon Myers and Doug Memering • Brewer: Jon Myers • Brewing System: Twenty-gallon morebeer.com brewing system and Blichman Engineering fermenter • Annual Production: 12 barrels • Tours: Yes, ask about availability. • Hours: Monday through Thursday 11:00 a.m. to 11:00 p.m.; Friday and Saturday 11:00 a.m. to 1:00 a.m.; Sunday 4:00 p.m. to 11:00 p.m. • Beer to go: Growlers are planned. • Food: The Power House Brewing Company's Columbus Bar is a full-service restaurant with an array of offerings from pub grub and salads to seasonal specials, such as grilled locally grown pork chops served with apricot-chipotle sauce. The Columbus tenderloin sandwich is a longtime house specialty.

Main Street Brewery
408 North Main Street
Evansville, IN 47711
(812) 424–9871
www.turonis.com

THE MAIN STREET BREWERY BEGAN IN 1996, not long after owners Jerry and Judy Turner witnessed the madcap success of McGuire's brewpub in Pensacola, Florida. The Turners were already running a successful Evansville restaurant operation, Turoni's Pizzery, which dated back to the 1960s. A warren of kitsch-encrusted, tin-ceilinged dining rooms with Italian music warbling through the air, Turoni's is located in a rambling old brick building. The Turners determined there was room for a microbrewery and decided to go for it.

Soon the Main Street Brewery emerged, a bright and airy space with a Canadian seven-barrel Specific Mechanical brewing system and four dish-bottomed

Jack Frey, brewer, the master of his Main Street rig.

open fermenters. The Turners' son, Tom, was the first brewer, aided by enthusiastic college students. Seibel-trained Eric Watson began overseeing the brewery in 2001 and ran it for three years. After a career in bank computing, the current brewer, Jack Frey, took over in 2004. "You've got a certain amount of fame here that you don't get in a bank," he laughed.

A blue-eyed guy with gold wire-rimmed glasses and a ready smile, Frey had been an award-winning home brewer when he made his career switch. The transition with Watson was smooth, as Frey continued to perfect Watson's recipes—for example, adding

Beers Brewed:
Vinny's Light Lager, a German-style Pilsner; Honey Blond Ale with an English accent and Indiana honey; Thunderbolt Red Ale, an alt beer with German hops; Blue-eyed Moose, a British-style IPA; and Ol' 23 Stout, a sweet style with bitter chocolate notes. There are twelve to fourteen seasonals annually, including Helles Bock lager; Wit's Up summer Belgian-style wheat ale with coriander, orange peel, and ginger; a German-styled Hefeweizen; the award-winning Black Light Lager; Octoberfest amber lager; and Rudolph's Revenge Belgian strong ale.

Fuggles hops to the British-style IPA that used only Cascades previously. "Our customers like malty beers," Frey said. Evansville's old brewers who worked for Indiana's last industrial breweries sometimes come into Turoni's. "A lot of them like the light American beers," Frey said, and find his Honey Blonde an agreeable craft lager. Through the years, Main Street beers have won numerous Indiana State Fair awards. In 2008 the Brewers Cup judges awarded Frey's Blacklight Lager a Gold Medal in the Schwarzbier category.

Frey's also a history buff, living in an 1888 Queen Anne-style house in one of Evansville's vintage neighborhoods. He remembers with chagrin when Sterling shut down. Besides his trove of Evansville brewing lore, Frey gives a great tour of Evansville's old brewery and beer garden sites, perhaps auguring his third career as a local brewing historian.

Opened: 1996 • Owners: Jerry and Judy Turner • Brewer: Jack Frey • Brewing System: Seven-barrel Specific Mechanical brewing system • Annual Production: 550 barrels Tours: Yes, ask about availability. • Hours: Monday through Thursday 11:00 a.m. to 11:00 p.m.; Friday 11:00 a.m. to midnight; Saturday noon to midnght; Sunday 4:00 p.m. to 11:00 p.m. • Beer to go: Growlers • Food: The Main Street Brewery is part of Turoni's Pizzery, an Evansville institution. The brewery serves a wide array of appetizers, salads, sandwiches, and pizza.

Great Crescent Brewery
327 Second Street
Aurora, IN 47001
(812) 655–2435
www.gcbeer.com

THE GREAT CRESCENT BREWERY is just around the bend from its historic namesake's old lagering cellars above the Ohio River. At one point in the late nineteenth century, the Great Crescent Brewery was Indiana's largest. The twenty-first-century manifestation of Great Crescent is located in an 1875 Italianate storefront with dark wainscoting that lends the brewery an air of an earlier day.

Brewer Dan Valas was brewing his first batch in September 2008 when he stopped to chat with townsfolk wandering in to see the town's new brewery. A grizzle-bearded guy wearing a Bass Pro Shop t-shirt with a leaping bass and an American flag, Valas has been home brewing for seventeen years. He's won numerous awards, including first prize at the Dayton beer festival for his Mild Ale, and a second prize at the Bluebonnet Brewoff, the nation's second largest, for his cherry ale made with Belgian tart cherries. Valas eagerly awaited the judges' notes. "We take those comments and constantly improve our beer," said Valas.

Beers Brewed:
A malty Great Crescent Blonde Ale; a crisp Witbier, with a hit of coriander and citrus; English-Style Great Crescent Mild Ale, made with five different malts; and Great Crescent Stout is made with American hops and dark-roasted malts. The Belgian-kriekbier styled Great Crescent Cherry Ale is a mildly hopped ale that is tinged with the tart cherries added during a second fermentation. It is sold only in bottles.

In his work as an aircraft maintenance manager, Valas has overseen aviation facilities all over the world, including in the brewing havens of Belgium, Germany, and Great Britain. "You see the farmhouse brewing, and think, 'Pfft, I can do that,'" he said. About a decade ago, Valas and his wife Lani hoped to open in the old post office in neighboring Lawrenceburg, but it did not work out. When the Aurora location became available, Valas jumped on it. "I just enjoy brewing. We got to the point where we thought you should be able to do something creative and fun," Valas said. He's studied with Chicago's Seibel Institute and Munich's Doemens brewing academy. "We just want to make good solid beers—to style," he said.

Opened: November 2008 • Owners: Dan and Lani Valas • Brewer: Dan Valas • Brewing System: Half-Barrel Sabco "Brewing Magic" system with six custom-made, one-barrel fermenters • Annual Production: Not available • Tours: Yes, ask about availability. • Hours: 10:00 a.m. to 10:00 p.m. Friday and Saturday. • Beer to go: Growlers, bottles, and mini kegs • Food: No

The New Albanian Brewing Company

Original brewery:	Bank Street Brewhouse & Brasserie:
3312 Plaza Drive	415 Bank Street
New Albany, IN 47150	New Albany, IN 47150
(812) 949–2804	(812) 725–9585
www.newalbanian.com	

The "cerebral guy"—Roger Baylor.

NEW ALBANIAN'S ROGER BAYLOR is a crusty intellectual, as apt to discourse on local history, the perfidy of electoral politics, or the virtues of the Trotskyite movement as he is to hold forth with his voluminous beer lore, some gathered during his long beer-biking tours of Belgium, Germany, and the Netherlands. Independent and well informed, Baylor is often singled out as the thinker of Indiana brewers—"the cerebral guy," as World Class Brewing and Indiana craft-beer expert Jim Schembre calls him.

Located in a low-slung suburban strip mall, the New Albanian Brewing Company is adjacent to its sister businesses, NABC Public House and Pizzaria. The Public House is famous for its thirty-four beer lines that Baylor fills with a staggering variety of the world's most interesting brews, including eight taps of his own. "We don't try to ape something else," Baylor said about his

New Albanian beers, "we try to do something else." Something else includes Cone Smoker, a hoppy rauchbier, Phoenix, a sour, dark beer that mimics an old-style Louisville brew, and Hoptimus, a double IPA that Baylor calls "stupid big."

Baylor's a fit fellow, with wire-rim glasses, a soul patch, and a baleful eye. With his breadth of knowledge and capacity to meld diverse interests into a coherent whole, Baylor brings to mind another New Albany iconoclast, Hew Ainslie, the nineteenth-century Scottish poet-brewer who parlayed his days with the utopian New Harmonists into a successful Falls City brewing career. Ainslie's dreams for a better world fueled his life, both in his work as a teacher in New Harmony and as a pioneer brewer in New Albany. Through his quirky marketing materials and his web-soap-box, potablecurmudgeon.blogspot.com, Baylor perpetually filibusters for a more beautiful and just world. Progressive, humanistic, episodically anti-clerical, Baylor's postings interweave his thoughts on beer, travel, art, politics, and Fall Cities events. "America's megabrewers have done for beer what Pol Pot did for Cambodia," is a typical Baylor pronunciamento. "I've always wanted to do something like Hew's brews," Baylor said wistfully. "Hew Ainslie was a different kind of brewer."

Beers Brewed:
The Community Dark is a light-bodied dark ale; the imperial red Elector ale; 15-B brown porter; Croupier English-style IPA; and the massive, dry-hopped Hoptimus that weighs in at over 90 IBU. There are typically fifteen seasonals per year, including smoked, spiced, and barrel-aged beers.

The New Albanian sprang from Rich O's Public House, a homey, den-like collection of snuggeries that began serving specialty beers in 1992. In 1994 Baylor and his partners decided to seize an opportunity and acquired the brewing system from the defunct Tucker Brewing Company. Then in 1999 they purchased the brewing equipment from the Oldenberg microbrewery in Kentucky. But it was not until 2002 that it all came together. Under first head brewer, Michael Borchers, the brewery primarily produced big, malty Belgian-style ales. In 2003 Indiana State Fair Judges awarded a Gold to Bourbon Daddy Stout, as they did in 2004, when the stout took Best of Show. The Elector IPA also won a State Fair Gold in 2003. In 2005 Jessie Williams took over as brewmaster. With his culinary arts training, Williams aimed the New Albanian toward a drier, hoppier style.

The future looks bright for the New Albanian. Loyal customers continue to flock into the NABC Public House to sample the latest offerings. A second location, the Bank Street Brewhouse and Brasserie, opened in 2009 with its own fifteen-barrel brewing system. With its sleek décor and upscale menu, it's a surprisingly bourgeois addition for bohemian NABC. Baylor chuckles, "We told people, 'It's going to be completely different,' and people came down and said, 'It's completely different!'"

But the NABC focus on great beer remains. "First and foremost," Baylor said, "the experience was about the beer we can brew." With its state-of-the-art, fifteen-barrel DME brewing system, NABC can now expand its beer distribution into the surrounding regions. But like most educators, Baylor still fusses about accomplishing his full mission: "It's frustrating because I don't have a lot of time to teach our customers about beer. I'm curmudgeonly enough that it's not just that we're making more."

Opened: NABC Public House and Pizzaria, 2002; Bank Street Brewhouse & Brasserie, March 2009 • Owners: Roger Baylor, Amy Baylor, Kate Lewison • Brewers: David Pierce, Jessie Williams, Jared Williamson • Brewing Systems: NABC Public House and Pizzaria system has a 4-barrel Elliott Bay and DME brewing system. Bank Street Brewhouse and Brasserie has a 15-barrel DME system. • Annual Production: 1,300 barrels 2009 (projected); 2,600 barrels 2010 (projected) • Tours: Yes, ask about availability. • Hours: NABC Public House and Pizzaria 11:00 a.m. to midnight Monday through Saturday; Bank Street Brewhouse and Brasserie 11:00 a.m. to 10:00 p.m. Tuesday through Thursday, 11:00 a.m. to 11:00 p.m. Friday and Saturday, noon to 8:00 p.m. Sunday • Beer to go: Growlers and kegs • Food: The NABC Public House and Pizzaria serves a full menu of appetizers, salads, sandwiches, pasta, and pizza. The popular Spinach Käse dip utilizes a spicy beer cheese. Bank Street Brewhouse and Brasserie presents a full Belgian-tinged, New American menu.

Women in Brewing

Women have been brewing from the beginning. Prehistoric women most likely invented beer ten thousand years ago, when they learned masticated and spat grain gives a nice buzz if stored for a while with some water. Under the Babylonian brewing goddesses Siduri and Ninkasi, "the woman who fills the mouth," female brewers called Sabtien were credited with taming the wild men and keeping the kingdom lubricated. The Egyptian goddess Hathor is credited with inventing beer, which was primarily brewed by women. It was the same in the Americas. Archaeologists recently unearthed a thousand-year-old brewery in southern Peru, where elite Wari Empire brewsters (female brewers) produced beer for the aristocracy.

From the fifth century well into the Middle Ages, European women were the brewers. When their beer was ready for quaffing, brewsters traditionally hung a broomstick garlanded with hops (called an ale stick) over their door to advertise. It took the emergence of the monastery breweries and their desire to control an increasingly profitable commodity to shake the female domination of the trade. The monks hit upon a diabolical scheme: Claim the brewsters were "brew witches," and their brooms a Satanic symbol. Any failed monastic brew could then be blamed on the brew witches, with bonfires soon after. The last burning of a brew witch was recorded in 1591. In spite of hostile work conditions, women persisted as brewers and pub owners. In 1509, all of the 152 brewers in Aberdeen, Scotland, were female. During the eighteenth century, 78 percent of the registered brewers in England were women. In America's early days, women continued to carry the brewing load, most often for household consumption. But by the late eighteenth century, the male-dominated brewing business supplanted the brewsters' home brewing.

Brewsters have been part of Indiana commercial brewing since at least the 1870s. While women such as Cecilia Hochesgang in Jasper, Elizabeth Ruhkamp in Ferdinand, and Anna Volver in Decatur ran small-scale breweries, a Hoosier woman headed up the second largest brewery in the state. Caroline Schmidt was the chief officer of Indianapolis's C. F. Schmidt brewery, which produced 25,000 barrels in 1876. She was not the last woman to run a major Indiana industrial brewery. When the Old Crown Brewing Corporation in Fort Wayne closed in 1973, Marjorie E. Aubrey had been the company's general manager for fourteen years.

During World War II, Rosie the Brewer helped the war effort. "My mother was one of them," Fort Wayne's Susan Berghoff Prowant exclaimed. When her father was drafted, Prowant's mother, Ethel Jauch Berghoff, pitched in at the Berghoff family brewery, where Prowant's great-grandfather was the first plant manager.

Eileen Martin is the dean of the Indiana women craft brewers, having started in commercial brewing in 1992. After home brewing, Eileen, or Ale-een as she likes to be known, began working in Louisville's first brewpub, the Silo Brewpub, where she subsequently served as head brewer. She later worked for three years as the head brewer at Brownie's Brewery at Louisville's Slugger Field. In May 2006 she joined Upland Brewery in Bloomington. "You have to be a Jill of all trades—mechanics, plumbing, chemistry," she said. "It's still pretty hands-on. I'm still climbing in to shovel out the mash tun. Still need to haul the hoses around. I'm in the best shape of my life." A small, green-eyed woman with spiky blond hair and a quick smile, Martin extols her brewing work, "For me, brewing is a passion. It's great to be able to go to work everyday and do what you love."

In 2008 Elysia Poor joined the Upland's distaff brewing team. A Plymouth native and Indiana University student, Poor is a graduate of the University of California, Davis's master brewing class. She was an intern at Upland before working for a short time as a brewer. "It's just that I believe that people should understand things they care about," Poor said. "I love beer, and I wanted to stay with it. It's a physical, creative job. That appealed to me."

At Alcatraz Brewery in Indianapolis, Belinda Short is the brewing assistant. Like many brewers, she got hooked with home brewing and just kept going. "I already knew a bunch of brewers, including the guys over at Ram. I took Anita Johnson's home brewing class at Great Fermentations. I'm very logical," Short said. While also fronting

MIKE SCHWAB

a rock band, Short has tackled craft brewing: "There's a lot of physical challenges, carrying things up stairs, stirring the mash tuns."

Liz Laughlin presides over her spotless Rock Bottom Brewery in Indianapolis's College Park area. "I have my baby," she said, looking around proudly, "I keep her clean." After her upbringing on Cape Cod, Laughlin relocated to the brewing hotbed of Eugene, Oregon, where she got her start working at Steelhead Brewery. Her first boss was Teri Fahrendorf, now famous in the craft-brewing world for starting the Pink Boots Society of women brewers. "Every job I've ever had has been in male-dominated fields," Laughlin explained. "You get more attention. 'Oh, she's a woman, that's weird!' You get more respect." She enumerates some of the advantages women have in brewing: "We can get in smaller spaces. There's attention to detail; cleanliness." And there is her rebuttal to the perennial dismissal of brewsters' strength: "Women can lift fifty pounds. Men shouldn't be commonly hauling around much more than that anyway."

Anita Johnson is the gregarious Queen Bee of Indiana craft brewing. Owner of Indianapolis's Great Fermentations home brewing mecca, Johnson is also the organizer of the annual Brewers Cup competition. "I've always loved good beer," she said. "Home brewing became a passion. Even my kids have read *The New Complete Joy of Homebrewing*." Since the store opened in 1995, Johnson has commingled being a cheerleader for Indiana home brewers with her own brewing. "There's the joy of creation. Gadgeteering. The science. The acclaim. You go to a party—'This is Anita, she makes beer.' Suddenly you're a rock star," she said.

No brewster has been more honored than Hoosier native Tonya Cornett. In 2008 at the World Beer Cup awards banquet, the judges honored her with the Brewmaster of the Year award, along with Gold medals for her Outback X and Black Diamond Lager. "I was the first woman to win," Cornett remembers. "It was so emotional for me. Tears were running down my face. People around me were so moved." Pink Boots Society founder Fahrendorf, herself a pioneer American brewster, remembered the crowd going wild. Women screaming and standing on chairs; brewers across the spectrum yelling their support as the tiny, pig-tailed Cornett accepted the award. The judge had said, "Sometimes great things come from the smallest places."

Raised in Marion, Indiana, Cornett began home brewing after

working in the early 1990s at a forty-tap Fort Collins, Colorado, brewpub, where she learned to appreciate craft beers. Soon she'd launched herself into all-grain batches, which led to part-time brewing at a couple of Fort Collins microbreweries. One brewer told the five-foot-two-inch, 105-pound apprentice, "You know, you're too little," before pitching in to help train her.

Cornett persisted. She returned to Indiana in the late 1990s, when she tried to get on at the newly opened Upland Brewery in Bloomington. The misogynist brewer at the time dismissed her, saying she couldn't lift a full keg. "I don't think guys should be lifting a full keg either," Cornett retorted. She soon found a position with the Oaken Barrel in Greenwood, where she worked as an assistant. "I think it really helped me with cleaning," she said, "I realized how important it was. I don't know any brewer who cleans as much as I do."

After three years, it was time to move on. "I realized I was going to be an assistant if I stayed there forever," said Cornett. In 2001 she enrolled in the World Brewing Academy, a partnership between the Siebel Institute in Chicago and Doemens Academy in Munich, where half of the course was taught. "That was great," Cornett said. "I got to see brewing traditions. That made an impact on me, for sure." Within a few months of her graduation in early 2002, Cornett accepted a brewmaster position at Bend Brewing Company in the Oregon craft-brewing country. "It got me in the area I wanted to be in—the Pacific Northwest, northern California. I figured you have to have good beer around to be able to understand what you're shooting for," she said.

There Cornett embarked on her development as a brewmaster, honing traditional recipes and creating unique new ones. Soon international awards began coming her way: three medals at the North American Brewers Awards; a 2006 Great American Beer Festival Gold Medal for her Hophead in the highly competitive American IPA category, and a Silver in 2007 for her Outback X. Then came the climactic awards at the 2008 World Beer Cup. "Now I'm brewing a bunch of beers from an artistic viewpoint, rather than from a stylistic viewpoint," Cornett said, going on to speak about the global attention being paid to innovative American craft brewers. "The creative process is just oozing out of us. The whole world is looking."

LiL' Charlie's Restaurant and Brewery

504 East Pearl Street
Batesville, IN 47006
(812) 934–6392
www.lilcharlies.com

THE GERMANS OF BATESVILLE and Franklin County finally have a brewery again. Housed in a steakhouse, LiL' Charlie's made a big hit with its opening. "Things are going great," says brewmaster Adam Israel. "Bar's been packed. People are loving the beer." It's a comfortable place with warm colors, fireplace, and a gleaming brewhouse tucked behind a plate glass window.

Beers Brewed:
Batesville Blonde Pilsner is made with two-row brewers malt and Liberty and East Kent Goldings hops. The coriander-tinged Father Franz' Hefeweizen, named for the German-Catholic town of Oldenburg's first priest, is hopped with Liberty and Chinook. Bull Ram Bock is a full-flavored beer made with dark malts. Fire House Red Wheat is a citrusy brew. Named for the building's first owner, a grocer, Harry's Pale Ale is LiL' Charlie's hoppiest brew. The brewers are planning a raspberry wheat beer for Halloween.

With Israel's Culinary Institute of America training, LiL' Charlie's is banking on his gastronomic abilities. Both of the brewers have a background in home brewing. "We're beginning brewers; we're taking it slow," Israel said. "But with my culinary background, I want to pair beer and food." Accordingly, the menu touts specialties such as the rosemary-hefé-glazed pork chop, sirloin with red ale jus, and beer-battered tiger shrimp, each with a recommended beer.

Opened: September 2009 • Owners: Kip and Tricia Miller • Brewers: Kip Miller and Adam Israel • Brewing System: LiL' Charlie's indicate they have a 30-barrel JW Kent system. • Annual Production: 720 barrels (projected) • Tours: Yes, inquire about availability. • Hours: Monday through Thursday 10:00 a.m. to 9:00 p.m.. Friday and Saturday 10:00 a.m. to 10:00 p.m., Sunday 11:00 a.m. to 9:00 p.m. (bar only). • Beer to go: Growlers and ½ barrels • Food: LiL' Charlie's has a full menu, including pizza, steaks, fish, sandwiches, and salads. It prides itself on its beer-food pairings.

Big Woods Brewing Company
60 Molly's Lane
Nashville, IN 47448
(812) 988–6000
www.bigwoodsbeer.com

THE BIG WOODS BREWING COMPANY put Nashville's Little Brown Jug on a growth plan, enveloping it in a new timber-frame building. The result is a doubled-in-size, hand-pegged structure housing Brown County's first brewpub. "We'd been home brewing for years and years," owner Jeff McCabe said. "Why not do what we've always wanted to do?"

Part of a family of Illinois tavern keepers, McCabe is a Nashville innkeeper and timber-frame contractor. Tim O'Bryan is a chef turned brewmaster. With the new brewery, they hope to provide a welcoming respite from Nashville's relentless shopping culture. Their daily food specials and focus on local ingredients will offer an alternative to the town's often predictable dining. How many tenderloins and fried biscuits can one eat anyway? And the attention to local ingredients extends to the brewery: O'Bryan is experimenting with a persimmon beer.

Beers Brewed:
Big Woods anticipates brewing Tim's Stout, Six-foot Blonde, "a tall cool drink," a Pale Ale, and an IPA, as well as several seasonals.

Opened: October 2009 • Owners: Ed Ryan, Jeff McCabe, and Tim O'Bryan • Brewer: Tim O'Bryan • Brewing Systems: Sabco System with Blichmann fermenters • Annual Production: 100 barrels (projected) • Tours: Yes, inquire about availability. • Hours: 11:00 a.m. to 10:00 p.m. • Beer to go: Growlers and kegs • Food: Big Woods plans on serving seasonal menus, with different specialties every day, including flatbread pizza, steaks, and sausages from the outdoor grill, and a shepherd's pie made with Tim's Stout.

Yummy!

Malt

Malted grain is the backbone of beer. Since Egyptian days, maltsters have been steeping, germinating, and drying grain to produce the basic ingredient for brewing. Full of the enzymes, complex carbohydrates, and sugars necessary for fermentation, malt is most often barley, wheat,

MIKE SCHWAB

or rye, though sorghum and spelt are occasionally malted for specialty beers. Cultivated for more than ten thousand years, barley remains the primary grain for brewing. With its germ-protecting hull, high-yielding starch-to-protein ratio, complete enzyme structure, self-adjusting pH, and neutral color and flavor, barley has proven to be an ideal brewing malt.

Contemporary brewers choose between two-row and six row-barley, so named because different barley varieties grow with either two or six rows of kernels. Six row is less expensive, but is often considered to have a harsher, grainier flavor. Two row is celebrated for its cleaner, smoother flavor, though the actual flavor profile varies by each individual crop.

Malt comes in two main categories, standard (also known as base or brewers malts) and specialty malts. Standard malts contain high amounts of the necessary enzymes, complex carbohydrates, and sugars. Maltsers craft specialty malts by adjusting time, temperature, and humidity throughout the malting process to develop unique flavors, colors, and characteristics. The intense heat needed for some of the roasted malts used in darker beers decreases the enzymes needed for fermentation, so specialty malts are often used in conjunction with standard malts. With a wide spectrum of roasted hues, specialty malts contribute color and distinctive flavors, including maltiness, caramel, nut, wood, and coffee.

Like hops, malt skyrocketed in price in the last few years, impacted by crop failures, farmers preferring to plant corn and other government-subsidized crops, farmland-devouring urban sprawl, as well as commodities speculation. There were more than four million acres of barley planted in the United States in 2008, seemingly a lot of barley until it is compared to more than eighty-five million acres of corn. Canada dwarfs our barley production, planting more than twelve million acres. But only a small amount of the harvest makes it to the mash tun.

CHAPTER THIRTEEN

Favorite Indiana Draft Houses

· · · · · · · · · · · ·

EVERYONE HAS THEIR FAVORITE draft house. Below is a highly subjective gathering of some of Indiana's top beer bars. In general, the choices are canted toward bars with a great draft selection, a commitment to Indiana beers, a knowledgeable and enthusiastic staff, and a unique sense of place that makes you happy to be there.

The Rathskeller
401 East Michigan Street
Indianapolis, IN 46204
(317) 636–0396
www.rathskeller.com

· ·

This book began with beers at the Rathskeller's Kellerbar. It's somewhat appropriate, as this Germanic bastion in the Teutonic Atheneaum building has been glorying beer since 1894. Today, a full array of German and Continental beers are available on twelve taps, including Weihenstephaner, the world's oldest operating brewery; Spaten; Warsteiner; as well as the Rathskeller Amber *alt*-style beer, for a taste of old German Indiana. There are also more than fifty fine bottled beers offered.

Shallo's Antique Restaurant and Brewhaus
8811 Hardegan Street (in Shoppes of County Line)
Indianapolis, IN 46227
(317) 882–7997
www.shallos.net

"They say we're the Cheers of the Southside," Shallo's partner Paul Zoellner laughed, going on to brag on his friendly bartenders' and waiters' enthusiasm for beer. "Our staff are really our beer snobs," he said. They should be: Shallo's has forty-two taps with everything from Breckenridge 471 IPA and five different Bell's to Franzikaner and Dog Fish 60 Minute. Shallo's has six hundred different beers from twenty-one countries, including high-end, high-alcohol brews that can run up to $300 a bottle. "We always had a lot of beer," said founder Paul Shellabarger, "but we just kept adding and adding and adding." Indiana is well represented with a wide array of Hoosier beers, including Upland, Three Floyds, Oaken Barrel, and Brugge.

The Heorot
219 South Walnut
Muncie, IN 47305
(765) 287–0173

It's Beowolf in a beer lust. Decorated with a Viking-meets-Black-Knight theme, The Heorot has more than fifty taps delivering a staggering diversity of brews, including Unibroue's Canadian-Belgian styles, Bells, Dogfish Head, Arrogant Bastard's Double Bastard, Rogues Old Crustacean and Dead Guy, Sierra Nevada's Bigfoot, Ayinger Celebrator, Reissdorf Kölsch, and rarities such as Sam Adams Chocolate Bock. The legendary cellar harbors a cache of extraordinary beers from around the globe—the bar typically has four hundred different bottled beers available. "We have a lot of beer here," owner Stan Stephens modestly said. A polymath with a master's degree in world history, Stephens obviously decided to explore the world of beer, including Hoosier brews such as Oaken Barrel, Three Floyds, and Upland. "Indiana beers are just outstanding," he said. The warm and knowledge-able staff are happy to parlay about the virtues of various brews. The beeradvocate.com raters veritably gushed praise on The Heorot, giving the place an A+ grade.

The Fickle Peach
117 East Charles Street
Muncie, IN 47305
(765) 282–5211
www.ficklepeach.com

The slogan reads, "Passionately dedicated to great beer," and the Fickle Peach follows through. The bar's twenty-five lines carry great import and American craft beers, including Hoegaarden, Ayinger, Grotten, Magic Hat, and Bell's. There's a full contingent of Indiana beers, including Brugge, Three Floyds, Upland, and Warbird. Housed in an old bank building, the bar emanates a handcrafted vision, with staff members who are ambassadors of good brew.

Chumley's Pub
122 North Third Street
Lafayette, IN 47901
(765) 420–9372

Housed in an 1850s building near Lafayette's wedding-cake of a courthouse building, Chumley's boasts fifty taps and more than a hundred different bottled beers. The draft beers include Arro-gant Bastard, Delirium Tremens, Bell's, and Rogue. The bar's thick beer list offers concise overviews of each beer to help guide thirsty patrons. Chumley's has a special connection to Indiana brews, often featuring Back Road (including its Blueberry Ale), Barley Island, Mad Anthony, Mishawaka, Oaken Barrel, Three Floyds, and Upland. They have a Saturday special on Indiana beers, for a gas-saving brew-trot around the state.

Fiddler's Hearth Pub
127 North Main Street
South Bend, IN 46601
(574) 232–2853
www.fiddlershearth.com

Fiddler's Hearth is a Celtic haven in the midst of downtown South Bend. Accordingly, the pub's taps are heavy with Gaelic brews, including Guinness (Fiddler's is a Guinness Gold Standard establishment), Harp, Murphy's, and Belhaven. Other Continental beers on tap include Chimay, Delirium Tremens, and Weihenstephan. American craft beers certainly are not stinted, with Founders, Bell's, Magic Hat, Rogue, and Dogfish Head among the selections. Three Floyds is commonly on tap at Fiddler's.

Yeast

We owe beer to yeast, those tiny, single-celled, vaguely spud-shaped creatures. "It's kind of like the black box of brewing," said David Bryant, president of Brewing Science Institute, a major yeast supplier to the craft brewing industry. "It's the magical part." Ceaselessly laboring, the yeast cells consume grain sugars, converting them into alcohol and carbon dioxide, which results in a nice buzz, good fizz, and a host of distinctive flavors, including butterscotch, bread, banana, apple, and pear. The warm, earthy flavor of ale is due in part to Saccharomyces cerevisiae, otherwise known as ale yeast. Lager's smooth taste comes partly from Saccharomyces uvarum, lager yeast. It takes 34 million of these hardworking cells to produce one pint of beer.

Before Louis Pasteur uncorked the secrets of yeast in his 1876 paradigm, *Studies on Beer*, brewers used the term Godisgood to explain the mysterious function of fermentation. Prior to Pasteur, brewers theorized that yeast was a by-product of alcohol, rather than the other way around. The Danish brewing chemist for Carlsberg Brewing, Emil Christian Hansen, first isolated a single cell of yeast and then did the groundbreaking work that allowed reliable propagation of lager yeast. To honor his work, Saccharomyces uvarum is often known as Saccharomyces carlsbergenis.

Many craft brewers turn to the Brewing Science Institute in Colorado and White Labs in San Diego for their yeasts. The companies offer hundreds of varieties of yeasts—Brewing Science has three hundred

Three Floyds Brewing Company
9750 Indiana Parkway
Munster, IN 46321
(219) 922-4425
www.threefloydspub.com

While best known as an award-winning brewery, Three Floyds is also home to a heralded twenty-tap draft house. Beyond offering a full assortment of Three Floyds standards and small-batch seasonals, the pub serves a wide-ranging array of beers, including Chimay, Lieffman, Lachouffe, Piraat, Unibroue, Einbecker, Victory, Reissdorf, Red Seal, and Stone. Indiana breweries that have cycled through the brewpub taps include New Albanian, Back Road, Mad Anthony, and Brugge.

different yeasts, more than fifty Belgian yeasts alone. For example, the ale yeasts include specific yeasts for Alt and Kölsch beer, hefeweizen, herds of different English-ale yeasts, American-style East Coast ales, Australian styles, Irish stout yeast, Scottish yeast, French yeast, a wild array of Belgian yeasts, wits and saisons and Trappist among them—the lists go on and on. The lager yeast offerings are no less complex. There's different types of Czech pilsner yeast, dozens of German yeasts, Danish yeasts, Swiss yeasts, Mexican yeasts—billions of little international guys ready to work for you. Little guys who are closer to us than you might imagine. "Yeast has a complex genomic structure," Bryant said. "Humans share about 40 percent of yeast's genomes."

Then there's the shadowy world of the yeast rustlers, yeast zealots who devote themselves to propagating very specific brewing yeasts, as in, say, a Belgian Trappist ale yeast swiped from the cask- or bottle-conditioned beer. Or the very yeast used for Pilsner Urquell, the holy grail of pilsners. It filters up to the commercial yeast labs. So the "Pilsen-style lager yeast" may bear an extremely close relation to the yeast used by an extremely large Saint Louis-based brewery. Or the "Irish ale yeast" may be darn close to identical to the one used by a particularly revered stout brewery in Dublin.

MIKE SCHWAB

Sonka Irish Pub and Cafe
1366 Wabash
Terre Haute, IN 47807
(812) 234–8802
www.sonkairishpub.com

Sonka's is a Terre Haute institution, started in 1933 by George Sonka, a Romanian bootlegger looking to go legitimate. Since then, the bar has had five owners, all of them Irish, including the current publican, Sandy Boyles-Gillen. Accordingly, Sonka's is an Irish-style gathering place for students, professors, working folks, and a white-collar crowd. Behind the Kelly-green façade, there are friendly bartenders serving from thirty-three taps (the number honors 1933, when Prohibition ended and Sonka's began). They pull from an Irish-coffin draft system that sits behind Sonka's original brass-railed bar. The Irish beers include Guinness and Harp, with other various Continental brands that include Spaten, Hoegaarden, and Chimay. American craft brews include Bell's and Red Hook. Three Floyds's Alpha King is among its biggest sellers. Brugge and Upland beers also rotate as draft selections. Reviewers at beeradvocate.com found Sonka's a great place, giving it a solid A.

Rich O's Public House
3312 Plaza Drive
New Albany, IN 47150
(812) 949–2804
www.richos.com

Adjacent to the New Albanian brewery, Rich O's is a quirky (occasionally cranky) old Lefty hangout devoted to spectacular beer. More than forty taps dispense classic brews and exotica: Spaten, Rodenbach Grand Cru, Schlenkerla *rauchbier*, Saint Bernardus, Saison Dupont, Stone, Dogfish Head, and Rogue among them. There are typically six to ten New Albanian brews on the card, with a selection of other Indiana beers, including Three Floyds and Upland. There additionally are three hundred different bottled beers in stock. Ratebeer.com has ranked Rich O's among the ten best beer bars in the world. Beeradvocate.com reviewers gave Rich O's an A grade. "This is the oddest, most beer-focused place I've ever been," one wrote.

The Schnitzelbank
393 Third Avenue
Jasper, Indiana 47546
(812) 482–2640
www.schnitzelbank.com

If you need a solid hit of southern Indiana *gemütlichkeit,* head to the cozy, convivial Schnitzelbank in the German enclave of Jasper. Open since 1961, the Schnitzelbank serves some of Indiana's best German food in a rambling building that looks airlifted from Bavaria. Not surprisingly, the bar serves a lot of beer from its fourteen taps, albeit heavy on the German brews. The bar's German draft offerings include Spaten Optimator, Paulander Hefe, Franzinkaner Dark Wheat, Hacker-Pschorr, and Warsteiner. There are additionally more than a hundred different bottled beers, including Three Floyds and Upland.

Columbus Bar
322 Fourth Street
Columbus, IN 47201
(812) 375–8800
www.powerhousebrewingco.com

Columbus Bar is another draft house-brewery combo, as the diminutive Powerhouse Brewery is located in the barroom. The vernacular art-deco bar has twenty taps, dispensing a range of flavorful beers from fine breweries, such as Belhaven, Guinness, Young's, Bell's, Founders, Stone, Rogue, Blackhook, and Left Hand. There are typically six to ten Indiana brews on tap, including Powerhouse, Barley Island, Mad Anthony, and Brugge.

Farm

108/110 East Kirkwood Avenue
Bloomington, IN 47403
(877) 440–FARM
www.farm-bloomington.com

While the bar in this *haut*-rustic downtown bistro only has eight taps, they dispense the good stuff, such as Bluegrass Brewing Company's Jefferson Reserve Bourbon-barrel-aged stout, Dogfish Head 90 Minute IPA, Rogue Dead Guy, and Stone Arrogant Bastard. There are typically two or three Indiana brews rotating on the taps. Brew Collared Mondays features half off local draft beers. There's another twenty well-chosen bottled beers available. The bar has become a hangout for local beer aficionados seeking new thrills.

Nick's English Hut

423 East Kirkwood Avenue
Bloomington, IN 47408
(812) 332–4040
www.nicksenglishhut.com

It's hard to write about beer in Indiana without at least mentioning Nick's, an Indiana University watering hole since 1927. The bar has quenched the thirst of generations of IU students and faculty, as well as luminaries who range from hard-drinking Dylan Thomas to temperate Barack Obama. While most of their more than thirty taps pour a river of industrial beer, the Bloomington Brewing Company and Upland both hold down two draft lines each. Nick's best-selling beer is Upland's wheat beer.

Indiana Home Brewing

. . . .

OME BREWERS ARE OFTEN the vanguard of Indiana brewing. "As we know, home brewers drive craft brewers," says Mike Deweese, proprietor of J. Gumbos, downtown Indianapolis's premier draft house. Spared the rigors of bottom lines and unadventurous customers, home brewers have the opportunity to experiment with wildly creative concoctions, sparing no expense to perfect the ultimate brew. "We can just go out on a limb, because we don't have to make commercial considerations," longtime home brewer Paul Edwards noted. Interest in home brewing has exploded over the last few years. Submissions to the Brewers Cup home brewing competition more than doubled from 2006 to 2008, when the judges graded 596 entries. And the entire Indiana brewing community benefits from it—especially those who get to drink the home brewers' many excellent beers.

There are numerous organized groups of Indiana home brewers. Here are some of them:

Angola: Homebrewers of Preferred Suds (HOPS)
http://groups.yahoo.com/group/hops2004

This twenty-brewer group in northwest Indiana began in 2004. Club members have won numerous Brewers Cup and American Homebrewers Association National Homebrew Competition awards.

. . . .

Bloomington: Saint Gambrinus Benevolence Society
Contact Marvin Keenan, (812) 988–0384

This close-knit group of twenty home brewers has been meeting monthly for more than twenty years.

. . . .

Bloomington: Bloomington Hop Jockeys
Contact Ryan Clarke, (812) 337–0196, homebrewer@pobox.com
www.hopjockeys.org

The Hop Jockeys started meeting in 2003, and between one to two dozen home brewers gather the second Thursday of each month at the Upland brewery to discuss zymurgic topics.

. . . .

Evansville: Ohio Valley Homebrewers Association
Contact Jack Frey, (812) 425–0392, brewer@tur_oris.com
www.ovha.net

This group meets on the last Wednesday of the month, usually at the Germania Maennechor. Additionally, the club has special events and road trips, such as the Brew-B-Q home brewing festival held each year at Great Fermentations in Indianapolis.

. . . .

Fort Wayne: Mad Anthony's Serious Homebrewers (MASH)
Contact Stephan Kelley, (260) 747–4525, skelley@logicos.com
http://groups.yahoo.com/group/mashfw

MASH meets the second Sunday of every month at 3:00 p.m. at Mad Anthony's brewpub for libacious discussions.

. . . .

Jasper: Dubois County SUDS Club
Contact Justin Rumbach, (812) 827–3497, jrumbach@hotmail.com

Organized in 2007, SUDS has about twenty active members, who meet monthly.

Kokomo: Howard County Homebrewers
Contact Tom Ferguson, (765) 628–2315, mrsoul12@yahoo.com
www.setbb.com/hchomebrew

The twenty-member club that began in 2006 meets monthly at a Kokomo brewpub. In 2008 two members were Indiana State Fair winners.

• • • •

Indianapolis: Foam Blowers of Indiana (FBI)
Contact Ron Smith, (317) 873–6976, info@MarketWiseSolutions.com
www.foamblowers.com

The FBI has approximately seventy members who meet three times a month. A cowinner of the Brewers Cup Indiana Homebrew Club of the Year, the FBI was recognized at the 2008 American Homebrewers Association annual meeting's Club Night. The FBI members showed up in Blues Brothers garb, replete with shades and fedoras. The Central Indiana Alliance of Beer Judges is an FBI subgroup.

• • • •

Indianapolis: MECA
Contact Bill Ballinger, (765) 544–2511, MECABrewers@aol.com

The central Indiana club, which started in 2005, has nine members, who meet once or twice a month to brew craft beer in one of the founding members' well-equipped brew-barns. In 2007 MECA was named the Brewers Cup Indiana Homebrew Club of the Year, an honor they also shared in 2008 with the Foam Blowers of Indiana. MECA members have won numerous individual awards.

• • • •

Lafayette: Tippecanoe Homebrewing Circle
Contact Linda Swihart, swihart@tippybrewers.org
www.tippyhomebrewers.org

This convivial and active club meets "approximately monthly" for brewing confabs. Tippecanoe brewers compete in many home brewing contests, and nine members have Beer Judge Certification Program credentials.

Michigan City: Duneland Homebrewers Association
Contact Bruce "Brews" Kehe, bkehe@adsnet.com
www.dunelandbrew.com

The Duneland Club began in 1995 and has about twenty members, including a number of state fair winners. Beyond their monthly meetings at Jackson Farms clubhouse at 600 East Highway 6 in Westville, Indiana, the group also takes road trips to breweries and brewpubs.

. . . .

Mishawaka: Michiana Extract and Grain Association
Contact Andy Walton, info@mega-brew.com
http://mega-brew.com

The club began in 2003. There are about forty members, who meet the second Sunday of the month at 1:00 p.m. at the Mishawaka Brewing Company.

. . . .

Muncie: Saint Munsee Order of Brewers
Contact St.Munsee@hotmail.com
http://munseebrewers.blogspot.com

Saint Munsee began in June 2007. The club meets monthly to brew, brag, and share, with junkets to such destinations as Three Floyds Dark Lord Day.

. . . .

Terre Haute: Wabash Valley Vintners' and Homebrewers' Club
Contact Neil Flatter, (812) 235–2682, neil.flatter@rose-hulman.edu

CHAPTER FIFTEEN

Recipes

. . . .

HERE'S A LONG TRADITION of beer-infused food recipes. And with the growing interest in artisanal craft beer, gourmet beer cuisine has likewise exploded, helped along by such books as Lucy Sanders's *The Best of American Beer and Food*, Leslie Mansfield's *From the Micro Breweries of America,* and John Schlimm's *The Ultimate Beer Lover's Cookbook.* Below are a few favorite recipes to get you going.

RICHARD SPAHR

Broad Ripple Brewpub's Beer-Cheese Crock

A beloved Broad Ripple Brewpub appetizer, adapted for easy home cooking

1 pound (1/2 block) Velveeta, shredded or diced
1/3 cup crumbled sharp blue cheese
1 cup amber beer, such as a Broad Ripple cask ale
1/3 cup dark beer, such as Broad Ripple's Monon Porter
Healthy pinch of dry mustard powder

Using a heavy-bottomed pot, bring beer and dry mustard to a boil. Add in cheeses, stirring constantly with a heavy whisk (mixture can scorch on the bottom in seconds).

Turn off heat just prior to complete melt and continue whisking until mixture is smooth.

Serve with hearty breads and/or crudités.

The beer-cheese mixture can be cooled and served later in smaller portions. Microwave to heat and stir with fork to desired smoothness.

Heartland Beer-Cheese Soup

A rich and hefty soup that is ideal for a cold winter's day.

1 tablespoon butter
1 pound smoked kielbasa sausage
2 cups minced onions
2 cups minced carrots
1 cup minced celery
1 teaspoon garlic
1/3 cup all-purpose flour
12 ounces (1 bottle) of lager, such as Back Road Brewery's Millenium Lager, which won the Brewers Cup Gold, or Bell's Lager that took the Bronze medal. For a more complex flavor, use a smoked beer, such as Schlenkerla Rauchbier or New Albanian's Cone Smoker.

3 cups chicken stock
1 bay leaf
2 cups pre-boiled diced red potatoes
2 cups milk
3 cups grated sharp cheddar cheese
1 teaspoon dried thyme
2 teaspoons Worcestershire sauce
2 teaspoons paprika
Pinch of cayenne
2 tablespoons tomato paste
Salt and black pepper to taste
Thinly sliced scallions

Boil potatoes until just soft. In the meantime, melt butter over medium heat in a soup pot or Dutch oven. Add sausage, cooking about 5 minutes. Add onions, carrots, celery, garlic, and potatoes and cook another 5 minutes. Stir in flour, coating everything well. Add beer, chicken stock, and bay leaf, bringing to a boil. Lower heat and cook about 5 minutes until soup thickens. Stir in milk, cheese, thyme, Worcestershire sauce, paprika, cayenne, and tomato paste. Continue stirring until cheese is melted and the soup stock is smooth. Season to taste with salt and pepper. Garnish with thinly sliced scallions. If desired, serve with Tabasco or other hot sauce, such as Melinda's.

Carbonnade a la Flamade
Flemish-style beef, beer, and onion stew
This is the classic Belgian dish that often defines traditional beer cuisine.

3 ½ pounds chuck roast, cut into 1" by 1" pieces, with fat and gristle removed
3 tablespoons vegetable fat
2 pounds of onions, halved and sliced ¼" thick
1 tablespoon tomato paste

2 teaspoons minced garlic

3 tablespoons all-purpose flour

¾ cup chicken broth

¾ cup beef broth

12 ounces of Belgian-style brown or red ale, such as Liefmans'
Goudenband or Rodenbach's red or Grand Cru. Brugge in Indianapolis uses their Black for their take on the stew.

4 sprigs of fresh thyme or 1 teaspoon of dried thyme

2 bay leaves

2 tablespoons of Dijon mustard

1 tablespoon of brown sugar

1 ½ teaspoons of cornstarch mixed with 2 tablespoons of red-
wine or malt vinegar

Preheat oven to 300 degrees if cooking stew in oven. Dry beef
with paper towels, then salt and pepper generously. Heat 2 teaspoons of oil in Dutch oven with medium-high heat until butter
just begins to smoke. Add ⅓ or so of beef to pot and cook for
2 to 3 minutes until pieces are browned. Turn and cook for
another 5 minutes. Remove beef to bowl. Repeat with more
oil and beef until all beef is browned. If drippings on pan bottom get very dark at some point during the browning, deglaze
with chicken stock and pour stock and pan scrapings into the
browned-beef bowl.

Add remaining oil to pot and reduce to medium low. Add
onions, ½ teaspoon of salt, and tomato paste, scraping pot bottom to loosen any browned beef. Cook about 5 minutes. Raise
to medium heat and cook another 12 minutes or so until onions
are browned, stirring occasionally. Stir in garlic and cook for 30
seconds. Add flour and stir for about 2 minutes until onions are
coated and flour is lightly browned. Add beef and chicken broth
and deglaze. Stir in beer, thyme, bay, mustard, and browned beef
with its juices. Salt and pepper. Cook about 2 to 2 ½ hours at
low heat on stovetop or in oven at 300 degrees until meat is very
tender. Drain cooking liquid into saucepan and skim fat. Add
cornstarch-vinegar mixture and sugar, stir for about 3 minutes,

and pour over the meat and onions.

The stew is typically served with egg noodles or boiled potatoes, but, hey, it's Indiana—mashed potatoes are the way to go.

Coq à la Bière
Northern French chicken braised in beer
A beer-based version of Coq au vin

2 tablespoons of butter
2 tablespoons of olive oil
1 3 ½- to 4-pound chicken, cut into serving pieces
1 small chopped onion
1 teaspoon of minced garlic
1 ½ cups of dark beer, such as Upland's Bad Elmer's Porter or Ram's Total Discord Porter, both Brewers Cup winners, or Three Floyds's hoppy Alpha Klaus Christmas Porter.
3 tablespoons gin
¼ teaspoon dried thyme
1 bay leaf
2 parley springs
20 juniper berries (optional)
Salt and pepper
2 pinches of cayenne
¾ pound quartered mushrooms
3 tablespoons heavy cream
2 tablespoons chopped parsley

Heat the butter and oil in heavy pot with medium heat, add chicken and brown on all sides. Remove to bowl. Add onions and garlic and cook until lightly browned. Return chicken to pot. Add gin and ignite. Add the beer, herbs, cayenne, salt, and pepper. Bring to boil, reduce heat, and simmer for 15 minutes. Add mushrooms and cook for 45 minutes. Transfer chicken and mushrooms to platter and keep warm. Remove bay, parsley, and juniper berries, if used. Add cream and reduce until sauce thickens. Salt and pepper to taste. Pour over chicken and mushrooms, sprinkle with chopped parsley, and serve.

Hoosier-Gaucho BBQ Beer Chicken

Evolved in Indiana from the barbecue-crazy southern Brazilian pampas where gauchos famously grill, this recipe provides a succulent chicken, rendered tender by its two-day beer marinade. The dark beer provides a malty undertone. Thanks to gaucha Flavia Bastos for the Brazilian inspiration.

1 3 ½- to 4-pound chicken, cut into serving pieces
2 cups dark beer, such as Back Road's Belle Gunness Stout and Bell's Expedition Stout, both 2008 Brewers Cup winners, or Broad Ripple's Finneen's Auld Sod Stout. Xingu Black Beer is the antipodal choice.
½ cup vegetable oil
½ cup Dijon mustard
1 tablespoon paprika
1 pinch cayenne
1 teaspoon black pepper
1 onion thinly sliced
12 chopped garlic cloves
3 bay leaves
Course salt

Combine beer, oil, mustard, paprika, cayenne, and black pepper and stir together. Add onion, garlic, and bay. Dry chicken pieces with paper towels and marinate, turning to cover all sides. Marinate in refrigerator for two days, turning occasionally.

Preheat grill. Remove chicken from marinade and blot dry. Season the chicken with liberal amounts of coarse salt. Oil the grill grate and place chicken skin down initially. During the first 10 minutes of cooking, brush the chicken generously with the remaining marinade. Turning as needed, cook until done.

Indiana Pork Loin with Kriek and Dried Cherry Sauce

This is a Hoosier variation of a Belgian-style pork stew made with kriek.

1 pork tenderloin, 3 pounds or so
12 ounces kriek, such as Lindemans, Upland's Cherry Lambic, or
Great Crescent's Cherry Beer
½ cup dried cherries
¾ teaspoon dried thyme
½ teaspoon rosemary
1 tablespoon black cherry preserves
1 large onion, minced
2 teaspoons minced garlic
2 tablespoons olive oil
1 to 2 tablespoons of malt, red wine, or balsamic vinegar
1½ teaspoons of cornstarch mixed with 2 tablespoons of water
Salt and black pepper

Marinate pork in beer, ½ teaspoon of thyme, and dried cherries
in the refrigerator for 6 to 24 hours. Preheat oven to 350 degrees.
Heat 1 tablespoon of olive oil in large skillet and sauté onions,
garlic, and ¼ teaspoon of rosemary on medium heat until soft;
do not brown. Remove mixture from skillet. Remove pork and
dried cherries from marinade, reserving the liquid for later.
Chop dried cherries (now softened) and add to onion-garlic mix.
Reserve ½ cup of the mixture to be used later for the sauce. Add
1 tablespoon of olive oil to skillet and sear pork on all sides. Salt
pork on all sides and place a layer of the remaining onion, garlic,
and cherry mixture between the two halves of the pork loin. Tie
the two halves together with butcher twine (white cotton twine).
Then pat the onion, garlic, and cherry mixture onto the outside
of the pork.

Using a two-part broiler pan, put an inch or two of water in
the bottom of the pan. Place the pork on the slotted top baking
sheet. Bake at 350 degrees for 20-30 minutes per pound. (More
boiling water can be added to the bottom pan during the cooking process if needed, pouring through the edge of the slotted

top baking sheet.) Let meat rest 10 minutes before slicing.

Place the marinade into a saucepan on medium heat. Bring to a boil, and cook for 4-5 minutes to reduce the beer and drive off the alcohol. Reducing the heat to a simmer, add the reserved ½ cup of onion, garlic, and dried cherry mixture to the sauce, along with ¼ teaspoon of rosemary, ¼ teaspoon of thyme, and 1 tablespoon of black cherry preserves. Simmer for five minutes. Add to taste 1 to 2 tablespoons of vinegar and stir. Stir cornstarch-water mixture into sauce to thicken. Adjust seasonings with salt and pepper.

Jets de Houblon
Hops Shoots with Poached Eggs

A Belgian specialty, hops shoots are the early thinnings of the vines. Often compared to asparagus, hops fanciers compare the flavor to a nuttier bean sprout or bamboo sprout. Should you have backyard hops plants, this can be a springtime dish. Hops rhizomes for the towering plants can be purchased at www.freshops.com.

4 eggs
8 ounces hops shoots
1 teaspoon lemon juice
2 tablespoons butter
Salt and pepper

Wash hops shoots (typically the tender first 2 inches of the shoot) and place in a saucepan of salted, boiling water. Add lemon juice and cook until tender, about 10 minutes. Briefly rinse under cold water and place on warm serving plate. Dot with butter. Poach eggs for about 5-6 minutes in simmering water with a few dashes vinegar added, until yolks are just firm. Place eggs on hops shoots and serve with hot toast.

Lager Pancakes

What to do with that flat half-bottle of lager the next morning? Lager pancakes! A fluffy, flavorful way to assuage the fear of waste.

3 cups flour
3 teaspoons baking powder
1 teaspoon salt
2 tablespoons sugar
3 eggs, separated
1 cup of flat lager beer
1 ½ cups milk
⅓ cup melted butter

Mix dry ingredients together. Beat egg yolks with a fork. Stir in beer, milk, and butter. Add dry ingredients and beat until smooth. Beat egg whites until stiff peaks form. Fold into batter. Add oil to hot skillet, and spoon batter into skillet. Flip when pancake rises and bubbles have popped. Makes about 20 pancakes.

Appendix

. . . .

Indiana Breweries Operating at the Onset of Prohibition, April 1918

Anderson	T. M. Norton
Evansville	F. W. Cook
	Evansville Brewing Company
Fort Wayne	Berghoff Brewing Association
	C. L. Centlivre Brewing Company
Hammond	West Hammond Brewing Company
Huntingburg	Monkhaus and Seubold
Huntington	Huntington Brewing Company
Indianapolis	American Brewing Company
	Citizens Brewing Company
	Home Brewing Company
	Indianapolis Brewing Company
	P. Lieber Brewery
	C. F. Schmidt Brewery
Lafayette	George A. Bohrer Brewing Company
	Thieme and Wagner Brewing Company
LaPorte	Guenther and Zerweck
Logansport	Columbia Brewing Company
Madison	Madison Brewing Company
Michigan City	Phillip Zorn Brewing Company

Mishawaka	Kamm and Schellinger Brewing Company
New Albany	State Street Brewery
	Southern Indiana Brewing Company
Peru	Peru Brewing Company
Richmond	Minck Brewing Company
South Bend	Muessel Brewing Company
	South Bend Brewing Association
Tell City	Tell City Brewing Company
Terre Haute	People's Brewing Company
	Terre Haute Brewing Company
Vincennes	Hack and Simon Brewing Company

Indiana Breweries, 1933–1997

Anderson	T. M. Norton Brewing Company, closed 1940.
Evansville	F. W. Cook Company, closed 1955.
	Sterling Brewers, Inc., acquired by Associated Brewing Company, 1964. Closed 1997.
	Wittekindt Brewing Company, closed 1940.
Fort Wayne	Berghoff Brewing Corporation, became Falstaff Brewing Corporation June 1954. Closed 1990.
	Centlivre Brewing Corporation, became Old Crown Brewing Corporation July 1961. Closed 1973.
	Hoff-Brau Brewing Corporation (originally Berghoff Brothers Brewing Company) Closed 1951
Indianapolis	Indianapolis Brewing Company, closed 1948.
	Lieber Brewing Company, became Phoenix Brewing Company, July 1937; Ajax Brewing Company, December 1937. Closed 1941.
Lafayette	Lafayette Brewery, Inc., closed 1953.
Marion	Kiley Brewing Company, Inc., closed 1949.

Michigan City	Zorn Brewing Company, closed 1937.
Mishawaka	Kamm and Schellinger Company, Inc., closed 1951.
New Albany	Southern Indiana Beverage and Ice Company, closed 1935.
South Bend	K. G. Schmidt Brewing Company, closed 1950
	Muessel Brewing Company, became Drewrys Limited U.S.A., Inc., 1936. Closed 1972.
	South Bend Brewing Company, closed 1950.
Terre Haute	Terre Haute Brewing Company, Inc., merged with Napco Industries in 1957; acquired by Atlantic Brewing Company in 1958. Closed 1958.